A SACRED ARGUMENT

"*A Sacred Argument* offers practical wisdom and hard-won guidance desperately needed to disarm hostilities and divisions in America today. Christopher Leighton demonstrates the promise that can emerge from disruptive encounters and difficult conversations about the things that matter most in our lives. It is a book that inspires struggle and learning, friendship and discovery, hope and compassion even in the midst of uncertainty and conflict."

—BILL MOYERS,
broadcast journalist

"This book illuminates an ongoing miracle: the story of a reversal that is changing the great world religions from enemies into partners. In recounting the difficult yet exhilarating work of the ICJS, Christopher Leighton guides readers into the labor required to turn religion from the habits of contempt and ignorance into a constructive force for good, a blessing for all the families of the earth."

—IRVING (YITZ) GREENBERG,
president, J. J. Greenberg Institute for the Advancement of Jewish Life.

"*A Sacred Argument* is a book for this searing moment in history. Each period of history calls forth visionaries like King, Mandela, Elie Wiesel, and Susan Sontag who shine light into the darkness. Chris Leighton is an American treasure with a moving and wise story to tell about hope, peacemaking, justice, and moral leadership in a religiously diverse and conflicted world. His message about forgiveness as an 'impossible necessity' is absolutely riveting and should be required reading for all thoughtful people."

—ROBERT M. FRANKLIN,
president emeritus, Morehouse College

"*A Sacred Argument* captures with gentle force the pain, challenge, and reward of interreligious encounters. Christopher Leighton tells the story of his own journeys in interfaith dialogue with captivating and disarming clarity and candor. His humanity and his kindness, his convictions and his courage, his certainties and his doubts, and his love and concern for all humanity appear on every page of this book. A Sacred Argument should be required reading for persons of all faiths!"

—DAVID ELLENSON,
chancellor emeritus, Hebrew Union College-Jewish Institute of Religion

"*A Sacred Argument,* beautifully composed by Christopher Leighton, is the powerful account of how a remarkable center of teaching and self-exploration came into being and now serves as an invaluable resource for interfaith engagement. But *A Sacred Argument* is not just a chronology of important milestones. Leighton invites us into the painful, humbling but ever-enlightening experience of coming to know the other—and he does so with a grace and warmth that soothes the soul."

—JOHN PETER SARBANES,
U.S. Congressman

"Eloquent and engrossing, intensely personal and insightfully profound, Christopher Leighton's *A Sacred Argument* maps the odyssey of Christian encounters with Jews and Muslims in post-Holocaust America. Dynamic and dialogical, this memoir—both scholarly and page-turning—wisely guides decisive steps that Americans need to take to advance religious understanding and to defend endangered democracy."

—JOHN K. ROTH,
professor emeritus of philosophy, Claremont McKenna College

"*A Sacred Argument* tells the remarkable history of the Institute for Islamic-Christian-Jewish Studies in Baltimore. From its beginnings in 1987 as a small circle of Jews and Christians to its present multi-faith staff and programs, ICJS is a model of a vibrant interfaith center that has evolved to address the broader challenges of our times. Chris Leighton has written a profound book about the importance of interfaith work for our democracy."

—VICTORIA J. BARNETT,
former director, Programs on Ethics, Religion, and the Holocaust at the United States Holocaust Memorial Museum

A Sacred Argument

Dispatches from the Christian, Jewish, and Muslim Encounter

CHRISTOPHER M. LEIGHTON
afterword by Heather Miller Rubens

WIPF & STOCK · Eugene, Oregon

A SACRED ARGUMENT
Dispatches from the Christian, Jewish, and Muslim Encounter

Copyright © 2024 Christopher M. Leighton. All rights reserved. Except for brief quotations in critical publications or reviews, no part of this book may be reproduced in any manner without prior written permission from the publisher. Write: Permissions, Wipf and Stock Publishers, 199 W. 8th Ave., Suite 3, Eugene, OR 97401.

Wipf & Stock
An Imprint of Wipf and Stock Publishers
199 W. 8th Ave., Suite 3
Eugene, OR 97401

www.wipfandstock.com

PAPERBACK ISBN: 979-8-3852-0051-1
HARDCOVER ISBN: 979-8-3852-0052-8
EBOOK ISBN: 979-8-3852-0053-5

VERSION NUMBER 01/25/24

A version of chapter 7, "Bach and the Indelible Stain," is reprinted with the permission of Orbis Books from: *With the Best of Intentions: Interreligious Missteps and Mistakes*, edited by Lucinda Mosher, Elinor J. Pierce, and Or N. Rose (Maryknoll, NY: Orbis, 2023). All rights reserved.

The icon *Captive Daughter of Zion*, by Brother Robert Lenz, courtesy of Trinity Stores, www.trinitystores.com, 800.699.4482.

In memory of Rabbi Joel H. Zaiman

"All real living is meeting"—Martin Buber

Contents

Preface | ix

Introduction | xi

Chapter 1　　In the Beginning | 1
Chapter 2　　The Bones We Carry | 9
Chapter 3　　Shaking the Foundations | 18
Chapter 4　　Leaving Home | 32
Chapter 5　　The Baltimore Declaration | 38
Chapter 6　　Paul Alexander and the Gospel of John | 51
Chapter 7　　Bach and the Indelible Stain | 61
Chapter 8　　A Sacred Argument | 70
Chapter 9　　Job and the Question of Suffering | 78
Chapter 10　 Bill and Judith Moyers and the Genesis Project | 91
Chapter 11　 The Jewish Scholars Group and *Dabru Emet* | 100
Chapter 12　 The Atlanta Project | 111
Chapter 13　 The Challenge of Israel | 118
Chapter 14　 Islam | 134
Chapter 15　 Religion in the Public Square | 153
Chapter 16　 Forgiveness—The Impossible Necessity | 173

Afterword by Heather Miller Rubens | 190

Acknowledgments | 195

Bibliography | 199

Preface

I meet Rabbi Joel Zaiman at the restaurant with every expectation of a delectable feast. Grilled salmon with mashed potatoes infused with garlic and herbs, topped off with warm chocolate bread pudding equally divided between the two of us! When our paths first crossed forty years ago, I must have looked a bit undernourished. He was alert to the rumblings of an empty stomach and clearly felt a moral obligation to make sure that I had a big meal under my belt. A pattern of monthly lunches began and continued for more than three decades.

I confide to Joel my intention to write a book. He gazes at me quizzically. There is an uncomfortable pause before he breaks the silence, "Really? Why would you want to do that?"

I am a bit defensive: "Because I have stories to tell, stories that need to be told." I cannot help it.

A wry smile appears as he digs deeper. "And who do you think will be interested?"

"Well, certainly my friends and family! The people with whom I have worked. Readers who care about the future and want to disarm religious hate."

A burst of laughter erupts. I have heard this outburst many times over the course of several decades. It bears no mockery, no malice, no denunciation. The laugh reveals a mix of delight, incredulity, and challenge. He tests my resolve—as usual. "Will this be a tragedy or a comedy?"

"I'm not sure. Some of both. Laughter and tears," I tell him.

"Nothing scandalous? Nothing that will make your readers uncomfortable?" He can never resist the urge to poke and prod. He is by nature and breeding a mischievous interrogator.

"Well, do you think I have learned nothing from you?" I volley.

"I think you want to be nice, and I think you are inclined to hide in the shadows," he observes.

"And what then would you have me do?" I try my best to deflect his provocations.

"Tell a story that makes you squirm, a story that brings uncertainty alive, a story your readers must finish themselves." I imagine him demanding this and more, his voice still echoing even after he was returned to the earth several years ago.

Introduction

Many of us have at one time or another been asked the question: if you could invite anyone to join you for dinner, whom would you bring to the table? Within my Presbyterian family, the answer was foreordained. The list would include grandparents, aunts and uncles, cousins, and an assortment of intimate friends. In our household, we gravitated to those we knew and trusted. We stuck with people who made us feel comfortable, people with whom we were at home. Our crowd inhabited a shared culture, told familiar stories, and learned to enjoy the same jokes. We had gone to similar schools and attended similar churches. In my case, these institutions were within easy walking distance of our house. The menu was fixed and the table was configured to maintain a formality that ruled out surprise, especially awkward disagreement.

This story is about the kind of disruption that occurs when the guest list is changed and an unfamiliar and often unruly cast of characters comes to the feast. The narrative is about the disorientation that arises when the rules of etiquette are no longer binding or known, when the menu features unorthodox dishes, and indigestion frequently follows. At this enlarged table, the talk routinely becomes loud and words go offensively rogue. The people next to you are inclined to raise their voices and sometimes storm out of the room in disgust, exasperation, or despair. The atmosphere is wildly unpredictable, like the weather in Maine during hurricane season.

This too needs acknowledgement: we come to a table that has in large measure already been set by ancestors who can also inflame the uproar. They are known to emerge from the shadows unexpectedly. When given the opportunity, they add their voices to the dining room babel and often give it a feverish pitch. Their opinions may bring depth and grandeur to the melee, but they can also provoke agonizing discomfort when enlisted to bolster arguments with the authority of the past. Cranky predecessors speak the loudest and have a habit of making guests wince—dredging up memories that produce awkward silence or thunderous protest—a skill parents unfailingly display when their children are out to impress a visitor. Once their spectral presence is recognized, it is difficult to moderate these ancestors. They demand respect, if not obedience.

I was not raised for this kind of dinner table tumult. My religious faith took aim at a peaceful kingdom where the music was soft and harmonious. My people pursued a vision filled with calm and contemplative quiet. Confusion and doubt and agitation were regarded as incompatible with the decorum expected at the messianic banquet.

Hospitality is a risky business when the seating is open, and neighbors of every stripe show up. Most within my kin were reared to distrust the stranger. The instructions were clear and non-negotiable: take no candy and accept no rides from anyone unknown. Caution and suspicion encircled the outsider.

Yet our cultures are brimming with stories in which the stranger is the bearer of blessings, and hospitality directed to the needy is regarded as an ethical imperative. Abraham welcomed strangers who, on closer inspection, turned out to be divine messengers (Gen 18). His generosity demonstrated his righteousness. Jesus consorted with the marginalized and dined with quislings like tax collectors (Luke 19). His behavior dissolved distinctions normally deployed to differentiate friends and enemies.

The virtue of hospitality is also enshrined in Greek and Roman mythology, as illustrated in Ovid's story of Philemon and Baucis. The myth portrays Jupiter and Mercury—poised to destroy humankind in response to its wicked ways. The two arrive disguised as weary travelers. Although rudely spurned by other villagers, Philemon and Baucis welcome these strangers. They share what little they possess with their visitors—thereby deflecting a disastrous punishment (*Metamorphoses* 8.631, 8.8720).[1]

And the treatment of guests within Islam is no less foundational, entailing a recognition of the triangular ties binding host and guest to God. Similar moral codes are etched into Eastern mythologies, underscoring the obligation to care for the vulnerable outsider, establishing hospitality as an expansive if not universal duty. In the precarious conditions around the world and for the better part of human history, the question has always been loaded with existential urgency: what if your life were to depend on the kindness of a stranger?

The claim that religion provides an ethical and theological basis for open-armed hospitality may nonetheless appear counterintuitive.

---

1. Note the narrative affinity with Gen 19:1-26, where three angels visit Lot and his family at Sodom and Gomorrah.

In the minds of many, religion is a source of division that pits insiders against outsiders, believers against nonbelievers, the righteous against the damned. Religious institutions are repeatedly viewed as bastions of intolerance, and they routinely define themselves in adversarial relationship to those who appear threatening and deviant.

In contemporary parlance, people who anger and annoy us are branded "toxic"—reflecting the more sweeping and intolerant temper of our times. The compulsion that prompts people to cancel anyone who causes offense is certainly not confined to religious adherents; there are powerful tendencies in our culture urging people to sever bonds with anyone who crosses the line and disturbs peace of mind. Increasingly, internet gurus counsel clients to break ties with those who have hurt their feelings or done them harm. We are advised to protect ourselves from anyone, including friends and family, who steps on our toes and undermines our self-esteem. We are encouraged to remain in safe spaces and cut off people who add negativity to our lives.[2] The results are plain to see. We are choking on grievances and distrust, if not outright hatred, of political, religious, and ethnic opponents. In ways that once seemed unimaginable, the demonization of adversaries is intensifying the threat of violence and the unraveling of our democracy.

The discovery at the heart of this book is that there are no safe spaces that can sustain moral integrity and human flourishing. Disruption and conflict, disorientation and confusion are inescapable, and people who remain at a table where no one spills their soup or no one squabbles end up with an empty heart and a vacant mind. Whether we can live in the disarray and build trust and compassion within mayhem remains an open question for us as individuals and for us as a nation. We are so polarized, and our identities so dependent on opposition. Breaking the habits that lock us into destructive antagonism requires resolve and practice that are undeveloped and in desperate demand.

The organization where I worked for thirty-three years, the Institute for Islamic, Christian, and Jewish Studies (ICJS), is devoted to an ethic of radical hospitality and has gone to great lengths to set a table where disruption is on the menu. While keenly aware that religion is often a source of dysfunctional conflict, the governing mission of the ICJS has resisted the temptation to cut and run in the face of toxic fallout. The challenge that animated its educational quest was to engage different philosophical and theological perspectives, break the grip of long-standing distortions,

---

2. Advisers on Twitter, Instragram, TikTok, and Reddit routinely offer instructions expressed in the following post: "There is no better self-care than cutting off people who are toxic to you." Tiffany, "That's It. You're Dead to Me."

and redeem the sacred bequests of our ancestors. The aim was and remains daunting: to neutralize the worst in our traditions and to nurture the best—all the while recognizing the task does not promise closure or guarantee success.

This work of reconstruction involves displacement, a movement from orientation to disorientation to reorientation, and most importantly cannot be pursued in solitary or communal confinement. No single tradition can develop the cure or acquire the wisdom to heal the fractures that afflict our society and the world at large. The sensitivities and skills needed to build compassionate connection and resilient trust compel people to step outside their familiar enclaves. While religious traditions often present themselves as self-sufficient, nothing could be farther from the truth.

Frankly, our religious communities are poorly prepared to meet the challenge. Congregational life remains—with precious few exceptions—insular and self-contained, caught up in the scramble to survive. Meanwhile, seminaries rarely expose their students to other religious traditions or equip them to engage adherents with divergent theological orientations. As Rabbi Harold Schulweis once noted, seminaries do a wonderful job of preparing their students to live in a world that no longer exists. And yet, a future that holds durable promise requires us as individuals and communities to leave home and enter foreign territory. This venture is riddled with risk because the path brings us face-to-face with failure as well as achievement—our own and our ancestors'. Insight and regeneration hinge on a willingness to see ourselves through the eyes of others, most especially those we have traditionally regarded with contempt or systematically ignored. Sooner or later comes a reckoning with our blind spots. The habit of neglect and the avoidance of creative conflict are reactive reflexes to religious, cultural, ethnic, and political pluralism—and they amount to a dereliction of a sacred obligation to our ancestors, our children, and the world at large.

I am hopeful my experiences with the ICJS over the course of thirty-three years—with its many steps and missteps—will embolden individuals and communities to welcome the stranger and embark on an odyssey of disruption. The road I have traveled has landed me in situations that repeatedly exposed my ignorance and challenged my sense of certainty. Although there are many ways to come to the realization that our cultural conditioning narrows our field of vision and constricts our awareness of others, my journey has entailed encounters with people from different religious and ethnic backgrounds, particularly Jews, Muslims, and other Christians.

INTRODUCTION

My fascination with religion is rooted in the conviction that our traditions have invaluable wisdom to offer if and only if we dare to contend with their flaws and foibles. In fact, I do not think we can escape the enduring impact of the religious legacies bequeathed to us. The values and norms that provide a sense of meaning and belonging have roots in this inheritance—and they require rigorous examination.

To be more specific, my commitment to my own religious tradition stems from its vision of transformation. Religions operate with the daring and extravagant conviction that change is possible, that hearts and minds are not necessarily fixed, that the wounds of the past need not define the future, that the conversion that opens us to the needs of others is a realistic hope. In other words, our religious traditions offer us resources to restore what is broken and mend the tattered fabric of our lives. They offer a necessary alternative to our tendency to cut and run—the natural impulse to retreat into the safety of the silo and turn away from our religious neighbors. At their best, our religious traditions advocate a spiritual discipline that can heal the fractures in our lives and give substance to the ideals of repentance and forgiveness.

Consider the options: a world without forgiveness leaves us to deal with those who bother, scandalize, and violate our norms and values by punishing them, expelling them, or eliminating them—hardly strategies that can sustain a healthy family or reinvigorate a divided country. In the rough-and-tumble encounters with peoples from divergent religious and ethnic backgrounds, we are afforded opportunities to discover the possibilities and limits of transformation. The credibility of our religious communities depends on the cultivation of this aptitude, and the formation of new habits of engaging our differences will determine the prospects for the human family.

Inquiries into the world of interreligious studies commonly involve surveys of the beliefs, rituals, practices, and history of different religious communities. They aim to develop religious literacy so people can better understand and engage their neighbors near and far. These accounts are assembled at high altitudes and rarely touch the messy business of implementation. This volume offers intimate and tumultuous dispatches from the front lines, and both the steps and missteps are disclosed in granular detail.

To illuminate the practical dimensions of this work, I toggle between personal experiences, biblical musings, and theological/philosophical reflections. It is the interplay of these modalities of exploration that brings out the complexity and urgency of interreligious engagement. Given my own proclivities for abstraction, I have tethered much of the narrative to particular relationships. Nothing is real unless it is local—or so the saying goes. In my case, nothing about the interreligious encounter is real unless it is relational. In this light I have directed a good bit of attention to my friendship with Rabbi Joel Zaiman, to whom this book is dedicated. He more than anyone taught me not to fear disruption and to search for opportunity in the midst of conflict. He turned conversation into a feast. May his memory be a blessing!

Chapter 1

In the Beginning

The city of Baltimore may not strike most observers as an auspicious location to launch a nonprofit organization devoted to interreligious education, especially in the years 1986 to 1989. Like so much of urban America, the lines of separation segmented the city into distinct ethnic and racial enclaves, and the divisions were generally fixed despite legal challenges to the restrictive covenants that preserved ancestral boundaries. Until the last decades of the twentieth century, Jews were largely relegated to an area east of Falls Road known as Pikesville, and Blacks were consigned to inner-city neighborhoods abandoned by more privileged white taxpayers, many of whom had moved to surrounding counties to enjoy lower taxes, better schools, safer streets, and a more homogenous and congenial community. The Black Muslim community either accepted or embraced a life separated from the dominant white culture, while Muslim immigrants often brought the academic and professional credentials needed to assimilate and blend into their own suburban neighborhoods.

Despite the economic and social chasm separating the inner city from the more affluent suburbs, Baltimore was nonetheless the beneficiary of inspired corporate and civic leadership. In response to a city in decline, a coalition of Jewish and Christian entrepreneurs came together and took daring steps to reverse the downward spiral. They revitalized significant commercial districts and then took measures to transform a deteriorating waterfront. Their collaborative engagement with local and state government led to a vibrant urban hub in the heart of downtown Baltimore featuring commercial plazas, tourist attractions, and public parks. In the late 1970s and 1980s, the success of the Inner Harbor garnered national acclaim and signaled the promise of urban renewal.

Visitors did not need to venture far before confronting a very different and more disturbing reality. In the words of one notable report, "There is rot beneath the glitter." A once robust manufacturing and shipping center had largely evaporated. Vast stretches of the city remained impoverished and grossly underserved. Wretched housing conditions, the proliferation of drugs and crime, an underfunded school system with an unwieldy bureaucracy, and a shrinking demographic clouded prospects of a brighter future.

Yet the Jewish and Christian businessmen and city planners who had combined their talents in the 1970s–80s to help revive the city had discovered one another. Friendships as well as partnerships developed, and a new and surprising impetus emerged for greater collaboration. The vision of James Rouse, a Christian who had planted his ideal of a self-sustaining city in Columbia, Maryland, had remarkable reach, and his dream of an alternative to suburban isolation inspired many civic leaders to take steps to overcome dysfunctional religious, ethnic, and socioeconomic divisions.

Of particular note, many of these corporate leaders believed that our religious communities were the most underrated and potent agents for social transformation. They were convinced a positive change in the city's physical and psychological geography would never happen until people discovered what Rabbi Jonathan Sacks called "the dignity of difference."[1] The ethical and theological mandate to care for the needy, pursue justice, and build an economy of mutual blessing resides at the heart of our varied religious traditions, but the ideals could never be realized as long as adherents remained isolated—suspicious, hostile, or simply indifferent to their neighbors. Serious and sustained effort was required to break the legacy of redlining and the exclusions of Jews and Blacks enforced by the dominant white culture. A deep change was needed to dispel the distorted perceptions of the religious outsider enshrined within our traditions.

During the early 1980s, a handful of dialogue groups were formed, comprised of prominent clergy and notable movers and shakers from the larger community. With the guidance of several rabbis, ministers, and priests, participants opened up conversations that led to greater literacy about the distinctive character of the Jewish and Christian heritages. As trust developed, more contentious issues were broached, namely, the ways in which Christians and Jews remained captivated by stereotypes of one another. The recognition began to take hold that Jews and Christians see and understand themselves and the world differently, however much they have in common. The vulnerabilities and the assumptions about our place in society pointed to different experiences and expectations. As participants gained

---

1 See Sacks, *Dignity of Difference*.

a deeper awareness of the disparities, the goal shifted from the promotion of greater tolerance—which is to say an ability to put up with and endure one another's idiosyncrasies—to an ideal of respectful reciprocity, vulnerability, and friendship. Almost everyone agreed that our religious communities had failed to provide guidelines for responding to the confounding reality of religious pluralism. And the blessing—given meeting after meeting—was the unexpected, exhilarating, and disorienting realization that Jewish and Christian participants were discovering something precious and noble in the other's community that could not be located within their own. A more daring educational model was sorely needed to capture this energy.

For more than a decade, the most ambitious and innovative interfaith dialogues were conducted at the National Workshops on Christian-Jewish Relations. These conferences rotated among cities around the country and were choreographed by professionals in agencies and organizations dedicated to deepening understanding between Jews and Christians. Their mission required the enlistment and mobilization of local communities to become actively engaged in the work. Distinguished scholars were recruited to attend the gathering and deliver lectures on a broad range of topics—illuminating the anguished history pitting Christians and Jews against one another, neutralizing distortions generated by biblical (mis)interpretation, and identifying theological challenges that necessitate ongoing exploration. Dialogue practitioners shared pedagogical strategies, and ample time was set aside to savor the music and culture of the host city. Leaders from Baltimore attended these gathering in increasing numbers, and then convinced the national organizers to hold the Ninth National Workshop in Baltimore.

The scale of planning that went into this conference was staggering. There was money to be raised not only to bring premiere scholars to Baltimore, but to provide support so that seminary and university students could attend. There was the need to design a sequence of presentations that would span the history of Jewish-Christian encounters and crack open contemporary theological challenges. These efforts required intense negotiations between local and national organizers. All the major Christian judicatories were recruited along with participation from the most influential Reform, Conservative, Reconstructionist, and Modern Orthodox synagogues. Regional colleges, universities, and seminaries were enlisted. Corporate sponsors and philanthropic foundations were lined up. Downtown hotels were secured, and city officials pressed into service. The list went on and on.

The Ninth National Workshop took place in May of 1986 and generated a buzz that reverberated well beyond the city. Baltimore emerged as a center for serious engagement in the burgeoning field of Jewish-Christian studies. The most far-reaching innovation to come out of the planning and implementation of this event was the decision to raise the funds to launch the educational initiative that would become the Institute for Christian & Jewish Studies (ICJS).

The reasoning was simple enough. A conference can pull a community together, and people can rally for three or four days, reap some new information, get inspired or at least agitated, and then slip back into familiar routines. The euphoria and resolve emanating from such massive undertakings tend to dissipate as the dust settles and inertia eventually has its way. The leaders in Baltimore—comprised of corporate, educational, and religious luminaries—believed the questions posed and the issues raised needed sustained attention and systematic follow-up. They dreamed of an educational venture that would raise the consciousness in and beyond the city of Baltimore by demonstrating that the health and vitality of our country hinges on a new era of interreligious cooperation.

The Christian and Jewish founders of the ICJS reached out to other colleagues and marshaled the business communities, and they assembled one of the most exceptional nonprofit boards in Maryland. These trustees gave the organization credibility and stature from its very inception. Coupled with the ardent commitment of key educational and religious leaders in Maryland, this fledgling coalition attracted trailblazers who gave the enterprise intellectual gravitas and spiritual legitimacy.

The mission initially revolved around a rigorous and unflinching examination of the religious roots of anti-Judaism, and this inquiry promised to upset and disorient Christians who were unaware of the depth and breadth of what Robert Wistrich identified as "the longest hatred."[2] The vision was grounded in the conviction that there could be no honest and sustained relationship between Christians and Jews without a reckoning with a history about which most Christians knew almost nothing. In retrospect, the ambition to disarm an antagonism with tentacles stretching all the way back to the church's beginnings was not only audacious but preposterously ambitious. The founders of the ICJS had yet to grasp a deeply entrenched pattern—the degree to which the identity of Christians was once and continues to be forged in adversarial relationship to Judaism and the Jewish people. They had yet to realize the chasm separating Jews and Christians— the difference in our readings of sacred scriptures, the enduring scars of an anguished history and the lingering distrust and fear, the incomprehensibility of divergent theological claims, and the sheer habit of avoiding the hard work of learning another's religious language. Admittedly, most people find it much easier to ignore and dismiss the spiritual endowments of the other

---

2. Wistrich, *Antisemitism: The Longest Hatred.*

than to embark on an uncertain and risky pilgrimage to a foreign land. All of this—the resistance and risk—did not dawn on our founders and our earliest supporters. The blend of optimism and naïveté and bold aspiration was the blessing that fired the imagination and gave birth to the ICJS.

What nonetheless defies easy comprehension is the utterly unpredictable path that led many of the founders and patrons of the ICJS to commit so much time, energy, and financial support to it from the very outset. This is the question I was asked repeatedly over the years: how did this nonprofit educational venture take hold and establish itself as one of Baltimore's most successful and well-endowed organizations, a national leader in the field of interfaith relations? Might the story of the ICJS provide other cities with a useful blueprint?

There is no simple answer to these questions, because the motivations among the founders varied considerably. Take Charlie Obrecht, a Presbyterian who in many ways was the indomitable force behind the ICJS. He was born into a well-established family and attended the Gilman School and Princeton University, where he distinguished himself as a stellar athlete and a dedicated student. Charlie was always a self-starter. At a young age, he proved his entrepreneurial chops, selling eggs to neighbors with his brother Fred. After college and a stint in the navy, the two of them resumed their business collaboration as real estate developers in East Baltimore. In light of his success, he was well positioned to settle into an insular life of privilege. He refused. He served on the governor's welfare commission and put his talents to work as an exemplary volunteer and board member in various organizations that aimed to better the world around him.

What happened that prompted him to move beyond the safe and circumscribed life into which he could have easily slipped? What led to his extraordinary determination to confront the problem of Jewish-Christian relations, a focus that must have mystified many of his peers? He claims Margaret "Peggy," the woman he married, should be held responsible. She grew up within a home surrounded by books and people with a deep love for learning, and Charlie was embraced as one of their own. No doubt Peggy's father, Clark Mock, was influential in view of his commitment to social justice and the ethical mandates of the gospel to ease the burdens of the poor. It is important to note that Peggy built on this legacy and went on to become the first director of what was then the Department of Church Relations at the United States Holocaust Memorial Museum.

No one in this family likes to talk about themselves, and Charlie, in particular, downplays his own achievements and directs attention to the accomplishments of others. Yet it was Charlie's vision and his tireless devotion that was especially pivotal in giving birth to the ICJS, an organization that exceeded everyone's expectations.

Charlie became absolutely convinced that the future of our world depended upon the work of disarming religious hostilities, and he insisted this task first required a commitment to uproot the anti-Jewish prejudices within the Christian tradition. The failure to confront this deadly dysfunction would rob future generations of religious ideals that he continues to believe are essential to forge the trust and the virtues upon which a democracy rests. An unflinching honesty about a shameful legacy with an ancient lineage was imperative to break the grip of theological arrogance and advance peace at home and around the world. Charlie approached the quest for interreligious understanding out of the conviction that this educational pursuit is a matter of life and death.

Bernie Manekin, Charlie's Jewish counterpart, shared Charlie's commitment, and he could not envision a healthy city in which people from different religious traditions capitulated to the forces of ignorance and hatred. In his role as the chairman of the Greater Baltimore Committee, Bernie had long demonstrated his capacious aptitude for friendship, and he built a web of connections in business that criss-crossed the city. His support of the ICJS was his way of honoring his family and the ethical mandates of his Jewish tradition.

Rick Berndt, the Roman Catholic chair, had relatives in Germany who were on the wrong side of history. Not only did he feel an obligation to his many Jewish friends to neutralize the dangerous distortions of the past, he was deeply committed to taking steps to make sure the failures of his own religious community were not repeated. His religious and political loyalties were inextricably bound together.

Rosann Catalano pursued her doctoral studies at the University of Toronto with an emphasis on the psalms of lament, and she found solidarity with a Jewish tradition that did not shy away from arguing with the divine and by extension any other authorities that sanctioned bigotry. She discovered Jewish approaches to reading and interpreting the Bible that opened surprising vistas, and her Jewish compatriots emboldened creative and daring responses to suffering and adversity. She became convinced that academic and spiritual integrity depended on breaking out of our silos.

Kathy Hoskins, a devout Roman Catholic, did the legal work to establish the ICJS as a legitimate nonprofit organization, and she remained a dedicated leader until her untimely death. Her husband thought that the initials "ICJS" stood for "I Just Can't Stop." And she was in the thick of every major decision about the scope of the ICJS mission and the labor required to advance disruptive education. The ICJS was not just an assignment but a vocation that tapped her deepest fealty.

Donna Lee Frisch, a cradle Episcopalian, was utterly flummoxed by anyone who held fast to hate. She was convinced that education had the power to dispel ignorance, and she both studied and taught with the intent of healing history's wounds. She was driven by an exuberant optimism and believed—despite all evidence to the contrary—every stranger had an irresistible wisdom to offer.

Mel Sykes, an Orthodox Jewish lawyer and scholar, claimed that Jews could help Christians become better Christians and that Christians could help Jews become better Jews. This was the chapter yet to be written, and the ICJS was vested with an indispensable educational role to make possible what once seemed unimaginable.

George Bunting was raised in a devout Roman Catholic family and attended parochial schools where both the students and faculty were immersed in the same theological waters. During the fifties and sixties in Baltimore, there were religious and racial lines that were not crossed. When George headed a New York Stock Exchange corporation and then served on several high-profile boards, he was exposed to talented individuals from very different backgrounds, not least among them Jews. Some of the prejudices ingested along the way did not align with his personal experiences, and his curiosity got the best of him. He wanted to know more, and the friendships that he had developed convinced him that change was imperative.

Bishop Frank Murphy was on the front lines of progressive activity within the Roman Catholic Church and had gained uncommon experience as the theological adviser to Lawrence Cardinal Shehan at the Second Vatican Council. In Maryland, he spearheaded low-cost housing in areas long neglected, and he gave voice to the impoverished and dispossessed. He was also outspoken in his advocacy for women in leadership. He took a keen interest in everyone who crossed his path and radiated kindness and generosity to an extent that I had never seen before. It came as no surprise that he became a champion of the ICJS from its tenuous beginnings. He insisted that he could not live in fidelity to his own religious heritage without standing in solidarity with the people and tradition into which Jesus was born, lived, and died. Antisemitism, he insisted, was a sin that not only stained the world, but sundered the heavens.

Joe and Nellie Birnbaum escaped the Nazi dragnet and found refuge in the United States. They simply could not believe a day would come when Christians would own up to their failures. I think they worried that their children and grandchildren lived under the shadow of the Holocaust and that the worst of the past might once again insert itself into the future. They were convinced that the ICJS espoused a vision that would safeguard their family and friends, their community, and the larger world from destruction. The depth of their gratitude for this work was humbling and underscored the sacred obligation we had undertaken.

Delores Kelley, an active member within the Black Protestant church, became a distinguished professor at Coppin State University and was later elected to the Maryland State Senate. She recognized that bigotry is rarely bounded. Hostility directed against one group sooner or later enlarges its scope and takes aim at other vulnerable targets. She insisted that it takes a diverse coalition of citizens to counter the human proclivity to elevate one community at the expense of another—and education holds the elixir to neutralize prejudice.

Tom Glenn, a Christian and one of the supporters of the ICJS from Atlanta, once remarked, "I have become intolerant of intolerance." Perhaps this was the conviction that animated those who became devoted supporters of the ICJS. I doubt many of the founders could give detailed reasons for their involvement other than it struck them as the right thing to do and the right time in which to do it. What moved me is the simple fact that virtually all of the people who gave of their time and treasure believed that the destinies of Jews, Christians, and Muslims, men and women, believers and nonbelievers, and peoples from all manner of ethnic backgrounds are interwoven. Everyone involved demonstrated a willingness to risk friendships with those who see the world differently and the courage to confront their own misconceptions. In the ICJS they found a sense of adventure and discovery that would define the substance and character of a shared future.

Chapter 2

The Bones We Carry

I first encountered Joel Zaiman in 1980 on his doorstep. He and his family had recently relocated from Providence, Rhode Island, after Joel had been appointed the senior rabbi of Chizuk Amuno, one of the largest and most influential Conservative synagogues in Maryland. His son, Ari, was a new student at the Gilman School, where I was serving as the chaplain and chair of the Religion Department. At that time every ninth- and tenth-grade student was saddled with two years' worth of religious studies, and Ari found himself surveying the wonders of Hinduism and Buddhism with me. No doubt Joel wanted to know who was filling his son's head with exotic enchantments.

Joel's wife, Ann, who was developing her considerable talents as a painter at the Maryland Institute College of Art, was in a class with my wife Betsy, and she reached out to invite us to a Sabbath dinner. When we showed up at the Zaiman home, Joel was there to meet us. The first thing I noticed: here was a big presence. Joel was not only large and imposing, he was a force, a patriarch accustomed to breaking the bread and carving the roast. He knew the ground on which he stood, and he was not one to blink in the face of battle. I had heard reports that he possessed a commanding and intimidating bearing. He did not become the president of the Synagogue Council of America because he showcased a timorous demeanor. Yet he was also gracious, engaging, and irrepressibly curious. As soon as we were seated, I found myself peppered with questions. He wanted to know what I was reading, what unexpected challenges I faced as a teacher and chaplain, and what issues and concerns kept me up at night. He drilled and then grilled with abandon. He went in search of my story, and he wanted things spelled out in detail. His habit was to dig deep without hesitation and to persist until he got to the heart of things. At the same time, he welcomed my rejoinders and was disarming in his honesty when I turned his questions back on him. For reasons beyond my understanding, I was neither overwhelmed nor rankled by his probing. I was enthralled. I had never met anyone remotely like him.

At one point during the dinner, Joel bumped his glass and spilled red wine onto the tablecloth. Perturbed by his own clumsy gesture, he blurted out the invective, "Jesus Christ!" He was immediately mortified that he had unwittingly offended me and began to apologize profusely. I told him the situation made an invocation of the divine perfectly understandable. In answer to my riposte, he let loose a belly laugh that rattled all the dishes on the table.

That episode was the beginning of a friendship that neither one of us could have imagined possible. Joel, the son of an Orthodox rabbi, grew up in Chicago. With the exception of our family doctor, I had no exposure to Jews during my childhood. Joel found the specter of Christianity more difficult to avoid. To ward off an alien intrusion, he was instructed as a child to cross the street and spit whenever his path took him past a church.

Joel was anchored in a tradition of rigorous Jewish education, and he clearly excelled. On one occasion a visiting scholar delivered a sermon that Joel—the precocious teenager—claimed was lacking originality. His father noted that innovation is not so easy when taking into account the scope and majesty of the Jewish tradition. Joel evidently shrugged his shoulders, and in response his father challenged him to deliver *d'var torah* (a "word of torah," i.e., the homily) for the coming week.

Joel poured heart and soul into his preparation, examining all sorts of commentaries and pouring over all manner of homiletical material. When he went to the bima to deliver his *d'var torah*, he was confident that he had composed a fresh and imaginative reading. In the aftermath of the service, he found himself rewarded with great acclaim. Here was a teenager with unbounded promise! He went to bed that evening with a swelled head and slept contentedly for the first time in several nights. When he awoke and headed downstairs for breakfast, he found a medieval codex on his plate opened to a textual commentary that tracked the same trajectory as his sermon. His creative leaps were anticipated long ago by ancestors who still frequented outhouses and read by candlelight.

Joel's father was clearly troubled by his son's arrogance, and there was an extended stretch when he only spoke to his son while they were studying Talmud together. I thought such tales were limited to the fiction of Chaim Potok. Not so! He told me of the time—long after he had gone through yeshivah and become a rabbi himself—when he delivered some remarks at his daughter Serena's wedding. He encouraged her and her husband to direct their gaze to the future and to pay whatever debt they felt toward their parents forward. She and her husband could best honor their parents by caring for one another and their children. Joel's father was in attendance and subsequently pulled his only son aside to contest this message. What about the commandment to honor mother and father—a much more counterintuitive and challenging orientation! Yes, but the way he and his wife, Ann, wanted to be honored was for their children to give their attention to the life ahead of them, not the world behind them. On this and many other matters, Joel and his father would not see eye to eye.

My father grew up on the outskirts of Cleveland with a silver spoon in hand. His father had launched five lucrative companies, which afforded the family an opulent lifestyle. So, upon graduation from Williams College in 1931, when my father enrolled at Harvard Business School, he was well poised to build upon the family fortune. The stock market crash, however, dashed this dream and the family moved from one of the largest mansions in Shaker Heights into a two-bedroom apartment. My father witnessed a breakdown that hollowed out my grandfather's trust in the world. The trauma shattered my father's tolerance for risk. He settled into a long and stable career as a salesman for the Campbell Chain Company. He kept his head down, avoided gambles, and sidestepped conflict. In his early sixties, my father took early retirement, a move that was precipitated by the onslaught of Alzheimer's disease. So both Joel and I were given fathers with whom wrestling was required, and we each faced the task of sorting out the entanglements of their complex legacies.

When the opportunity arose to apply for the position of director of the ICJS, it was my turn to do a risk assessment and determine the feasibility of a drastic shift in my career. Naturally I sought Joel's counsel, and true to form he posed his first question: "Why in the world would you want to leave a job you love?"

"Well, this is a groundbreaking opportunity." Since Betsy and I had received the diagnosis of infertility, we had no concerns about paying for diapers and college tuitions. Indeed, had we been given a prophetic message that we would eventually become the parents of Ben, Hannah, and Sam, we would have joined Sarah in her laughter of disbelief (Gen 18:12). "Besides, I am up for a new adventure," I replied.

"And what about the long-term prospects?" He wanted me tethered to the ground and carefully weighing the options.

"Well, the organization plans to go out of business in three years. Once we demonstrate the importance of Jewish-Christian relations and convince denominational leaders to move this challenge from the back burner to the front, the ICJS will have done its work. The Christian community will take the baton and pursue the work on their own," I explained.

"Really? You think you can persuade Christian clergy, educators, and lay leaders to invest their time and energy and money in an examination of a problem they don't even know they have?" Joel queried. "And you expect them to welcome the disruption—especially when they discover the surgery to remove the cancer may prove life-threatening?"

"I do not think the challenge can be avoided. The integrity and credibility of my tradition are on the line," I shot back.

Joel was incredulous, not only because I was convinced anti-Judaism was an affliction that a fledgling educational organization (the ICJS) could confront and actually remedy, but because I was seriously considering a job with a very limited future. It was not exactly the kind of move my own father would have recommended—and deep down I had my own doubts. He pressed me to assess my underlying motivations, and I shared two formative experiences.

Shortly after I arrived at the Gilman School, I was required to meet with the personnel committee of the Baltimore Presbytery. They needed to assess the legitimacy of my ministry as the school chaplain and determine if they would accept the transfer of my membership from the Pittsburgh to the Baltimore Presbytery. I took my seat at a large conference table to face a contingent of five senior ministers and the executive presbyter. One of the interrogators was a cantankerous man endowed with an excess of confidence. The words he spoke I will never forget: "It is my understanding that the Christian presence at the Gilman School has been diluted by the influx of Jews."

I was indignant and shot back, "If the Christian presence is so fragile it cannot withstand the presence of the Jewish people, then it is a faith that deserves to be shattered."

For many years I congratulated myself for biting his head off, because I normally fail to hit upon a blistering comeback until hours later in the grip of nocturnal brooding. While I have no doubt that this officious character was discharging a deeply engrained prejudice, I now think that I could have and should have been more generous in my response. At the time, the incident struck me as the outburst of a bigot who had rarely ventured beyond his barracks. What I failed to appreciate was that his attitude was widely shared and reflected the conventional conviction that Jews posed a serious threat. I had written him off and hastily concluded this was a man impossible to educate or redeem—a supposition that needed more extensive testing. And this was precisely the kind of judgment I would need to temper if the educational enterprise I was soon to embrace was to hold any promise.

The second experience was more profound and redirected the trajectory of my career. My wife and I had barely unpacked our bags at the Gilman School when the headmaster instructed me to meet with a trustee named Charles Obrecht, who—as I have already noted—turned out to be the visionary who would later become the principal founder of the ICJS. He wanted us to discuss the work of the Human Relations Committee. This group arose in response to a series of antisemitic incidents and was composed of students, faculty, trustees, and parents. The mission was to design programs that would confront the prejudices embedded in our society and to implement learning that would inoculate the school community against all manner of bigotry. In keeping with a practice he repeated over the next forty years, Charlie came to the table with an audacious idea. He wanted to see the Human Relations Committee develop an initiative to explore the Holocaust, and he dreamed of a comprehensive inquiry that would include upper school students and their parents, the trustees, as well as the faculty.

The year was 1978, and the "incident" at the Three Mile Island Nuclear Generating Station loomed just over the Pennsylvania border. The Soviets had invaded Afghanistan; the hostage crisis in Iran presaged a new era of global conflict. In those days, a gallon of gasoline had climbed to eighty-six cents, fueled by shortages and uncertainty. Within the confines of our insular academy, I had no idea that this project would pose questions and present challenges the magnitude of which would reverberate for many years to come—in my life and the world around me.

The Human Relations Committee met over the course of the next several months, and we lined up scholars, selected films, and developed curricular resources. I became acutely aware of major gaps in my own education. The fact is I never encountered a single Jewish scholar or rabbi during my entire three years at Princeton Theological Seminary. While the school buzzed with lectures and programs featuring African, Middle Eastern, and Asian theologians and church leaders, the educational horizons of the seminary did not extend into the troublesome domain of interreligious encounters. Not one to allow ignorance or naïveté deter me from a project with such scope and ambition, I joined Charlie and embraced the Holocaust program with abandon. I was mightily unprepared for what was to come.

The keynote speaker, Dr. Franklin Littell, from Temple University in Philadelphia, was a scholar who played a catalytic role in establishing Holocaust studies as a field of urgent import. In his presentation to a packed auditorium, he argued the Shoah posed two credibility crises for us to examine. In the first place, we needed to reckon with the fact that German universities at the time could boast of unparalleled standing in the world. The most daring and innovative scholarship in virtually every academic field was blossoming within the German educational system. He challenged us to consider what it meant that its universities were cranking out "technically competent barbarians," highly qualified graduates who were willing to do anything as long as the price was right. He wondered if our own schools were doing any better today.

The second credibility crisis revolved around the fact that the genocidal assault on the Jewish people took place in the very heartland of Christendom. Baptized Christians designed and built, operated and maintained the death camps. The trains that ran flawlessly on schedule and delivered victims to their doom required the services of thousands of functionaries, almost all of them baptized in churches. Lawyers, doctors, and engineers weaned on the Christian catechism greased the machinery of mass murder. Had Christianity shown itself to be spiritually and ethically bankrupt? And lest we get smug, we might consider whether Christians today still harbor a contempt for Jews and Judaism, a contempt that renders them indifferent if not actively hostile to those regarded as other.

The symposium generated some of the most intense and searching interactions that I had yet experienced. Conversations and disputes spilled from the lunch room into the locker room. Telephone chatter and late-night bull sessions brought together students and faculty and parents, pulling them into inquiries and debates. Not all of the chatter proved creative or reassuring. Some parents and students wanted to know why we were singling out the Jews for special treatment. Hadn't indigenous peoples and other racial minorities also suffered from discrimination and persecution? What about women and poor people? Weren't we teaching Jews to regard everyone outside of their ethnic tribe as antisemites, while instructing Christians to disparage, if not altogether reject, their own heritage? One parent was convinced that Jews had orchestrated the program to bolster support for the State of Israel, evoking sympathy and military aid from Americans in response to the oil embargo and belligerent Arab neighbors.

This educational venture exposed troubling fault lines. During a viewing of Alain Resnais's film masterpiece, *Night and Fog*, which documented atrocities against the now-abandoned landscape of the Auschwitz and Majdanek concentration camps, two seniors sat next to each other as they had on many occasions. One was Jewish and one Christian, but neither thought this distinction counted for much. They shared aspirations of an Ivy League education and high hopes for the raucous prom fast approaching. While the spectacle of methodical murder flashed before their eyes, the Christian boy did what he often did if he could get away with it. He ate his lunch. When the lights came up, the Jewish boy poured his outrage onto his Christian classmate. "How could you eat your sandwich while watching dead bodies bulldozed into mass graves? Some could have been my relatives." The Christian fired back defensively, "If you Jews want to hold a pity party, that is fine. But don't force me to attend." They did not speak to one another for the remainder of the year—if ever.

Nothing in my education had equipped me to plumb the depths of the Shoah, either its historical antecedents, its theological underpinnings, or its aftermath. I was utterly unprepared to sift through and decipher the complex of feelings and thoughts the Holocaust raised for me and the larger school community. The disorientation forced me to reexamine my assumptions about the unalloyed achievements of Western civilization—and prompted me to begin eight years of study at Baltimore Hebrew University as well as a summer intensive at Yad Vashem in Jerusalem and course work at the Jewish Theological Seminary in New York.

Joel was well aware that my heart and mind were aligned with the mission of the ICJS, and he ended up encouraging me to apply for the position of founding director. Just as important, he made it clear that he would help me and the ICJS roll out its vision. He was keenly aware of the asymmetry of this enterprise and the incommensurate agendas that would bring Jews and Christians to the table. He wanted nothing to do with the bland exercise of sharing commonalities, the frivolous exchanges that elide difference and disagreement. He bristled at interfaith dialogues in which Jews and Christians narrate holiday customs and claim that deep down they are all the same. The assumption that Jews and Christians are interchangeable because they have overlapping ethical commitments struck him as frivolous. I can still hear the echo of his voice: "What an exercise in narcissism to look in the mirror and imagine the reflection is actually your neighbor!"

As we ruminated about the possibilities of a pioneering educational venture, he would occasionally remind me of an episode in my family history and take great delight in the ironic reversal embodied in my own vocational trajectory. A half-century ago, while crafting my application for seminary, I noticed an opportunity for prospective students to list relatives who were legacies. My mother combed through her genealogical records and found a potential ally, a Reverend Alexander Heberton, who had run the academic gauntlet and survived. I dared imagine that he would provide the key to unlock the door to my admission. So I joined in the research and learned that his most notable achievement seems to have been the fact that he had outlasted his peers, living until the ripe age of ninety-two, the oldest member of his presbytery. Although I was not confident that longevity would count as a virtue, I was poised to beef up my pedigree with this citation when my mother advised caution. On closer inspection, she discovered he had driven a mule team up the steps of Princeton University's Nassau Hall to contest an unspecified administrative policy. His protest did not achieve its intended result—he was tossed out of the seminary. The documentation does not specify how he managed to refurbish his tarnished image, nor did it mention the amount of labor needed to recondition the hallways. However, he did manage to pay his dues, gain readmittance, and graduate. The details of his subsequent ministry were murky, excepting one perplexing footnote. He was evidently involved with an organization entitled the American Society for Meliorating the Condition of the Jews.

I assumed that this organization was devoted to offering comfort and economic aid to Jewish immigrants who had recently escaped discrimination and persecution in Europe. Only later did I learn that this ministry targeted vulnerable Jewish arrivals for conversion. Instead of outreach that centered on the distribution of food and shelter, the Society handed out tracts and the promise of eternal life. This evangelical commission was no doubt an improvement over the abuse received on the other side of the pond, but clearly the assistance delivered to Jewish arrivals hinged on conversion and assimilation. The May edition of *The Occident and American Jewish Advocate*, which was published in 1843, issued the following response to the American Society's missionary activity:

> Our readers will see that the weapons are changed, but that our religion is nevertheless to be attacked. Flattery and money are to do what violence in old, and coarse rudeness in more modern times, failed to accomplish . . . Of one thing our Jewish friends may rest assured, that if money can purchase souls, they will be dearly paid for; because we see that there is a false species of philanthropy spreading over the land, which is anxious to catch every straggler and to take away any wandering sheep that has missed our fold. As far as we are concerned we regard as inimical every one who comes to deprive us of our religion.[1]

With Joel's nudging, I often found myself pondering my ancestor's legacy, and I continue to wonder what my forefather would have made of my ministry. I suspect he would find little solace in the fact that so much of my life has revolved around the Jewish community. While he strove to bring Jews to the Christian faith, I have endeavored to convince and inspire Jews to reclaim and deepen their connections to the Jewish tradition. Perhaps he tosses in his grave, contemplating the bitter irony that his own flesh and blood is undoing the achievements of his generation and those who came before him.

1. "American Society," http://www.theoccident.com/Occident/volume1/may1843/meliorate2.html.

Curiously, I found peculiar solace in a midrash about Moses that some rabbinic colleagues brought to my attention. I was reminded that Moses did not depart from Egypt and cross the sea until he had first retrieved the bones of the patriarch Joseph (Exod 13:19). Joseph had demanded assurances from his children that his body would be returned to the land of his ancestors rather than remain entombed in a foreign land. According to Jewish lore, Moses not only fulfilled the promise made several hundred years before, he also recognized that there was no way to chart a path into the future without carrying the remains of his ancestor. Without a living and active memory, Moses realized his community would be doomed to endless wandering in the wilderness. The promised land could only be reached with a deep understanding of the condition from which they had escaped.

But there is more to this act of retrieval. In digging up and transporting Joseph's bones, Moses signals a bold act of rejection. By recovering and relocating the mortal remains of a patriarch who had become an Egyptian administrator—a powerful overseer whose function was to amass power and wealth—Moses symbolically rejected the project of cultural assimilation that Joseph had embodied. In other words, he honored his ancestry in the very act of repudiating values and a lifestyle that made Joseph a notable success.

I have yet to visit the graveyard and dig up my ancestor's bones, but I do bear his memory. I cannot discard his remains even though I labor to repudiate his missionary legacy. I have come to believe that this is what it means to belong to a family and to embrace a tradition. The good, the bad, and the ugly are entangled, and the task is to identify and live into the best while resisting the proclivities to reenact the worst. A tradition is alive insofar as the demand to preserve the past does not rule out the imperative for change.

I suppose Reverend Heberton and I would need to learn how to enter into a sacred argument if we were to maintain civility. At this point it is not clear how we could sit at the same table without engaging in mortal combat. I often wonder what it would take for me to convince my ancestor that the ministry I chose, and the changes I continue to advocate, are a timely and fitting response to our fraught circumstances. Might my experiences and discoveries, my friendships and feuds, convince him to reorient his own reading of the scriptures and his own understanding of the Christian faith? It is difficult for me to imagine that he could maintain his dogmatic certitude—the conviction that God will only grant eternal life to those who proclaim Jesus as their Lord and Savior—if he had the opportunity to spend time with Joel Zaiman and my other rabbinic colleagues. This was the challenge that haunted me as I began my work at the ICJS.

Chapter 3

Shaking the Foundations

The ICJS office was perched on the third floor of the parish house at Brown Memorial Church in Bolton Hill, an urban neighborhood notable for its grand mid-to-late-nineteenth-century townhouses in the middle of Baltimore. With Meyerhoff Symphony Hall and the Maryland Institute College of Art on one side and the squalor of urban slums only a stone's throw in the other direction, our headquarters straddled Baltimore's extremes. My first order of business was to outfit the office, a task performed with the acquisition of an ensemble of furniture from a bankrupt eatery by the name of Chicken George. For a total of $471, I decked out our base of operations with furnishings rich in the aroma of french fries. I have little doubt I made my Scottish Presbyterian ancestors—as well as Charlie Obrecht—very proud.

There were no blueprints or manuals to guide me, and the job of contesting and transforming the dogmatic certainties of clergy and their congregations offered the stuff out of which sleepless nights are made. I began by knocking on the doors of ministers, priests, and rabbis. I did my best to gauge their interests and needs, and I was not particularly surprised to learn that each Christian denomination had its own peculiar organizational structure and its own approach to education. I also found a conspicuous divide between the governing concerns of Christians and Jews.

Virtually every rabbi with whom I met—and they ran the gamut from Reform and Reconstructionist to Conservative and Modern Orthodox[1]— expressed support for an organization with the mission to trace the roots

---

1. Traditional Orthodox rabbis discouraged fellow Jews from entering into theological dialogue with Christians, although there were a number of exceptional Orthodox scholars who have contributed significantly to the field.

of antisemitism and to take steps to weed out the distortions planted deep within the Christian tradition. The hope was that the ICJS would (1) confront prejudices and dismantle stereotypes that continued to imperil the Jewish community; (2) counter evangelical Christian efforts to proselytize among the most vulnerable members of the Jewish community, namely, students, recent immigrants, and the unaffiliated; and (3) provide a more balanced and nuanced portrait of the State of Israel. The Jewish posture was understandable and took the form of a defensive crouch.

At the conclusion of each meeting, I would ask my male and female colleagues in the rabbinate if they could imagine any constructive spiritual or theological contributions coming out of their encounter with Christians. Was there anything of religious significance for Jews to learn from their Christian counterparts? My query was met with incredulity, if not indignation. Again and again, I was told Christianity rests on the bedrock of Judaism. The Jewish tradition and its adherents have no reciprocal need for Christianity. Who could deny the asymmetrical conditions, the unbalanced burden of guilt and responsibility, and lopsided vulnerability of a minority among an uninformed and indifferent majority? The rabbis were more than willing to help Christians disinfect their mess, but more often than not I felt like the proverbial canoeist headed upstream without a paddle. I became accustomed to what Ogden Nash called "a one-way conversation on a two-way street."

The early forays into the Christian community were also fraught and called for careful strategic planning. Charlie Obrecht and I approached one denominational head after another with an unconventional and unsolicited proposal. Fortunately, Charlie could charm birds from their comfortable perches, and the ease with which he connected with others and garnered trust made him an indispensable ally in our recruitment efforts. Rather than move directly into an interfaith conversation, I was convinced Christians needed to do a good bit of homework before coming to the table with their Jewish neighbors and colleagues. As Edward Flannery—a Catholic priest who was the first director of Catholic-Jewish Relations for the US Bishops' Committee for Ecumenical and Interreligious Affairs—famously observed, Jews know best the pages of Christian history that Christians have frequently torn out. Without firmer footing in the complex and twisted saga of the Christian-Jewish encounter, there was little chance of productive and respectful engagement.

When we approached judicatory heads and denominational leaders in the region, we asked if their communities would participate in an endeavor we called the Maryland Interfaith Project. In 1987, Islam was lamentably not even on our radar screens. The request Charlie and I put on the table was brazen: we asked each denomination to select ten to twenty of their most talented and inquisitive ministers, priests, educators, and/or lay leaders to join in a three-year study initiative. Participants would meet once a month and grapple with demanding assignments. The course was designed (1) to explore the multiple factors that led Christians and Jews to part ways, (2) to survey scrupulously the ensuing history, and (3) to consider pressing theological problems confronting Christians in a religiously plural world. Not only did the credibility of Christians require us to face the legacy of the Shoah, but we needed to contend with the ways religion continues to polarize people around the world and foment bloody conflict. To our astonishment, ten different denominational groups along with a coalition of African American clergy and educators signed on to the project—and these participants tackled the readings and attended faithfully from start to finish.

At the outset, we drew upon the "Dialogue Principles" formulated by Professor Leonard Swidler.[2] These ground rules delineate the terms for respectful and honest learning among peoples who see the world quite differently. Participants are exhorted to set aside their preconceptions and develop a healthy aptitude for self-critical engagement. They are to abide by the principle that dialogue can take place only between equals and can only take place on the basis of mutual trust.

When the Maryland Interfaith Project was launched, each group reviewed the "Dialogue Decalogue" and participants agreed to operate in accord with the guidelines at least while we were in session. I insisted that we were not in the business of converting anyone, and any effort to demonstrate the inadequacies of another tradition was out of line. On those occasions when we invited rabbinic colleagues to join in group discussions, I did not want my zealous Christian brethren to evangelize our guests, and I did not want them subjected to polemical interrogations. I saw myself as a guardian warding off embarrassment and protecting our Jewish visitors from cringeworthy inquisitions.

In retrospect, I do not think that it was realistic to expect people to come to the table as practitioners of Swidler's rules, or even to agree with these guidelines as a necessary passport to gain entry. In many respects, the dialogue principles now strike me as conclusions that many participants reach only after they have been involved in searching and sustained interreligious encounters. I also discovered quickly that my rabbinic colleagues

---

2. Swidler was Professor of Catholic Thought and Interreligious Dialogue at Temple University, and author of several brilliant books. For a full version of these principles, which were originally called the "Dialogue Decalogue," see Swidler, "Dialogue Principles," https://dialogueinstitute.org/dialogue-principles.

did not need me to protect them. They were quite capable of fending off Christians who insisted Judaism is incomplete without Christ.

On one occasion, I welcomed a rabbi to a discussion group. He was reflecting on Jewish responses to the Shoah when one of the Christian members interrupted with the suggestion that Jews had been swept into a deadly whirlwind and needed the theological reassurances that came from the love of God made known in Jesus Christ. My rabbinic colleague responded calmly and firmly: "You must excuse me and my fellow Jews if we are less than enthusiastic about your analysis of our need. What you consider a generous invitation strikes many of us as an offensive demand—indicative of either ignorance or contempt."

Had all of us abided by the dialogue principles, we might have avoided a very awkward and upsetting moment. Yet this discomfort was profoundly instructive and prompted everyone around the table to pause and reconsider the assumptions with which each of us operated. The occasion was one of many that led me to believe that embarrassment is the gateway through which the interfaith conversation must pass. There are few better settings in which we are brought face-to-face with our own cluelessness—our limitations and our shortcomings. As Thomas Merton wisely stated, "If I insist on giving you my truth, and never stop to receive your truth in return, there can be no truth between us."[3] Most of us have to learn the veracity of this maxim the hard way, stumbling and bumbling and tumbling into the realization that we do not know nearly as much as we imagine.

Many remarkable exchanges took place over the course of these three years. There were, for example, a number of individuals in the Southern Baptist study group who were profoundly disoriented by the inquiry. One fellow, named Homer, announced that he dreaded each session. He knew something disruptive was going to occur, and yet he described himself as a moth who anticipated the burn but could not resist the light. He was close to retirement age and wore the expression of someone who was more accustomed to giving advice than receiving it. Yet without fail he drove three hours for every meeting. He came time and again because we were drilling into the foundations of his faith every time we picked up the Good Book. For him, the Bible was absolute bedrock. So, what was he to make of texts that seemed to authorize the denigration of Jews?

A case in point: how can we remove the polemical venom in numerous passages in the Gospel of John? In an address directed at "the Jews," Jesus asks and then caustically answers his own question: "Why do you not understand what I say? It is because you cannot accept my word. You are from

---

3. Merton, *Collected Poems*, 383.

your father the devil, and you choose to do your father's desires. He was a murderer from the beginning and does not stand in the truth, because there is no truth in him. When he lies, he speaks according to his nature, for he is a liar and the father of lies" (John 8:44).

There are various tactics that more liberal-minded Christians use to soften if not neutralize the vitriol of such passages. They are quick to point out that this kind of rhetoric is commonplace among prophets who accuse their people of idolatry and moral decadence. Jesus is simply revealing his bona fides as a Jew speaking in a manner his compatriots could understand. The hyperbole reflects a rhetorical practice that strikes modern readers as harsh, but the imprecations would not have been alien to Jewish ears. Or, so the argument goes.

Others suggest that we should attribute this verbal assault to the author of the Gospel, not Jesus. The exchange reflects the strife felt by the followers of Jesus. They were no longer welcome in the synagogue, and they drew upon the overheated language of an apocalyptic crisis to account for their rejection. Jesus would not have deployed generic categories and directed sweeping assaults at a group to which he himself belonged, namely, "the Jews."

Still others insisted that Jesus was addressing a particular gathering of Jews, not all Jews—not Jews from different lands or Jews from different times. We rehearsed these and other hermeneutical tactics that aim to temper the verbal rancor. Yet none of these literary and historical approaches offered Homer much satisfaction. The question of the Bible's inerrancy suddenly put him in an existential bind. "What if the Bible harbors a profoundly mistaken notion? What if Jesus and by extension the Gospel are responsible for planting the seeds of hate?" Homer insisted this was not just an academic problem, but an earthshaking quandary for him.

Our inquiries not only stretched our historical horizons, but evoked soul-searching conversations about ordinary liturgical practices easily overlooked. Why, asked Roman Catholic and Episcopal participants, do we sit for the readings from the Old Testament, but stand for the Gospel lesson? How do the lectionary readings shape our understanding of the relationship between the Old Testament and the New? Is the logic of a Christian faith that renders the Jewish tradition obsolete and nugatory etched into the weekly juxtaposition of lessons from the Old and New?[4] Does the pairing of Old and New lead Christians to disparage Jews because they apparently are unable to recognize that what is promised in the Old finds its fulfillment in

---

4. See Heb 8:13.

the New? The lectionary readings around Christmas and Easter struck one and all as especially problematic.

In a report to the ICJS board, Carl Edwards, a priest and leader of the Episcopal study group, and Bob Albright, priest and member of the Roman Catholic study group, described our inquiries into treasured hymns that Christians sing. One of the most beloved carols, sung during Advent, is "O Come, O Come Emmanuel," which has roots stretching back as far as the 1500s. It is difficult to convey the power of this plaintive melody, its atmospheric authority to orient Christians to the mystery of an astonishing birth. One of my earliest memories situates my father next to me in church, and his tenor voice flowing into the communal harmony. This was the hymn that he chanted in the shower and hummed while doing the dinner dishes— it heralded the approach of Christmas. Small wonder that it remains one of my favorite carols. A great many Christians share my attachment. Yet the lyrics enshrine a troubling message. Carl and Bob invited the assembled ICJS board to brood on the meaning of the words.

> O come, O come, Emmanuel,
> And ransom captive Israel,
> That mourns in lonely exile here,
> Until the Son of God appear.
> Rejoice! Rejoice! Emmanuel
> Shall come to thee, O Israel.
> O come, Thou Rod of Jesse, free
> Thine own from Satan's tyranny;
> From depths of hell Thy people save,
> And give them victory o'er the grave.
> Rejoice! Rejoice! Emmanuel
> Shall come to thee, O Israel.

For the next thirty minutes, the board reckoned with the perception of the Jewish people and Judaism conveyed by these lyrics. The hymn disclosed a message that Jews have no hope of salvation apart from the arrival and intervention of Jesus Christ, whom Christians proclaim as the Son of God. It was shocking for the Christian members of the board to consider that this music might immortalize a supersessionist worldview.

Was there a different and more positive way of interpreting the words of this Advent carol? Could Israel be understood as a metaphor for all of humanity? Could the hymn announce that it is not just the Jews who stand in need of rescue, but the entire world? Or does the redefinition of Israel in these more inclusive terms simply incorporate the Jewish people into a

Christian narrative—a reframing and universalizing of language that ensures the Jews are lost in translation?

The conversation was searching and demanding, but the impact of the discussion did not fully register until one of the Jewish members of the board asked if we would sing the hymn to help him appreciate the conundrum. The suggestion was unexpected, bold, and potentially fraught—especially coming from an Orthodox Jewish lawyer! So, from one corner of the room, Bishop Frank Murphy gave us a note, and then the room filled with song. Some of the Jews who had attended elite Christian schools knew the tune well and added their voices to the chorus. The entire assembly was reminded—or first discovered—the soaring power of the tune, tapping feelings somewhere deep within, usually unquestioned. A musical talent that had never been known or expressed in this group gave rise to an elegant performance that threw everyone off kilter.

The Jews in the room felt the majestic intensity of the music, the elemental longing in the melody. The Christians recognized that their Jewish neighbors were squeezed into a narrative plot that authorized attitudes of condescension and disrespect. In each other's company we experienced both the dissonance and the grandeur. The Jews understood the distress, if not the implausibility, of simply hitting the delete button. The Christians grasped the problem of anti-Judaism, which is deeply embedded in the tradition and resides even in the midst of its most sublime oeuvres. The challenge involved complexities that went well beyond rearranging the living room furniture. Change that honors the blessings of the past while simultaneously contending with its curses requires structural adjustments and repairs, a rigorous inspection and a radical modification of the very foundations on which we Christians rest.

During the coming months, the ICJS board heard reports from other Christian study groups, and they discovered the magnitude of the challenge extended farther and deeper than Christian hymnody. For instance, there were learned pastors comprising the Lutheran study group with a vast knowledge of history, theology, and Bible. At the outset of our investigations, these pastors were vaguely aware that Martin Luther had some nasty things to say about Jews. They knew and had studied with Bible scholars and historians of the Reformation who had noted how Luther's anti-Jewish legacy became deeply entrenched in polemics that highlighted the distinction between the deadening power of "the Law" and the liberating grace of "the Gospel," but his rants in the 1543 treatise entitled *The Jews and Their Lies* evoked shock and outrage—and demanded a forceful rebuttal.

First to set fire to their synagogues or schools and to bury and cover with dirt whatever will not burn, so that no man will ever again see a stone or cinder of them. This is to be done in honor of our Lord and of Christendom, so that God might see that we are Christians, and do not condone or knowingly tolerate such public lying, cursing, and blaspheming of his Son and of his Christians. . . .

Second, I advise that their houses also be razed and destroyed. For they pursue in them the same aims as in their synagogues. Instead they might be lodged under a roof or in a barn, like the gypsies. This will bring home to them that they are not masters in our country, as they boast, but that they are living in exile and in captivity, as they incessantly wail and lament about us before God.

Third, I advise that all their prayer books and talmudic writings, in which such idolatry, lies, cursing and blasphemy are taught, be taken from them.

Fourth, I advise that their rabbis be forbidden to teach henceforth on pain of loss of life and limb. . . .

Fifth, I advise that safe-conduct on the highways be abolished completely for the Jews. For they have no business in the countryside, since they are not lords, officials, tradesmen, or the like. Let them stay at home. . . .

Sixth, I advise that usury be prohibited to them, and that all cash and treasure of silver and gold be taken from them and put aside for safekeeping. The reason for such a measure is that, as said above, they have no other means of earning a livelihood than usury, and by it they have stolen and robbed from us all they possess. . . .

Seventh, I commend putting a flail, an ax, a hoe, a spade, a distaff, or a spindle into the hands of young, strong Jews and Jewesses and letting them earn their bread in the sweat of their brow, as was imposed on the children of Adam (Gen 3:19). For it is not fitting that they should let us accursed Goyim toil in the sweat of our faces while they, the holy people, idle away their time behind the stove, feasting and farting, and on top of all, boasting blasphemously of their lordship over the Christians by means of our sweat. No, one should toss out these lazy rogues by the seat of their pants.[5]

---

5. Luther, *On the Jews and Their Lies*, part 11, quoted fron https://www.jewishvirtuallibrary.org/martin-luther-quot-the-jews-and-their-lies-quot.

Although the road to Auschwitz is long and twisted, Luther's polemical assault provided a playbook that to a disturbing degree informed Nazi policies and practices. When placed within its historical context, Luther's rage was directed first and foremost against the Roman Catholic establishment. The Jews were the indispensable trope in Luther's assault and gave incendiary fuel to his indictments. According to his accounting, both the Roman Catholic Church and the Jews mirrored one another's failings. Both were trapped within legalistic systems that blinded them to the divine blessings given as an expression of God's unconditional love. The failure shared by Jews and Roman Catholics stemmed from an inability to recognize that God's grace is not earned by works. In both cases, "false teachers" had drained the scriptures of its spirit and subjected followers to the "killing letter" of a corrupted tradition. These judgments were loaded with metaphysical significance, for Luther imagined that both groups were careening into the eternal flames of the underworld.

While the Lutheran study group was busy scrutinizing and then agonizing over Luther's anti-Judaism, the Roman Catholic study group was investigating Rome's indictments of the Reformation. Protestantism was historically seen at its core as a Jewish heresy. Its critique of the tradition and its reliance on the Hebrew scriptures, its evisceration of institutions, customs, and teachings central to Roman Catholic piety and authority—all were regarded as a return to the failings of Judaism.

The unsettling pattern became clear. Whenever Christians are pitted against one another and struggling to find bedrock that will resolve doubts about their identities, Jews are dragged into the middle and find themselves caught in the crossfire. They are the indispensable foils over and against which one Christian group exalts itself by means of defining and denouncing its opponents as a resurgent Jewish heresy. In the course of three years, the same point emerged time and time again: Christians cannot get clear on who they are, how they are to live, and what determines their ultimate destiny without reference to the Jews. Christians quite simply cannot leave Jews alone—and this constitutes an inescapable predicament for both.

This dynamic came into sharp focus for the Greek Orthodox study group when they encountered the collection of sermons delivered by St. John Chrysostom, "the golden-tongued" church father whose liturgical contributions and exegetical works remain celebrated, most especially among Eastern Orthodox Christians. The study group examined a series of eight homilies delivered in Antioch from 386 to 387 as chilling examples of *Adversus Judaeos* literature.

During this period, Antioch was a major metropolis bustling with competing religious cults and home to thriving Jewish communities.

Scholars such as Robert Louis Wilkens offer incisive portraits of the historical context, and they elucidate the rhetorical chops that any religious leader needed to display.[6] Preachers who dished out insipid homiletic platitudes were evidently pelted with rotten tomatoes, deluged with jeers, and drummed out of the pulpit. Chrysostom secured an unassailable reputation as a stellar orator, and he won the approval of the masses not only because of his rhetorical gifts but because he refused to indulge in the lavish festivities of the wealthy. He lived a simple life in solidarity with the common people, but he did not hesitate to rail against any whom he thought had compromised the integrity of his flock.

In the *Adversus Judaeos* sermons that our study group examined, Chrysostom deployed a rhetorical strategy known as *psogos*—an early form of trash talk that public orators were taught so that they could efficiently discredit and debase their opponents. To wage a successful linguistic assault, there were standard elements that students of rhetoric were taught to draw upon—a rhetorical storehouse teeming with stock insults. When precisely crafted and directed against one's rivals, the polemical offensive called into question the opponents' moral, intellectual, and religious integrity. The objective was to win support for one's own agenda by assassinating the opponent's character.

Chrysostom was a master of this art, and in this series of sermons he unleashed verbal assaults on his adversaries that subsequent generations of Christians would put to more insidious ends. Ostensibly, the target of this series of sermons was the Jewish people, and when heard against the backdrop of the Shoah, the virulence of his speech is harrowing. A sampling from his first discourse in 386 framed a challenge for the Greek Orthodox study group, most especially because this church father occupies a prominent place in the pantheon of saints.

> Part I (5) The festivals of the pitiful and miserable Jews are soon to march upon us one after the other and in quick succession: the feast of Trumpets, the feast of Tabernacles, the fasts. There are many in our ranks who say they think as we do. Yet some of these are going to watch the festivals and others will join the Jews in keeping their feasts and observing their fasts. I wish to drive this perverse custom from the church right now.
>
> Part II (1) Do not be surprised that I called the Jews pitiable. They really are pitiable and miserable. When so many blessings from heaven came into their hands, they thrust them aside and were at great pains to reject them.... From their childhood they

---

6. See Wilken, "Jews as the Christians Saw Them," and *John Chrysostom and the Jews*.

read the prophets, but they crucified him whom the prophets had foretold. . . . But see how thereafter the order was changed about: they became the dogs, and we became the children...

(5) But what is the source of this hardness? It comes from gluttony and drunkenness. Who says so? Moses himself: "Israel ate and was filled and the darling grew fat and frisky." When brute animals feed from a full manger, they grow plump and become more obstinate and hard to hold in check; they endure neither the yoke, the reins, nor the hand of the charioteer. Just so the Jewish people were driven by their drunkenness and plumpness to the ultimate evil; they kicked about, they failed to accept the yoke of Christ, nor did they pull the plow of his teaching...

(6) Although such beasts are unfit for work, they are fit for killing. And this is what happened to the Jews: while they were making themselves unfit for work, they grew fit for slaughter.

Part III (1) Where a harlot has set herself up, that place is a brothel. But the synagogue is not only a brothel and a theater; it also is a den of robbers and a lodging for wild beasts.

Part VI (4) The Jews practice a deceit which is more dangerous (than the pagans). In their synagogue stands an invisible altar of deceit on which they sacrifice not sheep and calves but the souls of men.[7]

Chrysostom's depiction of the Jews offered a horrifying litany of imagined crimes that would seem to demand swift and harsh punishment. Yet there is no evidence that his congregation took violent action against the Jews of Antioch. Indeed, the Jews of Antioch in this period continued to thrive. Perhaps the reason that these homilies did not carry deadly repercussions is that the rhetoric was well understood as hyperbolic and wildly exaggerated. But more significantly, the audience understood that Chrysostom's opponents were actually not their Jewish neighbors, but members within or associated with their own congregation. These individuals were apparently attracted to Jewish practices and wanted to participate in rituals that were most likely woven into the ritual life of Jesus and his early Jewish followers.

What Chrysostom feared and intemperately denounced was a resurgence of Jewish customs amongst his own congregants! As the High Holy Days approached and opportunities to attend synagogue services abounded, Chrysostom went on the attack. But his real opponents and the true threat to his own community came from Judaizing followers of Jesus, not the actual

---

7. John Chrysostom, *Eight Homilies against the Jews*, Homily 1, https://en.wikisource.org/wiki/Eight_Homilies_Against_the_Jews.

Jews of Antioch. Once again, we see the construction of the imaginary Jew who is thrust into the middle of an intra-Christian battle being waged between adversaries struggling for domination within the church.

While members of the Greek Orthodox study group took some solace from our efforts to appreciate the historical and literary context of John Chrysostom's world, there was also the disturbing recognition that a text can live many lives. The words of one generation can be dug up and repurposed in ways the original authors could not have dreamed possible. The church fathers laid a foundation on which classical Christian traditions were built, but the seeds of contempt were cemented into the edifice, wittingly or unwittingly. This is the legacy that presented participants in the Maryland Interfaith Project with an inescapable burden. We began to reckon with the habit of dragging the Jewish people and Judaism into the middle of the internecine struggles among Christians, a practice that echoes down the corridors of Western history into our own time.

Of course, there were those who maintained they were not complicit in either creating or perpetuating anti-Jewish prejudices. For good reason, many in the African American study group reframed the challenge and concluded that the problem was at its core an issue for white Christians to sort out. I remember my efforts to recruit Curtis, a highly respected African American minister within the Presbytery of Baltimore. He had serious doubts about the entire enterprise, because he suspected our inquiry would deflect attention away from more urgent obstacles besetting urban America. The task of tracing the roots of antisemitism and recalibrating the relationship between Christians and Jews struck him as little more than a white middle-class pastime, an academic exercise with minimal relevance to the plight of Black and Brown communities.

"How might this intensive investigation help my congregation understand and respond to a broken justice system, or help address the scourge of drug addictions, or counter the inequities built into Maryland's public and independent education? What relevance does this study have for a community with a high rate of teenage pregnancies and single-parent households, and what impact will this initiative have in confronting the pervasive poverty and unemployment that is dismantling hope? Tell me how this educational venture will make a difference in the life of my community," Curtis asked me.

His questions were repeated by other African American pastors, and required answers that could not be developed without an immersion in the struggle for racial justice. There was an understandable resistance to solutions offered from a white man on an academic pedestal. Once again, I was reminded of my parochial background, and I did my best to wiggle out of my blinkered condition with three defensive responses. First, I was unwilling to accept the assessment that African Americans had escaped the pathological grip of anti-Judaism. They did, after all, read the New Testament and could hardly avoid the stereotypes enshrined in the Good Book. In the second place, I suspected resistance to our inquiry involved a dysfunctional rivalry between traumatized communities. Both understood themselves as victimized by the dominant culture, and efforts to lift up the suffering of one group seemed to eclipse the pain of the other. As I heard on a good many occasions, African Americans were worn ragged with accounts of the Holocaust in Europe while their own country had failed to recognize and come to terms with the enduring consequences of slavery and the depravations of Jim Crow. Finally, I maintained that the refusal to participate was rooted in a failure to recognize the larger web of hatred, the intersections that bound discriminated groups together.[8] I believed that contempt for one community sooner or later redounded on the other. The destinies of Jews and Blacks here and around the world are interwoven.

While there were elements within my defensive retort that merit further consideration, I needed to get outside my academic enclave and greatly expand the circle of white Christians and Jews that had claimed my undivided attention. The complexities turned out to be far more tangled and intractable than I appreciated. Among these conundrums, the issue emerged: do Jews fit within the rubric of being "white"?[9] Many Jews, based on their own experience and their communal history, saw themselves as racially defined and marginalized. Yet the road to assimilation and "passing" as members of the white majority remained open—thereby raising key questions about the categories used in America to ground ethnic, racial, and religious identity. As will become evident, the circle of participants needed expansion and a large dose of disruptive education.

As the project unfolded, I often wondered how much adrenalin was required to instigate change—and whether an even larger quantity was required to resist it. For some of us, the investigation into the origins of anti-Judaism turned the world inside out and flipped everything about the Christian tradition upside down. The earth started to shake beneath our feet, and the rotation of a familiar world spun out of control. On occasion there were those among us who felt they had been sucker punched by historical forces they never knew were lurking just beneath the surface.

---

8. This intersection is examined in great detail in Teter, *Christian Supremacy*.

9. It is important to note that there are Blacks in America who are Jews, and Jews from Africa and beyond who would not fit into the category of "white."

What if the claims of the gospel are inseparable from the repudiation and denigration of Judaism? What if the proclamation that Jesus is Lord is inextricably bound to the declaration, "And the Jews be damned!" Indeed, what if the reach of the problem extends into nearly every corner of our culture? The magnitude of the challenge is difficult to exaggerate—at least for a good many of us. For the first time in the lives of many Christians, participants at the ICJS began to reckon with the verdict David Nirenberg articulated: "Anti-Judaism should not be understood as some archaic or irrational closet in the vast edifice of Western thought. It was rather one of the basic tools with which that edifice was constructed."[10]

---

10. Nirenberg, *Anti-Judaism*, 6. To appreciate both the depth and breadth of anti-semitism, also see Teter, *Christian Supremacy* and *Blood Libel*.

Chapter 4

Leaving Home

As the ICJS was getting its bearing, Dr. John Gager came to Baltimore to deliver a lecture, and he framed a challenge of pivotal importance. As the author of a pioneering book, *The Origins of Anti-Semitism*, and long-standing chair of the religion department at Princeton University, he gave an unsettling specificity to the work the ICJS had launched. He wondered, "Can a religious tradition think a new thought?" More precisely, "Can Christians break the habit of building their affirmations of faith on the negation of Judaism and the Jewish people? What will it take for Christians to face an anti-Jewish legacy, a legacy about which most Christians know little, have willfully ignored, and from which they have benefitted?"

Gager probably wondered if any of us would live long enough to see such a radical reformation. There are solid grounds for disillusionment when the challenge is placed within a wide-ranging historical context. Of course, Christians are not the only religious adherents who have provided a warrant to hold outsiders in contempt and to devise justifications for savage abuse. Nor is religion alone responsible for the bloody rampages that continue to disfigure societies and, in the most extreme cases, foment genocide. Jews and Muslims, Hindus and Buddhists—to mention the most obvious contenders—are also susceptible to movements that fuse nationalism with religious zealotry and that join economic and political domination with mystical fanaticism.

The focus on anti-Judaism, however, was our starting place, because a faithful audit of the bigger question requires the dominant religious community in the United States to begin with an examination of itself before turning attention to the curses and blessings emanating from other traditions. For me and the founders of the ICJS, we needed to investigate the basement of the religious home that shaped the Christian imagination, that gifted us with its story and song, and that inspired its adherents to labor, risk, and hold fast to an extravagant promise of redemption. The failure to grapple with the excesses and shortcomings of the Christian tradition would render the possibility and promise of a more global inquiry empty. How could Christians ask others to dissect their own religious communities without first surgically cutting into their own?

As our earliest forays into the origins of anti-Judaism made clear, our investigations were not only intellectually demanding, but existentially charged—disruptive, disorienting, and also cathartic. The inescapable sense of dislocation involved a great deal more than the acquisition of new information and new methods of inquiry. Almost all Christian participants felt their foundational assumptions shaken. The upheaval rattled the heart as well as the head. When fully entered, the inquiry delivered us into what the Jewish writer Martin Buber called "the kingdom of holy insecurity."[1]

One of the most difficult challenges I faced was maintaining an empathetic appreciation of the dislocation, commotion, and disarray induced by the experience of seeing our own tradition through the eyes of our Jewish neighbors. We were asking participants to step onto the knife edge, and I needed to hold fast to memories of this kind of disruption. I was compelled to return to a time in my own life when the world was turned upside down and inside out. I also needed to contend with the fact that my parochial background did not make the leap into the ICJS either natural or easy.

I was born twelve miles down the Ohio River from Pittsburgh in an affluent suburb called Sewickley. In many ways it was an ideal community in which to grow up. The Presbyterian church to which our family belonged and the private school I attended were within easy walking distance, and almost every classmate was only a bike ride away. However bucolic and serene, our security came at an unacknowledged price. We were encircled by privilege, utterly oblivious to the plight of the urban decay upstream, including the ravaging demise of the steel industry. The African American population in our village was small, and Blacks were simply known as "the help." Our school was totally segregated excepting its two janitors. We had only one Roman Catholic in our class, and the rest of us were exclusively consigned to the Presbyterian and Episcopal tribes. The political culture was Republican and consistently monochromatic.

When I graduated from middle school, most of my classmates headed off to prestigious boarding schools. I followed in my brother's wake and

---

1. Buber, *Daniel*, 27.

shipped off to an Episcopal prep school called South Kent School with a total enrollment of 150 students. Nestled into the rolling hills of western Connecticut, I entered an academic setting defined by its monastic ideals. The school took pride in a countercultural ethos and embraced a lifestyle very much at odds with the fashions of the times. Other schools referred to us as "the farmers" and there was truth in this designation since we picked our own potatoes every fall. Students were charged with all manner of chores—cleaning toilets, washing dishes, raking leaves, shoveling snow, and sweeping floors twice a day. These labors were performed by underclassmen and supervised by seniors.

Simplicity was lifted up as a cornerstone virtue. There was no gymnasium and no auditorium. No radios or televisions. All sports were held outside. Everyone played ice hockey in the winter on the nearby lake. This bare-bones lifestyle enabled the administration to direct its funds into scholarship programs, and a surprisingly diverse student body was a powerful expression of its religious mission.

News of the world traveled slowly to our cloistered habitat, and the upheavals of the times rarely interrupted daily routines. But the winds of change were increasingly reaching our campus and presaged a gathering storm. A trickle of graduates returned on alumni days with horror stories of warfare in Vietnam and the military draft cast a heavy pall on our futures. Rioting at the Chicago Democratic Convention exposed a growing generational and political chasm. The Civil Rights Movement was on the march, but the tensions between those who advocated nonviolence and those who raised the specter of bloody confrontation heightened the sense that we were on the verge of an uprising. The assassinations of Martin Luther King Jr. and Bobby Kennedy struck us as a turning point, a pivot into war at home as well as abroad. The music of Jimi Hendrix, Jefferson Airplane, James Brown, and The Rolling Stones was drastically changing the cultural tempo, and we heard intoxicating rumors of a sexual revolution, which we worried would never reach our dormitories. We tried to keep time and find a rhythm in the noise.

During my final year at South Kent, I was assigned a roommate named Earl, a Black teenager who came from the streets of Harlem. The distance between his experience and mine was vast and uneasily bridged. We came to know one another gradually and cautiously, thanks in large measure to our placement in the same section of American History. This course increasingly prompted spirited conversations and opened the door to a vulnerability that took us by surprise.

The march through the American Revolution generated mild agitation, but Earl was apoplectic by the time we concluded the section on the

Civil War and the Reconstruction Era. He insisted we live in the shadow of this legacy, and he was outraged our history books managed to keep his people in the dark. We learned of great men and great battles, and there was not a Black face to be found. The song of American freedom that echoed in the pages of our anthology rang hollow and false. The rude truth Earl refused to let me sidestep was that my experience and education were leading me to regard significant sectors of the American population as people who are not players, people to whom nothing is due, people who in fact—when you come right down to it—don't really matter.

He claimed my schooling was a narcissistic exercise that revolved around an assortment of interlocking myths—stories of individuals who just happen to be white and who overcome all manner of obstacle through self-discipline and natural talent. He insistently claimed, quite to the contrary, that we do not simply invent or create ourselves. We are saddled with a past that is packed with curses as well as blessings, and the patrimony is unevenly distributed. We do not all carry the same load, and we do not all inherit the same possibilities for the future.

I did not like the picture Earl painted. He pushed me to reckon with the advantages that came from an unacknowledged birthright—my white skin. He argued I took for granted benefits that were obtained either by way of subtle or savage exploitation. I tried to shove back by arguing he was embracing a narrative that now served to elevate his moral status. My people were perpetrators of a massive crime while his own community was cast in the passive role of victims. Would this revised narrative lead him to go through life with the conviction that every white person owed him something? Was he conveniently absolving his community of the responsibility for the creation of a new and better reality? He pointed to the papers and the urban rioting. The year was 1968. Did I not see a relationship between the anger in the streets and the demands of justice?

Earl was routinely amazed by my inability to hold hallowed assumptions in check and loosen my grip on the comforts and certainties bequeathed to me. Remarkably, Earl did not give up on me, and he even believed I might someday come to my senses and surprise him.

Earl was one of my best and most important teachers. He convinced me that a genuine education begins when we are willing to go to uncomfortable places and when we learn to read and interpret the world through the eyes of the people whose experience is radically different from our own. Our relationship mattered to me, and because it mattered, I began to think and feel new and disruptive thoughts. Earl pushed me into an unexpected and not altogether welcome discovery: insight is a gift that comes when we are thrown off balance and when we subsequently realize that we have been flat-out wrong.

*

During my tenure at the ICJS, I needed to hold fast to this tempestuous memory and remember the necessary disruptions that factor into an education. Hard labor goes into the construction of a worldview, and a great deal of effort is required to maintain and bolster order, confidence, and conviction. And this was the experience I had over and over again: no sooner had I fashioned an ideological home that promised shelter, certainty, and security than I encountered a teaching or underwent an experience that exposed inadequacies etched into my assumptions. The new discovery subverted conclusions I had imagined were settled and trustworthy. There was exhilaration and adventure in reaching new heights and scanning open vistas; yet learning also entailed costs that strained the mind and taxed the heart. The humbling encounter with my own ignorance and the collision with my own mistakes were essential elements within the curriculum.

The thrill of victory and the agony of defeat were touted as basic to the wide world of sports, but they were also etched into philosophical and theological investigations. I needed to acknowledge and honor the pendular swing, the fear of losing control, and the terror of stepping into thin air because this leap into the unknown was what the ICJS was asking its participants to do. The venture suffused participants with a sacred discontent, a restlessness to break out of their familiar quarters and discover more spacious and hospitable dwellings. There was a danger in this educational enterprise, namely, that people would get lost in the dark message that our past was incurably mired in failure, that the legacies of our ancestors were morally culpable and incapable of rehabilitation, and that hope was nothing more than delusion.

A balanced education is exceptionally difficult to maintain when the task entails a reckoning with the deficiencies of the past as the obligatory gateway to a more just and life-affirming future. While the ICJS offered new treasure at the other end of the rainbow, our educational enterprise began with experiences that delivered a wrenching sense of loss. Who in their right mind wants to enter a battle that guarantees defeat—even with the hazy assurance that the collapse is only temporary? Who welcomes learning that induces heart-breaking grief? Without keeping the experience with my roommate Earl in mind, it was too easy to forget the perils as well as the elation of leaving home and entering uncharted territory. The ICJS offered an education that called for sacrifice, and I had great difficulty bearing this in mind when I found myself and the ICJS embroiled in an unexpected controversy with the Baltimore Declaration.

CHAPTER 5

The Baltimore Declaration

In the fall of 1990, I received an invitation from one of the parishioners of Old St. Paul's Church, who was alarmed to discover I was going to give a presentation at a large Baltimore synagogue, entitled, "Is the New Testament Antisemitic?" He wanted me to meet with his priest, Bill, in the hope that a diplomatic intervention would blunt the edges of a presentation that promised to inflame negative attitudes about Christianity before a Jewish audience.

Bill's home office was nestled into a bucolic setting at the edge of Roland Park in northern Baltimore. His office was tastefully appointed and bore all the vestiges of a highly cultured and affluent cleric. His manner was smooth and refined, dignified and reserved. He assumed a lofty perch, initially revealing little about his own views on this delicate subject.

I noted that the title of my presentation would no doubt raise eyebrows among members of his congregation, but the relationship between the New Testament and antisemitism was not a new or shocking subject for the overwhelming majority of Jews. Indeed, I had lifted the title for my presentation from a book by the Jewish scholar Dr. Samuel Sandmel, a work composed some years earlier. Bill expressed concern I might exacerbate anxieties among my Jewish listeners, deepen distrust, and further alienate the Jewish community from its Christian neighbors. He probed deeper to determine just what manner of Christian I claimed to be. Was I a prosecutor or defender of the gospel?

I tried to assure him that the debates about the origins of anti-Judaism within the New Testament were contested among scholars, and I was still trying to understand how this ancient antipathy took hold. However, beyond any doubt, there was this simple fact: the New Testament had frequently been deployed as a menacing weapon. When a sacred text frequently resides in close proximity to violence, aren't we obliged to assess its meaning and develop new understandings? Doesn't a text acquire a negative charge; doesn't it take on new properties when it is found time and again near the scene of the crime? It is difficult to hold a hammer the same way after it has been used repeatedly as a bludgeon. He listened with cards held closely to the chest, and I suspect that he had decided by the end of our conversation that when the world is separated into two categories—friends and foes, sheep and goats—I would be assigned a seat among the damned.

Beneath his composed demeanor lurked a conglomeration of anxieties, frustrations, and resentments that deserved a fuller airing. If he had given a full-throated broadcast of his unease, I suspect he could have mounted an important argument. I can easily imagine him exclaiming: "You are tearing down the Christian tradition when you falsely claim to be building it up. You are undermining confidence in a religious tradition upon which the American way of life is built and continues to depend. In highlighting the Christian teachings of contempt for Jews, you are teaching Christians to disparage and reject their own ancestry, their own faith, their very selves. You are also reinforcing suspicions and encouraging the Jewish community to keep its distance. This work is destructive, and your demolition project leaves the glories of the Christian past in ruins. Whether you admit it or not, you have played into the hands of cultural despisers and are greasing the slide into a secular society. The cynics will unseat the saints in your kingdom. What Christian institution will remain standing when your work is done? Frankly, there is something suicidal in a critical onslaught that undermines religious authority and shatters trust in the very moral and theological teachings that for generations bound Christians together in a community of faith. The opinions that you are spreading are a betrayal of the truth revealed to us in Jesus Christ."

I may be attributing greater precision to his indignation than this Episcopal priest deserves, but many of the apprehensions that fuel this kind of denunciation became apparent with the publication of a document known as "the Baltimore Declaration," issued in May of 1991—several months after my visit—and signed by six Episcopal priests from the Diocese of Maryland, including the Reverend William (Bill) McKeachie.

They challenged clergy and lay leaders to reaffirm in unambiguous language the essentials of doctrinal orthodoxy and to repudiate the false teachings infiltrating and corrupting congregations.[1]

---

1. At the 207th annual convention of the Diocese of Maryland, a resolution was submitted to "Reaffirm Our Orthodox Christian Faith" for the next General Assembling in Phoenix in July 1991. The proposal sought to "reaffirm our faith in Jesus Christ

According to his own account, Father Alvin Kimel received an urgent telephone call from his colleague, the Reverend Phil Roulette, who declared, "The Diocese of Maryland [at its annual convention] has denied our Lord . . . We must do something."[2] A resolution that called upon the diocese to affirm Jesus as the way, the truth, and the life had been submitted to the convention—and the majority of delegates had rejected the inclusion of this particular New Testament text. In protest, a monthly support group of Episcopal priests hammered out their declaration and sent it to all active bishops and priests within the Episcopal Church in America.

The Baltimore publication was modeled on the 1934 Barmen Declaration, which was adopted by a group of Protestants who risked their lives in opposition to the Nazi regime. The confessional document from Barmen was a denunciation of the German Christian movement, and it boldly protested ecclesial compromises that facilitated collaboration with the Nazi regime. Their refusal to cede the church's authority to the Nazi state put them on a collision course with an implacable and deadly foe.

The parallel between the plight of Maryland's Episcopalians and the life-and-death crisis of German Christians under the boot of the Nazis infused the Baltimore Declaration with a puffed-up grandiosity. However inflated the appeal, these priests gave voice to the fear that the integrity of their denomination was under siege. They were convinced that the church was collapsing under the pressure of liberal incursions and political correctness. Rather than fall under the spell of what Russell Reno calls "the three dogmas of modernity: inclusivity, relevance, and ambiguity"—their self-appointed mandate was to protect and preserve.[3] A few excerpts give expression to the gravity of their concerns.

> We repudiate the false teaching that Jesus Christ is only one revelation or manifestation of God, that there are other revelations and other experiences (political, ideological, cultural, or religious) to which we may look or must look to gain knowledge of the true God.

---

as the Son of God, that He is the Way, the Truth and the Life and no one comes to the Father except through Him." The proposal to accept the resolution was passed on the condition of a significant modification: a motion to eliminate the reference to "the Way, the Truth, and the Life" was approved by a vote of 139 to 102. This vote was the trigger that led to the Baltimore Declaration. Thanks to Mary Klein, the archivist at the Episcopal Diocese of Maryland, for tracking down the minutes from this Episcopal convention.

2. See Kimel, "Baltimore Declaration," https://afkimel.wordpress.com/2014/11/17/the-baltimore-declaration/.

3. See Gatta, review of *Reclaiming Faith*, 751.

We repudiate the false teaching that the salvation of humanity by the sovereign action and grace of God is unnecessary or that salvation may be ultimately found apart from the atoning death and resurrection of Jesus Christ. We repudiate the false teaching that Jesus is merely one savior among many – the savior of Christians but not of humankind.

We repudiate the false teaching that the Jews may be persecuted by Christians and we especially repudiate the repugnant and fallacious charge of "Christ-killers," which has been used by Christians down the centuries as an excuse for hatred, bigotry, and violence against the Jews. All anti-Semitism in thought, word, or deed is vicious and is to be decried and condemned by Christians. But we also repudiate the false teaching that eternal salvation is already given to the chosen people of Israel through the covenant of Abraham and Moses, independently of the crucified Christ, and the inference that the Gospel of Jesus the Messiah need not be proclaimed to them.

We repudiate the false teaching that the Old Testament is not to be interpreted in light of its messianic fulfillment in the person of Jesus Christ as witnessed in the New Testament, or that the Old and New Testaments stand hermeneutically, materially, and formally independent of each other.

This initiative called into question the leadership of Maryland's bishop, "Ted" Eastman, and sought to arrest the theological drift of the larger Episcopal community. In many respects the Baltimore Declaration mapped out the front lines of an embittered battle—a theological and ecclesiastical clash that would eventuate in the Anglican realignment. Here is a platform that would provide a scriptural and ecclesial bulwark against the election of the first gay bishop, Gene Robinson, and against the move to a more inclusive and less patriarchal establishment.

The storm provoked by the Baltimore Declaration revealed the complexities of change and the multitudinous forces that generate hardline divisions. The language of the Baltimore Declaration was disputatious and hyperbolic, splitting the larger community into factions and cutting off any detours around the conflict. You were either for or against. Lines were drawn so sharply that few dared to cross over, and the barriers grew increasingly twisted and barbed. If there was a blessing buried in the discord, the publication provoked important theological conversation not only in Episcopal circles, but also within the ranks of other Christian and Jewish groups. The condemnations at the heart of the Baltimore Declaration demanded a coherent and cogent response.

How are faithful Christians to understand the meaning of John 14:6, where the evangelist attributes the following words to Jesus: "I am the way, and the truth, and the life. No one comes to the Father except through me"? If a person affirms the unimpeachable authority of the New Testament, does this require a repudiation of other religious and secular traditions as sources of redemptive wisdom that accurately reveal the nature of the "true God"? Does adherence to the Christian scriptures require faithful Christians to proclaim "the Gospel of Jesus the Messiah" to Jews? Does the eternal salvation of the Jews depend upon "the crucified Christ" and their conversion to Christianity? Are the promises of Old Testament inseparable and dependent upon an understanding and acceptance of the teachings in the New Testament?

The authors of the Baltimore Declaration offered a template for the Christian life that remained resolutely aligned with "supersessionism," the theological claim that the church has replaced the synagogue as the covenantal locus of divine favor. Christianity has rendered Judaism obsolete at best, inimical to God's purposes at worst.

The writers strove to square the circle by denouncing antisemitism, but they continued to regard Judaism as essentially deficient and insisted upon the ongoing evangelization of the Jewish people. Judaism was treated as a failed religion because it is incapable on its own terms to deliver on the promise of salvation. The denial of the covenantal integrity of Judaism leaves intact biblical and theological (mis)understandings that have long sustained contempt for the Jewish people. By ignoring one of the most overlooked and dangerous taproots of antisemitism, the authors of the Baltimore Declaration unwittingly perpetuated the very prejudice they simultaneously decried.

The series of repudiations at the heart of this declaration exalt the church's exceptional status as the sole proprietor of the truth. As the defenders and guardians entrusted with "the deposit of faith," they occupy a position of privilege that enables them to call the errant to account. In retrospect, I suspect the sharp polemical edges might have been blunted had the authors—all well-established white men in positions of authority—involved a more representative cross section of the community. Yet consultations with other members of the larger Episcopal family as well as Jewish neighbors was unthinkable because the declaration was not interested in compromise or theological accommodation or ecclesial reconciliation between contentious factions. The anxieties dictated the drawing of sharp lines to distinguish the faithful from the reprobate, the pure from the culturally contaminated.

The Baltimore Declaration moved against the grain of liberal ideals that celebrate pluralism, the rights and autonomy of the individual, and the equality of one and all. Yet the primary thrust of its repudiations calls into question the substance and character of the Christian community. How are those Christians denounced in this declaration to respond to the charges of apostasy and betrayal? What are the scriptural and theological warrants to justify and secure a well-grounded and faithful alternative to the dogmatic stance represented in the Baltimore Declaration? Without new ways of reading and interpreting the church's sacred scriptures and contending with the supersessionist dispositions built into its foundations, the habit of defining Christian identity in adversarial relationship to the rest of the world would be impossible to break.

Efforts to neutralize a combative arrogance routinely circle back to John 14:6 and yield countervailing interpretations. Consider the exposition developed by the German-Jewish philosopher Franz Rosensweig (1886–1929). He acknowledged that the proclamation in John's Gospel may be true; Jesus may be the only way to the Father; but for those who are already covenantally conjoined with their heavenly Father, there is no need to go anywhere. The Jewish people are already with the One who called them into a divine partnership and have remained with God ever since. The conversion of the Jews is unnecessary. Indeed, it is a foolish redundancy—a failure to recognize and affirm that God keeps God's promises. To push this position further: if God abandoned those with whom he was covenantally bonded because of their faithlessness and idolatrous propensities, then on what ground could Christians stand with confidence? On the other hand, if God's love is unconditional, then Jews as well as Christians have good reason to trust God will not abandon them—or anyone else with whom God is covenantally attached.

The American Episcopal theologian Paul Van Buren offers another take on John 14:6. He notes the language of the Bible takes many forms and serves multiple purposes. The literary range within the Bible extends from history to mythology, from prophesy to law, from prayer to parables, from genealogies to sermons. Van Buren urges us to consider John 14:6 as the evangelist's love poetry.

While I would unabashedly proclaim my wife the most beautiful woman in the world, there are those who might contest my opinion. I doubt I could validate my claim on empirical grounds or by an appeal to a global survey. What I am declaring is that my wife is the one and only for me, that I have pledged myself to her and will live in fidelity with her. The Gospel writer is making an analogous, albeit far more lofty and theologically loaded affirmation. What he knows of God has come through his relationship with

Jesus. He insists there is no other to whom he could pledge allegiance, and he cannot imagine how anyone would be able to understand the depth and breadth of God's love except through the kind of relationship into which he has wholeheartedly plunged. To read John's poetic praise as a binding legal injunction to bring the entire world into the Christian fold is to misconstrue the meaning and intent of these words. The evangelical dream of universal conquest and consolidation entails consequences, and they are abhorrent. As the Jewish philosopher Sir Isaiah Berlin once noted, "The craving for unity—the regeneration of mankind by recovery of a lost innocence and harmony, the return from a fragmented existence to the all-embracing whole—is an infantile and dangerous delusion: to crush all diversity and even conflict in the interest of uniformity is to crush life itself."[4]

A third approach to John 14:6 captured my imagination during a Sunday Bible school session at Brown Memorial Presbyterian Church conducted by Dr. Van Hunter, a revered Presbyterian Bible scholar at St. Mary's Seminary and University. When the class landed on this verse, an elderly lay woman by the name of Meg declared, "Having gone through Father Raymond Brown's commentary on John's Gospel and having reviewed other analyses of this passage, I do not believe that Jesus actually said these words. I think those who redacted the Gospel attributed the statements to him for their own theological purpose." And then comes the kicker; she calmly but insistently concluded her appraisal: "And, if he did say these words, he was wrong!"

I like to imagine a follow-up exchange between Meg and the champions of the Baltimore Declaration.

> BD: Who do you think you are to question the authority of our Lord and rebuff his teaching? Aren't you repudiating the supremacy of the Scriptures?

> Meg: Actually, I am not interested in delivering repudiations. I am committed to teeing up a good argument. After all, if Abraham has the audacity to challenge God over the destruction of Sodom and Gomorrah, I figure I might share some serious reservations about the ultimate destiny of non-Christians. That strikes me as a challenge very much in keeping with our Scriptures.

> BD: And do you imagine that you would offer Jesus some valuable instruction?

---

4. Berlin, *Crooked Timber of Humanity*, 49.

Meg: Well, take the story of the Syrophoenician woman, a gentile, an outsider, who challenges Jesus (Mark 7:24–30). She enters into a spirited exchange with Jesus, and she ends up prodding him to think and behave differently. She teaches him to see the world through the eyes of people routinely avoided and dismissed.[5]

BD: So you would overturn the economy of salvation and jettison one of the most fundamental claims of our tradition—the proclamation enshrined in our liturgy that Jesus Christ is the Savior of the world?

Meg: I am not exactly clear what this proclamation means. Is this a statement of fact or an aspiration or an affirmation to bind a community together? A declaration of praise or an exhortation to evangelize the world? Does this mean that God will only save those who declare Jesus their Lord and Savior, or does it mean that Jesus is devoted to the health and well-being of the entire world and excludes no one from his compassionate embrace? Does this liturgical affirmation aim at inclusion or threaten exclusion? And how do you imagine these words might be heard by those who dwell in different religious tents—or those who have given up on religion altogether? Do we ignore the fact that what we proclaim as the "good news" is heard by many others around the world as menacing "bad news"?

Shortly after the publication of the Baltimore Declaration, I wrote an op-ed piece for the *Baltimore Sun*. I was nowhere near as charitable or irenic as Meg would have been. In a fundamental sense I mirrored the very dispositions of imperious intolerance that I ascribed to the authors. They and I were unfurling our war banners and fixing our bayonets, and each of us aimed at exposing the deficiencies of the other and puncturing each other's pretensions. I now realize the authors of the Baltimore Declaration and all those who shared their apprehensions and outrage needed to be heard, and neither they nor I were up to the hard work of compassionate listening.

Don't get me wrong. I think the positions they staked out are misguided and incompatible with a Christian community that aims to flourish —loving and honoring the wild and unruly mess of humanity from top to bottom—while opening itself to creative and unanticipated transformation. However flawed the effort to reconnect the Episcopal tradition to its

---

5. This parable is often misinterpreted in ways that present Jews as xenophobic, thereby ignoring the fact that the temple featured a court to the gentiles and was welcoming of non-Jews known as "godfearers." See Levine, *Difficult Words of Jesus*.

essential tenets, the advocates of the Baltimore Declaration exposed fault lines needing serious and sustained examination. Their inquest touched nerve ends and revealed feverish struggles roiling the larger community—making painfully clear that our traditions have not developed the discipline of sacred argumentation. One and all believed a battle was being waged for the very soul of the church, and the instinct—now as well as then—was to take no prisoners.

I frankly do not know if we Christians can break the destructive quest for supremacy, but as a first step it is vital to map out the divides and underscore the gravity of the problems. All the while, I wonder if there are enough people who will leave their settled quarters and relinquish their attachment to certitude long enough to fall into the hands of the great unknown, or what the Yale Divinity School poet Christian Witman calls "the bright abyss."[6] If enough of us from across the theological spectrum were willing to take this risk and brave the ensuing discomfort and irresolution, we might give greater substance to our character and might even learn something new.

Invariably the most contentious debates among Christians circle back to dogmatic affirmations at the heart of the Christian tradition. These articles of faith have historically given rise to some of the most ferocious and ruinous clashes within Western civilization. Curiously enough, the overwhelming majority of Christians would have tremendous difficulty parsing the nature of the doctrinal battles or delineating the terms of the debate with any precision. Take one of the most central doctrines of classical Christianity, the doctrine of the Trinity. Few mysteries generate as much head-scratching and exasperation among the Christian rank and file. How is it that Christians espouse their belief in the Father, Son, and Holy Spirit—one God in three persons? Jewish and Muslim colleagues often suspect that Christians have difficulty with basic mathematics. Three in one produces a fraction, if not an idolatrous formulation. The additions amount to a blasphemous subtraction.

Appeals to Greek philosophy, Neoplatonic categories, and the contentious, often vicious debates of the third and fourth centuries entail recondite excursions—more often than not generating bewilderment and commotion among faithful Christians today. Insofar as we Christians manage to approximate an intelligible account, we claim a name for the divine mystery that signifies a dynamic and relational essence. Christians strive to identify the experience of God as a disclosure that expresses the Divine's immanence and transcendence, a Presence active and concrete in our lives and simultaneously a Reality beyond our reach.

---

6. See Wiman, *My Bright Abyss.*

The mathematical rules of operation—addition, subtraction, multiplication, and division—often invoked to question and discredit the Christian status as a legitimately monotheistic tradition misconstrue the character of Christian theological discourse. Trinitarian language names something crucial about the Christian experience and understanding of God—the indivisible dynamism, the processive movement, the dialectic tension between holy presence and incommensurable otherness, the paradoxical compatibility binding the unknowable God to God's creation.

The Christian formulation of "unity within diversity" entails a reading of scripture, tradition, liturgy, and piety—and the language ultimately implies that the reality of God cannot be contained within any conceptual framework. The infinite can manifest itself in the finite, but the finite cannot contain or circumscribe the infinite. Trinitarian language is the complex mother tongue in which the vast majority of Christians learn to speak and sing and pray and reach into the Great Unknown. It is the ideational cathedral in which they dwell.

I tried to interest Joel in this theological investigation and urged him to explore the metaphysical jungle. He thought Christians were lavishing far too much attention on dogmatic speculations that did not seem to anchor or orient ethical behavior. Christian efforts to name the divine mystery and give greater precision to our understanding struck him as excessive, if not presumptuous.

"But my impression is that liberal Jews don't like to talk about God and so the Divine is reduced to an inaccessible abstraction. God certainly has a lead role in the scriptures you read every week, but in what sense does God show up here and now?" I heckled.

"You say this just because we don't talk incessantly about God. We affirm and honor God through a life of Torah observance—a life that recognizes and enlarges a sense of holiness all around us. Every Sabbath we enter into what [the Jewish theologian] Abraham Joshua Heschel calls 'a cathedral of time'—and we greet the *Shekinah* (the presence of God) in our homes and at our table week after week. The study of sacred texts is prayer. Our calendar and our ritual life are steady reminders of a holy obligation," Joel countered.

"Well, I heard you tell the story of Bernstein, who comes to the synagogue week after week to talk with God. But Silverman goes to synagogue week after week to talk with Bernstein. If I were to take a poll after a worship service and ask each individual if they had an experience of God, what do you think would be the result?" I pressed.

"Probably not very different from your Presbyterian church. You recite creeds every Sunday. Do you think most members of your congregation understand the words—or agree with the meaning of the doctrines? Christian worship moves through a set of puzzling and abstract concepts, and where does it land? Faith often seems to be reduced to a vague intellectual assent," Joel observed.

"Wait a moment! Trinitarian language is not just a matter of the head. The way Christians sing and pray, the readings and the preaching engage the heart as well as the mind. Worship informs and shapes holy affections—hope that gives us courage, joy that sparks celebration, gratitude that inspires generosity, and love that orients us to the needs of our neighbors," I insisted.

"Well, I think we provide a great deal more latitude in our refusal to lay down dogmatic injunctions. What counts boils down to Torah observance—living in the light of the *mitzvoth* [the commandments]! We place more emphasis on communal practices and duties—we have clear behavioral expectations, which you are inclined to characterize as legalistic. Our religion means nothing if it is not embodied," Joel declared.

"Sure. I've heard Jews insist repeatedly that they are about 'deeds not creeds.' This strikes me as an evasion. What does a deed mean if it is not linked to a theology? Can a community endure if it does not have a reasonable or at least articulate foundation on which actions are based? In the case of a religious tradition, doesn't that mean solid grounding in metaphysical affirmations?" I contended.

"Well, my congregants are not very interested in your metaphysical leaps. Jewish education hinges on other aptitudes, for example learning Hebrew. This is more elemental than your theological speculations. Learning a language requires American Jews to step outside of the dominant culture—not only to speak but more importantly to listen—to develop an ear. Learning Hebrew enables us to pay attention to ancestors whose voices would otherwise get lost in translation. Jews can then read their way into a community. The meanings they discover unfold as they build a vocabulary, appreciate the syntax, and then interpret the disputes of the sages. By the time they become adults, my hope is that they have become active participants in the foundational struggles of our tradition. It is this engagement with a distinct community, comprised of the living and the dead, that shapes a manner of living. I don't think you get it because you do all your thinking in English and do not really appreciate how another language can open the door to holiness."

"You may be right. But aren't you actually using Hebrew to separate yourselves from other communities. Hebrew becomes your way of declaring independence and keeping the outside world at a safe distance. No wonder there are so few Jews who are deeply committed to theological inquiries with

Christians. Your tradition seems to work with an ideal of self-preservation and self-sufficiency, and I keep hearing your rabbinic colleagues argue that they do not want to confuse their congregants with Christian thought when they do not have an adequate grasp of their own tradition. Is this isolation really possible or desirable?" I pressed.

Joel responded: "Well, you don't really get it—our community's need to protect itself and safeguard our tradition. You don't know or appreciate the depth of our vulnerability! And so let's take another look at where your metaphysical speculations take us. Jews are at best mystified by your notions of the Trinity, and it takes too much labor to get a handle on this doctrine. We don't find this study appealing or relevant. Furthermore, it is your claim about the incarnation—your insistence that Jesus Christ is the Savior of the world—that presents an even more serious stumbling block. This is the dogma Christians use as a club, and most Jews are tired of being told they are incomplete or lost or damned without getting right with Jesus."

There is no doubt that Joel was naming one of the biggest stumbling blocks within Christian theology, namely, the doctrines dealing with Christology. The logic behind the ways in which Christians think and talk about Jesus Christ all too often follows a rigid pattern. Since the church has traditionally insisted that Jesus Christ is inseparable from God the Father and the Holy Spirit, to deny the divinity of Jesus entails a denunciation of the one true God. You cannot be related to God without being bound to Jesus Christ. They are a package deal. You cannot have one without the other. Thus, anyone who does not hold fast to the incarnation has an inadequate or fallacious understanding of the Godhead. And if salvation depends upon right understanding and right relationship, non-Christians are adrift and blindly careening into the abyss. So of course, the argument goes, Christians are obligated to reach out to the entire world and rescue as many souls as possible. The refusal to evangelize Jews and Muslims or anyone else would amount to an act of disdain.

I am haunted by the words of the Jewish philosopher Franz Rosenzweig: "Christian love of one's enemy becomes reality and can be nothing else the moment the church or the individual follows the original command of Christianity to proselytize. Then the love of one's enemy becomes the strongest weapon with which to conquer the world, for the enemy is loved as one who will become a brother."[7] The goal of this kind of love entails a seduction, a conquest, a transformation of the beloved into one's mirror image. Although this is bad enough, the narcissism built into this Christian mission strikes me as a total betrayal of the life and teachings of Jesus.

---

7. Rosenzweig, "Love of One's Enemies," 348.

So much for love that entails radical acceptance, love that is given without condition or the expectation of reciprocity, love that responds to need and hurt, love that elevates and empowers. If Christian love is used as a means to an end, as an instrument for the transfiguration of the beloved, then its deployment is broken and manipulative and pernicious. Is this kind of love the driving force of the gospel and the logical offspring of its core doctrines?

An enormous amount of theological effort has gone into reinterpreting and reconceptionalizing both the Trinity and the incarnation so that the logic of supersessionism is blunted. To summarize and assess these developments would require another book. And yet I cannot overstate the importance of this enterprise, because these doctrines in large measure continue to define Christians' understanding of their mission in the world. The prospects of advancing peace and promoting justice in the world at large hinge on a revision of the ideal of Christian supremacy.

Joel pressed me on this theological challenge, and I admit I never came up with a response he found satisfactory. He did not want long and rambling expositions, but a succinct summation, one that was clean and clear. In retrospect and in no small measure due to his influence, I am reminded of an observation made by the Episcopal theologian Paul Van Buren. He noted we do not have any reliable records of Jesus' physical attributes. We do not know if he was tall or short, burly or skinny, handsome or homely. There is only one feature about which we can be certain: he was circumcised. He bore the covenantal marking of a Jew. What might this detail mean?

To take this fact seriously necessitates an acknowledgment that Jesus was born a Jew, lived his life as a Jew, and died a Jew. If he was a Jew and in some deep and abiding way stands in fidelity to being a Jew, it means that Jesus comes to us Christians as an outsider. Christians cannot authentically claim him as their own, or at least not exclusively. As Jesus declared, "Foxes have holes and birds of the air have nests, but the Son of Man has nowhere to lay his head" (Matt 8:20 and Luke 9:58). It is the homeless stranger who knocks at the door and is unrecognizable who may lure us into the presence of the Divine. This Jewish Jesus refuses domestication and renounces assimilation. If Christians hope to encounter their Lord, they cannot avoid ongoing encounters with a tradition that they cannot and should not attempt to encompass or possess. They are obligated to honor a divide and affirm the gap as a blessing. We are made wonderfully different and irreducibly distinct. A celebration of Jesus' outsider status does not yield a doctrine so much as a disposition that might incline Christians to embrace a more robust ethic of hospitality. An infusion of compassion and humility might enable the crusaders to beat their swords into a plowshares, while inspiring all of us to pursue dreams beyond the realm of conquest and domination.

CHAPTER 6

Paul Alexander and the Gospel of John

As the ICJS conducted inquiries into the conflicted history of Christians and Jews, the ICJS encountered a good bit of resistance from people who were convinced the antagonisms of the past had in large measure been overcome. Some notable country clubs now made accommodations for a select contingent of Blacks and Jews. The line that once isolated the Jewish community and confined it to the neighborhood of Pikesville had become blurred, and Jews could now be found in locales once defined by "covenants" excluding them. The doors of schools and businesses were opened to those once classified as unacceptable. Anti-Judaism may have ravaged communities in Europe, and occasionally spilled into the rants of demagogues like Father Charles Coughlin and infected the views of magnates such as Henry Ford. Yet the problem was frequently and mistakenly dismissed as an anachronism, a negligible relic of a bygone era. The prevailing sentiment was to avoid conversations that would reignite anxieties in the larger Jewish community and burden others with the failures of the past.

The work of the ICJS troubled the waters and called into question the self-satisfied complacency within a significant cross section of Christian communities in and beyond Maryland. There were increasing numbers of Christians who began to pay close attention to noxious passages in the New Testament. They suggested more needed to be done to identify and disarm prejudices enshrined in their holy book. The reactions to these suggestions were predictable. Stalwart pillars of the church refused to acknowledge the Gospels could be pressed into the service of hate, at least not within their churches. They insisted the message of love constituted the immutable core of their worship. Traces of anti-Jewish attitudes were brushed off as the lamentable result of distortions layered onto the Christian scriptures—bad Christians doing bad things to a perfectly good and divinely inspired text! My colleagues and I were repeatedly told that we were making much ado about nothing.

A couple of public events did much to rattle people out of their dogmatic slumbers. It was more than thirty-five years ago when I was informed that an actor by the name of Paul Alexander would perform the Gospel of John in the basement of St. Vincent de Paul, a Roman Catholic Church in a beleaguered quarter of downtown Baltimore. Mr. Alexander was trained as a Royal Shakespearean actor and had committed the entirety of the Gospel to memory. He was heralded as a gifted performer of a spellbinding narrative. So, I made my way downtown and joined about thirty others for the evening's program. Although I had low expectations, I was deeply moved and equally troubled by his brilliant rendering.

The next day I was able to track Paul down for a coffee and conversation. I wanted to know if he had ever performed this piece in front of a Jewish audience. No; he confessed his programs were normally conducted in churches and public settings attended by Christians. I then asked him if he would he be willing to come back to Baltimore and give a dramatic recitation to an audience comprised of an even mix of Christians and Jews. "Most certainly," he insisted. "Do you think that there would be a problem?"

I noted that "the Jews" are cited on seventy-one occasions, and they certainly do not come off very well. Tellingly, he had never really thought there was anything particularly offensive or troubling about the portrait of Jews in John's Gospel, but he was intrigued to explore the issue.

In 1988, Paul Alexander returned to Baltimore and performed the Gospel of John at St. Mary's Seminary before an audience of approximately two hundred: an even mix of Jews and Christians, with a heavy infusion of ministers, priests, and rabbis, along with professors, educators, and community leaders—and the entire board of the ICJS. As the recitation unfolded, the atmosphere grew increasingly charged, even agitated. The words rang out loud and clear, and the verbal assaults encircled the audience. "The Jews started to persecute Jesus . . ." (5:16). "The Jews were seeking all the more to kill him . . ." (5:18). "No one would speak openly for fear of the Jews . . ." (7:13).

Up until this point, I suspect, most of the Christians and many of the Jews in the audience had regarded the problem of anti-Judaism within the New Testament as an abstraction. They were vaguely aware of hazardous material, but assumed the complications could be cleaned up or at least sidestepped with some fancy homiletical footwork. Yet, in the thick of the event, the audience was startled by an awareness in the pit of the stomach. As the tension and the tempo mounted, a text Christians had heard many times in a liturgical context suddenly became unfamiliar and emotively charged. A moment of disorientation gave way to a more persistent feeling of awkwardness and crested in an acute embarrassment—and beneath this discomfort there was an inchoate sense of dread, the haunting apprehension that the ground on which we stood might no longer support us.

I doubt the realization of the problem could have taken hold were it not for the fact that many of the Jews and Christians at this gathering shared a history, had dealings with one another, and even considered each other friends. There they sat, huddled together around a talented performer, as the recitation swept them up and landed them in a partitioned landscape. They became acutely aware, perhaps for the first time, they inhabited different domains, which amounted to a staggering realization of a gap—a sense of a vast, unbridgeable separation.

Upon the conclusion of the performance, the audience broke for dinner and subdued conversation at the refectory tables. When the attendees reassembled in the conference room, Father Daniel Harrington (1940–2014), a prominent Roman Catholic Bible scholar, placed the Gospel of John in its historical context and helped a startled audience get its bearings.

Here it might be worth taking an excursus, because most Jews and a great many Christians are unfamiliar with the tools of biblical exegesis, and a few brief comments will better equip us to assess both the promise and the limitations of disarming toxic texts with literary and historical criticism.

In the first place, there is a tendency on the part of many contemporary readers to approach the four canonical Gospels as though they were newspaper accounts about the life, death, and resurrection of Jesus of Nazareth. While the Gospels contain significant historical details, the authors did not compose these narratives so that a neutral audience could access a factual chronicle of events and retrieve a detailed biographical record. They were intended to be read and interpreted as theological portraits serving to orient and reassure specific communities of Jesus' followers as they faced massive struggles within their ranks and threatening opposition from the outside world. All four Gospels are literary narratives intended to acclimate these communities in the midst of extreme uncertainty. If people fail to appreciate the nature of this genre and the underlying theological purpose, the complexities of biblical interpretation will elude readers, and they will misconstrue the meaning of the gospel.

Most people are unaware that they conduct a sophisticated literary feat every time they read the morning newspaper. The challenge of interpretation is inescapable. If they encounter the headline "Chiefs Murder Cowboys," it makes an enormous difference whether they are holding the front page, the sports section, or the book review of a recent work on American history. They make exacting judgments about the meaning of a statement based upon the author, the audience, and the circumstances that occasion the writing. A visitor who floats on the surface of the heading might reach the mistaken conclusion that Missouri is not a safe city for cattlemen to visit. The problems of interpretation become even more daunting as the gaze is directed to sacred texts shaped in ancient times and in distant places.

When individuals examine an episode from the Gospels, they are challenged to dig beneath the surface of the text, excavate the neglected fragments, sift through the evidence, and configure and reconfigure the data with the creative imagination of a literary detective. First, readers need to recognize that they are handling a sacred document that has multiple layers and is brimming with a confounding mix of clues. The earliest stratum of the Gospels offers access to the words and actions of Jesus. These memories were passed along to subsequent generations of his followers, but in the process of transmission the accounts were adapted to address the concerns of a beleaguered minority that found itself in constantly changing circumstances. The Gospel writers, or evangelists, did more than receive dictation. Their overriding purpose was not defined by our contemporary strictures about biographical accuracy, but stemmed from the quest to discern the meaning of Jesus' life, death, and resurrection for the followers of Jesus. So, the evangelists stitched together oral traditions dating back to Jesus and his earliest disciples and then combined these accounts with a variety of other sources. Gospel writers edited and redacted these received materials so that they might speak authoritatively to the questions and concerns of the followers of Jesus living at least forty years after Jesus' death. The critical reader therefore needs to acknowledge overlapping layers within the Gospels and glean insights into both the life of Jesus and the life of the early church. The Gospels are a complex mix of narratives that provide meaning and give direction over a period of time within a shifting context—where the struggles of one generation may diverge from the conflicts of the next. Furthermore, this literature delineates a sacred vocation that is then nested within the larger story of Israel and endowed with cosmic significance for the future.

To come to terms with a tradition of denunciation and repudiation known as anti-Judaism within the Christian tradition, readers are obliged to ponder the historical circumstances out of which the early church emerged, especially the underlying conflicts that defined these fledgling communities. Many of us are acutely aware that some of the world's ugliest fights are waged within a family. Proximity often amplifies rather than moderates friction. People who have a stake in a common inheritance all too often vie for control over the same religious symbols and stories, and in the struggle for custody they are swept into passionate rivalries. The closer people stand to one another, the more likely they are to mangle one another's toes.

The problem of a family rivalry is reflected in many of the conflicts within the New Testament. To appreciate the intensity of this identity struggle, we do well to remember that the Jews were confronted with a massive challenge when the Romans destroyed the temple in Jerusalem (70 CE), and conflicts escalated even more drastically in 135 with the Bar Kochba revolt. These national catastrophes prompted the evolving rabbinic movement to temper the fervor of political revolutionaries and to recenter communal life on written and oral traditions, a process that transfigured the temple's sacrificial system.

The vast majority of Jews rejected the messianic claims that a small minority of Jews attributed to Jesus. The communal clash with the Jewish followers of Jesus was then exacerbated with the influx of gentiles into the Jesus movement. While gentile followers—frequently referred to as "godfearers"—may have felt an affinity with key philosophical and theological aspects of the Jewish life, they were not full-fledged converts who adhered to those ritual aspects of Torah observance that distinguished Jews from neighbors, most notably circumcision and dietary restrictions. Scandalous to many of the Jewish followers of Jesus was the claim that the status of full membership was possible apart from practices that defined the boundaries of a movement, which eventually evolved into Rabbinic Judaism.

Turning attention directly to the Gospel of John, Daniel Harrington noted that this text is a layered historical document, generally thought to have been redacted at the end of the first and early part of the second century of the Common Era. Composed for a community living in Syria, Palestine, or Transjordan, the evangelist is responding to an existential dilemma that purportedly arose with its eviction from the local synagogue (John 9:22).[1] Therefore, the crisis of separation and identity formation lies at the heart of the Gospel of John. To authenticate its proclamation and account for its rejection, the evangelist situates the communal plight within an apocalyptic worldview. The new world is envisioned as crashing into the old; the forces of good have entered into mortal combat with the forces of evil. God has intervened and is finally on the verge of overthrowing the powers of darkness and falsehood. The final outcome turns on the axis of belief.

Jesus and his followers are portrayed as the champions of divine truth who must engage in holy warfare with opponents allied with the

---

1. The Jewish scholar Adele Reinhartz, who has written extensively on the Gospel of John, notes that this singular allusion indicates expulsions were exceptional, if indeed they took place at all. See her *Cast Out of the Covenant*.

principalities of evil. The evangelist envisions a world tottering on the edge of history, and he frames the crisis as a moment of decision. On which side of the divide will individuals take their stand? Everything is at stake; all depends on the decision for or against Christ. In this cosmic war, "the Jews" who refuse to acknowledge Jesus as the Messiah become the archetypal enemies.

There are seventy-one references made to "the Jews" (in Greek, *Ioudaioi*). At times the term is simply used to designate people who live in Judea as opposed to Galileans and Samaritans. On one occasion Jesus declares that salvation is from the Jews (John 4:22), although more problematically the passages goes on to show that Jewish geography is now irrelevant as is ethnic Israel. Furthermore, the vast majority of allusions identify "the Jews" as malevolent rivals who are consistently opposed to the truth that Jesus embodied. At an early stage in the narrative, "the Jews" are described as those who persecute and seek to kill Jesus (5:16–18; 7:1), and the pattern continues from the fifth chapter to the seventh, and then again from the tenth to the eleventh chapters (10:31; 11:18). This antagonism is buttressed by another motif that runs through the Gospel, namely, the fear of suppression that Jewish hostility instills in Jesus' followers (7:13; 9:22; 19:38; 20:19). The vilification is amplified by portrayals of the Jews as untrue to their own faith and tradition. They do not keep the Torah (7:19) and they fail to comprehend the spiritual truth within their own scriptures (5:39–40; 10:31–39).

The unbelief, rejection, and hostility of the Jews are further intensified when the narrator turns his gaze upon the Jewish authorities and the Pharisaic movement. They are characterized as blind, and together with the council and chief priests they plot Jesus' death.[2] The chief priests, who are appointed by Rome, conspire to have Lazarus killed so as to undercut Jesus' support (12:10); they cry out for Jesus to be crucified (19:6); and they

---

[2]. Ellis Rivkin noted in his 1978 study, *A Hidden Revolution*, that the Pharisees served to democratize biblical Israel, elevating the rabbi to a position of authority rather than confining leadership to a hereditary priesthood. They made the synagogue a center for communal life and thereby established an institution that enabled Jews to thrive even after the destruction of the second temple. They gave great prominence to table fellowship and in the process transformed the home into a sanctuary that echoed key dimensions of the temple. Finally, they developed ways of reading and interpreting the Bible that opened up the vast riches of rabbinic Judaism embedded in the Oral Law. All of this suggests that Jesus was profoundly indebted to the Pharisaic movement and may very well have identified with its teachings. Rivkin's work is rather dated and the depiction has been explored in much greater depth by subsequent generations of scholars. Of particular importance is the volume *The Pharisees*, edited by Joseph Sievers and Amy-Jill Levine, which features presentations delivered at Rome's Biblical Institute in 2019 by outstanding Jewish, Protestant, and Roman Catholic scholars. They demonstrate the vital importance of correcting a dangerously distorted portrait.

declare that Jesus is not their king (19:15). The polemical thrust of John's passion narrative leaves the impression that the Jews bear the responsibility for the arrest, conviction, and death of Jesus. John portrays Pilate as crumbling under the pressure of the Jews, for he declares on no less than four occasions that Jesus is innocent. Even the execution itself appears as a deed performed by the chief priests: "So in the end Pilate handed him over to them (the chief priests) to be crucified" (19:16).

The anti-Jewish edge of John's Gospel cuts deeper still as the narrator indicates the many ways in which Jesus displaces Judaism and fulfills its covenantal promises. In chapter 6, shortly before the Passover, Jesus multiplies the loaves for a multitude, substituting the bread of heaven for the manna of the exodus. The freedom from Egyptian tyranny that was granted to Moses and his followers is represented as paling in comparison to the promise of spiritual freedom offered by Christ. The pattern is repeated in chapter 7, where Jesus eclipses the significance of the Feast of Tabernacles, and again in chapter 10, where the messianic promise delivered by Jesus overshadows the Feast of the Dedication or Hanukkah. Indeed, the meaning of temple is transposed from a geographical place to the person of Christ, whose own sacrificial death is understood as rendering the Jerusalem temple obsolete—a theme that becomes particularly prominent in another New Testament work, the Letter to the Hebrews. In both cases, the audience is left with the impression that Jewish life and practice were temporary—incomplete, inadequate, and antiquated. In the words of Arnold Toynbee, Judaism emerges as a casualty of evolution—it is a "fossilized religion."

The dynamics of Christian supersessionism within the Gospel of John are conspicuous from start to finish, but this negative portrayal is augmented by some especially pernicious imagery. In chapter 8, Jesus is embroiled in an acrimonious debate with "the Jews" about their status as children of Abraham, and the following accusation is attributed to Jesus: "The devil is your father, and you prefer to do what your father wants. He was a murderer from the start; he was never grounded in the truth; there is no truth in him at all . . . The reason that you do not hear them (the words) is that you are not of God" (8:44, 47). While this virulent trope reflects literary conventions that were used in both pagan and Jewish rhetoric, this conflation of the Jews and the devil mutates over the centuries in Christian culture, giving rise to malignant fantasies of a demonic enemy whose death-dealing ambitions are global.

Professor Harrington was keenly aware of the complex swerve from Christian anti-Judaism to modern antisemitism, which in large measure accounted for his rigorously honest examination of the supersessionist dynamics within the Gospel of John. He framed a fundamental problem that lingered long after this event concluded. How can Christians remain faithful to their sacred scriptures without falling captive to anti-Judaism? A deep understanding of the historical and literary context in which the Gospels were composed may blunt the supersessionist assault, but this intellectual project is apt to undermine scriptural authority by rendering the text fully human and therefore fallible. On a more visceral level, what happens to the driving narrative force, the agonistic struggle for truth, the existential drama of this Gospel's proclamation when stripped of its anti-Jewish dynamic—when there is no longer an evil antagonist over whom the protagonist must definitively triumph?

Upon the completion of Harrington's commentary, Rabbi Mark Loeb took the stage and noted the problems of religious triumphalism are not a pathology to which Christians can claim exclusive ownership. He took stock of dangers woven into the core of the Exodus story and brought into focus a troublesome feature of every Passover celebration. He suggested that many might read this narrative as establishing the underpinnings of a binary worldview, a bifurcation of humanity into two irreconcilable camps. On one side stands the descendants of those who escaped Pharaoh's enslavement, and on the other side loom enemies who continue to threaten the subjugation, if not the annihilation of the Jewish people. In this life-and-death contest there are winners and losers. There are the divinely chosen ones, who are delivered, and there are those whose heinous schemes are thwarted. The Exodus account attributes the rescue operation to God's gracious intervention. God's decisive action provides good reason for Jews to celebrate the liberation of Moses and the Hebrew slaves—while simultaneously rejoicing at the destruction of Pharaoh and his minions.

Rabbi Loeb cited a midrash (rabbinic interpretation) that recognized and attempted to neutralize unbridled jubilation. The exposition wrapped around the Exodus account imagines the ministering angels united in song with all those who had crossed to safety. Together they were given a ringside seat to witness and rejoice at the devastation of Pharoah's army. According to the midrash, God reprimands the angelic choir: "My creations are drowning, and you are singing before me?" (b. Megilla 10b). This interpolation becomes so central that it is woven into the annual Passover ritual. When remembering the ten plagues during the seder meal, Jewish families pour out some wine from each glass to demonstrate that the cup of joy cannot be full as long as others—even enemies—are suffering.

Rabbi Loeb noted that the rabbinic sages recognized some biblical narratives need to be tempered. An uncritical reading of passages in the Hebrew scriptures can deliver a warrant for violence. The community needs to hold fast to the well-known teaching from the Babylonian Talmud,

Sanhedrin 39b: "The Holy One, Blessed be He, does not rejoice over the fall of the wicked." One and all bear the imprint of the Divine, and the destruction of the oppressor may be necessary but should not be an occasion for gloating.

The challenge posed by Rabbi Loeb revolved around the question: "What kind of midrash, what kind of interpretation, what kind of commentary would Christians need to develop in order to invalidate, if not redeem anti-Jewish readings of the Gospels?"

This summons continues to unnerve Christians, especially during the liturgical season leading up to Easter. Year after year the lectionary readings delivered on Good Friday immortalize vile portraits of the Jews. The renowned Roman Catholic Bible scholar Raymond Brown (1928–1988) declared a flat and uncritical reading of New Testament accounts of Jesus' crucifixion is irresponsible and indefensible in light of our anguished history. These scriptural proclamations have functioned as "texts of terror" and they need to be placed within a historical context that disarms them. Lamentably there are still a good many priests and ministers who gloss over this disagreeable material, brush aside the polemical fallout, and make haste to Jesus' glorious resurrection. A direct confrontation with our anti-Jewish legacy casts a pall over a liturgical moment that has traditionally served as the climax of the Christian calendar. Yet to ignore or conceal the ominous undercurrent of the narrative makes the proclamation of good news for Christians a blessing that is repeatedly purchased at the expense of the Jews. How then are Christians to find a way out of this dreadful bind?

The dramatic recitation of the Gospel of John marked a turning point for the ICJS by underscoring the difficulties of attentive listening and discernment. Familiarity all too often breeds complacency, and congregants and clergy alike filter out words and images that generate discomfort and embarrassment. Most Christians assume they already know the meaning of the story, and any messages that do not fit the predetermined template are dismissed as irrelevant. Christian communities become embedded in ritual performances that reflexively rule out the possibility that their routinized reading of the sacred text may have concealed an unacknowledged and deplorable truth—the triumph of the cross signals a murderous Jewish predilection. The way out of the impasse required the ICJS to discover that deep listening is not a solitary act but relies on the presence of others who prompt individuals and communities to plunge beneath the surface and discern important content they would have otherwise missed or avoided. The ICJS realized an essential educational dynamic: our job was to shake the foundations and call into question habits of mind that offer refuge in self-satisfaction and indolence. In the wake of this experience, the ICJS realized that deep listening and transformational learning are a dialogical discipline.³

---

3. This dialogical practice became a standard feature of ICJS programs for years and decades to come. For example, when Mel Gibson's film *The Passion of the Christ* was released in 2004, the ICJS hosted a showing at the Senator, the last remaining big-picture theater in Baltimore. With an audience of approximately eight hundred, from both Jewish and Christian neighborhoods, we orchestrated a panel discussion after the viewing that featured Jewish and Christian scholars who examined the disturbing dimensions of the portrayal. We also provided supplementary curricular materials for further study and discussion in dialogue groups.

CHAPTER 7

Bach and the Indelible Stain

Back in 1990, another path opened up through an unlikely and circuitous course of events. In the early years of the ICJS, our office was tucked into the third floor of the former manse of Brown Memorial Presbyterian Church. The Baltimore Choral Arts Society housed its office directly below us on the second floor. Its executive director and choral conductor was Tom Hall, a fellow Presbyterian, celebrated maestro, charismatic schmoozer, and treasured friend. One afternoon Tom knocked on the door in the hope that I might shed some light on a baffling dilemma.

He had submitted a request to a Jewish philanthropic foundation known for its support of cultural programming. The Baltimore Choral Arts Society aspired to perform Johann Sebastian Bach's masterpiece *St. Matthew Passion*, a daunting three-hour work that features two choirs, a double orchestra, and several soloists. The scale of the production, the proposed venue at the Meyerhoff Symphony Hall, and the marketing of the event would require significant support from the larger Baltimore community.

In the appeal for funding, the Baltimore Choral Arts Society provided a synopsis that underscored the work's import in the canon of classical choral music. In terms of its historical context, Bach composed this devotional music in 1727, and the work was first performed in Leipzig at St. Thomas Church on Good Friday. The Lutheran minister had the formidable job of wedging an hour-long sermon in between its two parts. In addition to texts drawn from Martin Luther's German translation of the Gospel of Matthew, chapters 26 and 27, the composition featured the poetry of Picander (pen name of Christian Friedrich Henrici) within the libretto and chorales. These commentaries opened and closed most scenes in the narration, adding to the devotional depth of this musical meditation. The dramatic centerpiece retraced the narrative flow of the passion, moving from the arrest of Jesus to his burial and the sealing of the tomb.

During the early eighteenth century, numerous composers, including George Frideric Handel and Georg Philipp Telemann, wrote musical meditations on the passion. The accompanying poetry in their compositions intensified the anti-Jewish polemics of the Gospel accounts by vilifying Jews for their collusion in the death of Jesus. Michael Marissen, now professor emeritus of music at Swarthmore College, has noted that these works are mercifully almost never performed or even studied since they are of far less interest and lack Bach's euphonic brilliance. The eighteenth-century choral music that revolves around the passion narratives has become Bach's domain. The good news, he explained, is that Bach incorporated commentaries into his compositions that moderate the anti-Jewish tenor of the passions. The bad news is that Bach set the biblical texts to music that amplifies the violence and heightens the drama of an already damning portrait of the Jews.

The luminosity and virtuosity of Bach's passions have established these works as classics that choral groups around the world frequently perform. The complexity of these masterpieces is now compounded by the fact that works once confined to ecclesiastical settings have migrated from the church sanctuary to the secular concert hall. Yet no matter the context, the questions raised by the Hirschhorn Foundation remain. To what extent do these choral works continue to perpetuate negative views of Judaism? How did Bach and Picander treat an evangelical message that had historically inflicted untold suffering on the Jewish people? What steps was the Baltimore Choral Arts Society planning to take to educate its audience about issues long ignored, cavalierly dismissed, or resolutely avoided? These questions, Tom and I concluded, demanded sustained attention.

And so began a collaboration that continued for many years. Tom and I responded to the challenge by configuring an educational program a week before the Bach performance that would examine the narrative underpinnings of Matthew's Gospel, unveil depictions of the Jewish people during the Middle Ages and the Reformation, and then attend to the ways in which Bach's passion situates Jews within the music. This was the first community-wide colloquy to open up the issue of anti-Judaism in Bach's passions. Over the years the format was replicated in a variety of cities, and it was an approach we incorporated in a series of local and national radio presentations. The scholars who participated in these programs included Michael Marissen, Jaroslav Pelikan, Robert Bergman, Eric Chafe, Paula Fredriksen, and Amy-Jill Levine. The rigor and intensity of these public forums framed an ethos for subsequent presentations of Bach's passions, and the framing of the problem in program notes and public forums has now become commonplace among choral groups willing to struggle with the challenge.

While these efforts broke new ground, there was considerable pushback, indeed outrage in response to these initiatives. At one end of the spectrum, a prominent Reform rabbi in Baltimore denounced the entire enterprise as a fruitless gesture. He claimed a great deal depended on the location of the performance. It is one thing to integrate Bach's passions into the church's liturgical calendar and confine the performance to the sanctuary, and it is an altogether different matter to perform these works in a public venue. The stain of antisemitism was indelible, inextricably embedded in the music. To showcase this work before an unsuspecting public struck him as morally indefensible. No matter what verbiage commentators used to surround the production, words of explanation could not compete with, much less annul, the damage. The conspiratorial role assigned to the Jews was integral to a plot powered by music that would overwhelm the audience's rational faculties. From his perspective, audiences feasted on an aesthetic masterpiece without acknowledging, much less reckoning with the poison they ravished.

Of particular concern was the moment in Matthew's Gospel when Jesus is brought before the Roman procurator, Pontius Pilate. Having found no justification for Jesus' death sentence, Pilate declares Jesus innocent. Invoking a custom of releasing a prisoner, Pilate then invites the assembled crowd, a group Matthew calls "all the people," to make a life-and-death decision.[1] Who should live—Jesus or the notorious criminal Barabbas? The crowd reveals the depth of its depravity in the rejection of Jesus and the demand for Barabbas's release. When Pilate asks what they want done with "Jesus who is called the Messiah," "all the people" clamor for his crucifixion. Pilate washes his hands of this sordid affair, while the people proclaim, "His blood be on us and on our children" (Matt 27:25).

This passage is arguably the most calamitous text in the entire New Testament, because the alleged crime becomes the basis for the deicide charge—the evil of attempting to murder God. The crowd is presented as willfully and knowingly responsible for this transgression, and, worse, they have enmeshed their children in their wickedness. The iniquity mirrors, indeed magnifies what Christians have traditionally referred to as the "sin of Adam"—a crime that implicates future generations. Through the centuries Christians considered the insidious nature of this act as a crime that

---

1 No such custom appears in any Roman or Jewish record. The so-called Passover amnesty, in which Barabbas (Aramaic for "son of a father") is set free while the innocent Jesus (for the Gospels, the Son of the Father) dies, is most likely theological instruction, not historical event.

reverberates in perpetuity, giving rise to the delusion of a demonic alignment—the Jews had joined the devil in a revolt against God's sovereignty, in a bid for global domination.

The depiction of Pilate as an indecisive and magnanimous arbiter of Roman justice conceals his true character. The Jewish chronicler Josephus presented a picture of a brutal ruler who enlisted the muscle of Rome to crush dissent and savagely impose civic order on an oppressed and aggrieved population. His practice was to execute prisoners by crucifixion, a public spectacle to underscore Roman domination. His exercise of power was excessive even by Roman standards, and the gruesome displays that he choreographed to intimidate the masses were conducted with such brutality that his Roman superiors ultimately relieved him of his position.

The discrepancy between the historical evidence and the sympathetic rendering of Pilate in the Gospels offers vital clues about the precarious conditions of the early followers of Jesus. Without an adequate appreciation of the political pressures under which the early church labored, audiences will fail to understand why the Gospels delivered such a negative portrait of the Jews while offering a relatively sanguine image of the actual power brokers, the Roman occupiers. Crucifixion was a Roman form of execution associated with sedition, and Jesus' death located his followers in the shadows of political revolution. In the midst of the First Jewish War, from 66 to 73 CE, the messianic dreams of the Jesus movement would have engendered suspicions, prompting Jesus' early followers to distance themselves from Jewish insurgencies.

To redirect the watchful eye of Rome away from the early church, the Gospel writers made two decisive adjustments. First, they insisted that the kingdom of God transcended the power politics of Rome. (Jesus insisted, "My kingdom is not of this world; if my kingship were of this world, my servants would fight, that I might not be handed over to the Jews; but my kingship is not from the world"; John 18:36). Second, they whitewashed Roman culpability for Jesus' execution and thrust Jews—already perceived as rebellious subjects—into the spotlight. This imaginative literary trope amounted to a historical inversion: the oppressive Roman conqueror was reconstructed as a feckless defender of the innocent while the oppressed Jewish populace was transformed into the murderous enemy.

What began as a politically expedient tactic of survival was read by subsequent generations of Christians as a faithful and accurate account of a malicious Jewish disposition, an essential character trait of a politically and theologically disobedient people. The image enshrined in Western civilization legitimized an indictment of Jews and called for a punishment that would echo through the centuries. Christians maintained that Jews bore the curse of Cain and were therefore doomed to wander with no land to call home. Anti-Jewish legislation was repeatedly framed as a defensive measure to counter the diabolical plot to overthrown Christendom, and this lethal conspiracy theory pulsed through the veins of the larger culture even after the deicide charge was officially condemned by a number of mainline Protestant denominations at the World Council of Churches in 1961 and most especially in the landmark declaration *Nostra Aetate*, promulgated by Roman Catholic Church at the Second Vatican Council in 1965.

Tom Hall has observed the Gospel text in which the Jewish crowd calls for Jesus' execution occupies less than two minutes of a three-hour performance. In that brief but spectacular span, Bach avails himself of a devotional discipline that identifies the congregation as the people whose sins are responsible for Jesus' death. The move to implicate the Christian audience goes a long way in deflecting the anti-Jewish thrust of these passion settings. Whether Bach's adjustments meet the challenge posed by Rabbi Loeb and heighten the audience's empathy for the Jewish people remains an unsettled dispute.

As Michael Marissen has noted, Bach determined that an obsessive preoccupation with the Jews avoided the deeper significance of Jesus' sacrificial death. Drawing upon a potent current of Lutheran theology, Bach underscored the doctrinal claim that all of humanity bears the stain of original sin. One and all are guilty. One and all stand in need of redemption, not least the German Lutherans who had access to a gospel they claimed had been emancipated from Roman Catholic captivity.

When the crowd demands the death of Jesus, the audience is swept into the story as an active participant in the crime, and the composer's intent is to rouse a spirit of repentance. Both Marissen and Hall insisted Bach "pours water, not gasoline" on the problem of anti-Judaism. Without minimizing the ferocious encounters or the intractable undercurrents of contempt within these classical masterpieces, they maintain Bach's passions concentrate on the redemption of the world from sin, not the so-called villainy of Jewish deicide.

A fundamental problem nevertheless persists. Since the scope of sin and redemption is universalized, Jews are incorporated into a story that expunges their own distinctive calling, their divine election, and their covenantal integrity. They do not recognize or appreciate the necessity of Jesus' redemptive death, nor do they understand and accept the expanded dimensions of salvation now open to them along with the rest of humanity. The Christian missionary's dream of Jewish conversion perdures, and their access to the heavenly kingdom depends on their willingness to be loved out of their communal existence.

Those who occupy a comfortable seat in the dominant culture are generally unaware or indifferent or hostile to efforts to underscore the vulnerability of those who live on the edges of society. My initial reaction to the criticism of the Reform rabbi was a mix of disappointment and exasperation. Didn't he recognize that Tom Hall, Michael Marissen, and I were taking bold steps to bring the problem of antisemitism into the open? Wasn't this one more instance of political correctness run amok, a cancel culture that was bound to provoke negative pushback? Wasn't his protest a symptom of a dysfunctional paranoia, the cynicism of critics who, in the words of Oscar Wilde, "know the price of everything and the value of nothing?" Now I am not so certain about my dismissal of his reservations.

From his vantage point, productions of Bach's passions fall within a continuum that includes Shakespeare's Shylock in *The Merchant of Venice*. Despite the humanity shining through Shakespeare's portrait of the moneylender, the dramatic power of this play promotes stereotypes that continue to circulate widely. The idolatrous fixation on money, the irreconcilable animus pitting Jewish legalism against Christian love, and the undying quest for domination are squeezed into a narrative package and circulated among all those who treasure great theater and/or conspiratorial intrigue. In the wake of the Shoah and the recurrence of bloody antisemitic rampages, there are compelling ethical reasons why this Shakespeare production is rarely staged.

My rabbinic colleague suspected that Bach's passion settings no less than Shakespeare's Shylock sow the seeds of contempt. Although I found myself at odds with his conclusions, I could not easily write off a man who took great risks to march on the front lines in the early days of the Civil Rights Movement. He would denounce performances of minstrels in blackface and the prejudices built into our legal and social codes. I have no doubt that were he alive today, he would rail against the practice of consigning Muslims to diabolical roles in pop culture. He would have loudly protested the conflation of Muslims with terrorists, malevolent infiltrators, homophobic misogynists, devious schemers, and aliens incapable of assimilation.

What my rabbinic critic helped me grasp is the fact that our most celebrated cultural achievements shape the social imagination and inform the ways in which we inhabit the world. Any and every artistic artifact that degrades and dehumanizes others—whether rooted in anti-Judaism, racism, Islamophobia, sexism, or gender discrimination—needs to be critically engaged and potentially removed from the public eye. These works operate beyond the confines of reason and exert a power that rational discourse cannot tame. There are boundaries of propriety that are under constant negotiation, and they constantly shift. Yet the guardrails are consequential because they safeguard norms essential for a decent society.

From the perspective of many non-Christians, the public square is cluttered with the religious trappings of the dominant culture. Who can avoid the Christmas kitsch that annexes department stores and malls, the plastic snowmen and Santa Clauses that swarm the public square, and the jingle-bell soundtrack of good cheer pumped into elevators and office parties? While many Christians lament the trivialization and domestication of Christmas and regard the commercial takeover as a betrayal of a sacred story, the cultural message to so-called outsiders is clear: they are considered guests in a Christian nation. Against this backdrop, efforts to keep Bach's passions out of public concert halls becomes more understandable.

The pushback from the other end of the spectrum was even more strident. Tom and I were repeatedly admonished by devotees of Bach that our educational efforts were besmirching the reputation of one of the world's greatest composers. The idea that this exquisite choral music, which elevated audiences to great aesthetic heights, contained an anti-Jewish bias struck them as a nefarious allegation. Not only were they incensed by the apparent assault on Bach's reputation, they reacted as though their enjoyment of this music was enough to implicate them in the dissemination of hatred. Their reaction reflected outrage and resentment: they were simultaneously being condemned and robbed of precious treasure.

Time and again Tom and I heard concertgoers contend they paid no attention to the words. The overwhelming majority of them noted they could not understand German, and that they did not dwell on the translations in their printed programs. We were evidently magnifying if not creating a problem better ignored. The interjection of our concerns into the program was not only an unwelcome distraction, but also an infringement ruining the pure joy they had once innocently relished. The inquiry amounted to a defilement of the sacred.

What difference does it really make if Bach's music is performed in a public symphony hall or a church? Can the context for the performance annul the theological intentions of Bach's music, its devotional core? At the time of the symposium, some concertgoers argued the secular setting transformed the music, delivering an aesthetic experience that muted the religious message and rendered the sacral dimension superfluous. I am not convinced the theological underpinnings of Bach's masterpieces can be so easily elided. Yet the expectations and the dispositions of the audience will undoubtedly influence what is heard and how it is appreciated.

Another position was staked out by one of Baltimore's distinguished lawyers, a devout Christian, who maintained "our interrogations" did not just call into question public performances but amounted to a project that defamed Christianity. If the passion narratives are laden with anti-Jewish animus and should not be aired in a public venue, shouldn't they also be banned in church settings? He argued we were oiling a slippery slope, and our critiques of Bach's passions would logically culminate in a summons to cancel Good Friday services. Since there can be no Easter celebration of the resurrection without the ignominious death of Jesus, our efforts to educate the public—wittingly or unwittingly—were undermining the moral and theological foundations of the church. He declared that he was "embarrassed for me. An ordained minister should be ashamed."

As the range of reactions makes painfully clear, Michael Marissen, Tom Hall, and I discovered our inquiry into Bach's passions landed us at a hazardous intersection where religious, political, and cultural allegiances collide. How can anyone adjudicate such vastly conflicting viewpoints? Who is vested with the authority to determine the acceptability of aesthetic works displayed in museums or performed in public spaces? And when does critical engagement swerve into repressive censorship?

I do not believe the resolution of these conflicting viewpoints is possible. My rabbinic colleague articulated a position I suspect is shared by others who are convinced the anti-Jewish bias lives in the marrow of the Christian tradition, and the best defense against its encroachment is a secular society that strives to confine faith to a private realm, limiting the spillage beyond the church sanctuary and the home. My aesthetically minded compatriots will argue for a boundary that insulates the work of art from political and theological meddling. Every effort to contextualize Bach's masterpieces detracts from the purity and beauty of the performances, transmuting an experience of artistic transcendence into an object for rational analysis. In this case, the educational enterprise is surgery that murders the patient. Meanwhile, my pious lawyer maintains the truth of Christianity is bound to offend those who are at odds with the tradition. These individuals need not patronize the concert hall or visit the church. If anyone is scandalized or affronted by the proclamation of the gospel, that is their misfortune, but the potential for bruised feelings should not induce compromise or censorship. A preoccupation with anti-Judaism tarnishes Christian confidence and undermines trust in the revelation made known through Jesus Christ. No wonder future generations are growing disenchanted and estranged from their religious communities!

Was it a mistake to mount a civic performance of Bach's passions in Baltimore? I think not. However, I do not wish to minimize the sense of threat or dismiss the profound experience of loss that our efforts precipitated. The experience we orchestrated underscored the fact that interreligious education comes with a cost—and it is not always clear whether the gains outweigh the heavy price. Whether our ancestors' gifts are etched into our sacred scriptures or find expression in sublime music, the bequest bears both the blessings and curses of the culture that gave form to our most hallowed treasures. I believe that, sooner or later, there comes a reckoning with the past, an inescapable imperative to contend with the flaws—our own as well as those our ancestors passed down. Each generation is called upon to redeem the inheritance; and future generations will discover that the work of rehabilitation is never finished.

Chapter 8

A Sacred Argument

There is a baseball story that helped me appreciate the conundrum emanating from our overlapping and conflicted histories. A sports reporter who was conducting research into Yogi Berra and his family came across an up-and-coming second baseman on a Pittsburgh Pirates farm team. The young man's name was Dale Berra, and remarkably his legendary father had also launched his career with the Pittsburgh Pirates at the same position. When this sports writer approached Dale Berra, he asked the young second baseman to compare himself with his father. The story goes that Dale Berra responded: "Our similarities are totally different."

When it comes to Christians, Jews, and Muslims, our similarities are not only different. It turns out what we thought was utterly different actually entails some surprising similarities, and what we imagined was similar conceals some deep differences. It was in the protracted interplay with my rabbinic colleagues that I first became aware of indissoluble distinctions.

I reluctantly confess I initially situated my rabbinic colleagues on a pedestal and conjectured that their team was better equipped and more competent than our Christian lineup. They seemed better educated, more eloquent, more sophisticated, more linguistically facile, more revered by their congregants, and more respected by the larger community than their Christian counterparts. They were certainly better paid and better dressed. Time and experience would eventually disabuse me of my romanticized portrait—confirming the verdict of Immanuel Kant that all of us are carved out of "the crooked timber of humanity." Spiritual lethargy and intellectual torpor are disabilities that cross every religious boundary.

I was afforded the opportunity to forge friendships with a remarkable array of rabbis. Our initial encounters pivoted on similarities and charted common ground—the books we shared, the people who threaded us together, and the stories of family and friends who kept us guessing. As we gradually came to know one another more thoroughly, I notice a shift in the dynamics. My rabbinic colleagues liked to push back, and there was a keen interest in knowing where our paths veered in different directions. What struck me was not just a willingess but a delight taken in the discovery of areas of disagreement. Whereas I was accustomed to mapping out a safe and cozy enclave where consensus and harmony warmed us uniformly, the rabbinic colleagues from whom I learn the most ventured into uncharted territory and were enthused to hack their way through prickly and forbidding undergrowth. They acted as though spheres of agreement were lifeless zones that offered no prospects for discovery and exhilaration. Not only learning but also intimacy is achieved in the thick of disagreement and conflict. Arguing as a form of respect—this is the tribute paid to people they take seriously!

I was not always certain if their disruptive manner was reckless and rude or courageous and principled—or a fusion of both dispositions. Only in time did I come to understand that they were aligned with a Jewish tradition known as *machloket*. Roughly translated, this Hebrew word means an argument, a conflict, or dispute usually related to legal questions. While most of us are accustomed to arguments that are resolved through debates that yield winners and losers, there is within the Jewish heritage a discipline that moves in a different direction and constitutes a sacred argument.

A sacred argument seeks the inclusion of divergent points of view and affirms an ethos of both-and rather than either-or. To conduct a sacred argument you must be able to accurately and empathetically articulate the position of the person with whom you disagree. Rather than treat your interlocutor as an enemy to defeat, your verbal opponent is affirmed as an ally who instructs you to see the world from a different angle. Your best teachers often turn out to be the very people with whom you passionately feud. A sacred argument does honor to difference.

For those of us raised in a different religious and political climate, the practice of sacred argument may seem implausible and at odds with our times. We are so accustomed to combat that results in carnage. Debate has all too often become a blood sport. Our religious communities are torn asunder because we do not know how to deliberate with those who hold opposing views. A cursory survey of conversations dealing with abortion, race relations, gender identity, or environmental policy—to name just a few of today's divisive issues—bespeaks a breakdown in civil discourse. While religious denominations are fracturing, our political parties are at each other's throats and seek resolution through impeachment and the demonization of opponents, who are increasingly branded as enemies. Compromise is cast as capitulation.

My rabbinic colleagues have convinced me that not only our religious communities but also our democracy depends upon learning how to conduct a sacred argument. While the majority will rule the day, the minority opinion must be respected and preserved. As circumstances change, the insights and convictions embedded in the dissenting position may become indispensable and offer fresh insights in the pursuit of justice. That may be the key criteria that we use. We cannot land on an immutable truth that will win universal consent. Instead, our quest is to develop policies that advance a just and equitable order, and this ideal requires novel interpretations of our predicament, ongoing modifications and adaptations in response to fluid conditions.

Both the possibilities and limitations of sacred argument are not learned in the abstract but require disciplined scuffling, a rambunctious and fearless testing of the boundaries that separate one group from another. Insofar as I learned something of this art, it was in the company of Joel Zaiman. Despite the warnings of his father, Joel did not concern himself greatly when people accused him of arrogance. He spoke his mind without hesitation, forcefully and with conviction. He expected others to match his directness and to claim their authority. He grew impatient with self-deprecating public displays and noted that a Christian show of humility often amounted to a fraudulent modesty—and could morph into a moral evasion.

Once when Joel invited my wife and me to join a Shabbat dinner with a newly installed bishop, we had hardly lifted our forks when Joel asked the bishop about his vision for the diocese. In what direction did he want his clergy to move? What challenges did he want them to take on? What did he hope to accomplish? The bishop responded, "I am a great believer in servant leadership. I will take my cues from those I have been called to lead and do my best to keep my own ideas under wraps." Joel pressed him to explain how this model of leadership was rooted in his tradition. The bishop pointed to Jesus as the great exemplar: "Whoever wants to be first must be last of all and servant of all" (Mark 9:35).

For the remainder of the dinner, Joel made little effort to engage the bishop. I later asked why he did not press the matter further. Had I delivered a similar response, he would have lambasted me to give a fuller account. He would have questioned me about the moral and theological character of my tradition and the principled exercise of power. He would have adjured me to compare models of leadership exemplified in the persons of Jesus and Moses. I know this because on numerous occasions this was conversational terrain we covered over grilled salmon and bread pudding. Joel replied that he did not think the bishop was a "serious" Christian. This was a biting allegation I did not think necessarily warranted. After all, a lack of seriousness was the harshest indictment I ever heard him level against a fellow Jew. He answered, "In the first place, I am not convinced that he has no agenda for his diocese. In second place, I think that his understanding of servant leadership is an abdication of responsibility. His ideal of Christian humility strikes me as a failure to challenge his community and a refusal to offer a vision that might provoke resistance." I think Joel stopped his interrogation when he saw fear in the bishop's eyes, when he concluded that this version of servant leadership was an expression of either cowardice or obtuseness. He did not believe a sacred argument was possible—at least then and there.

There were plenty of times when Joel poked and prodded his conversation partners in ways a good Presbyterian would never dare. He asked embarrassing questions without embarrassment. He did not shy away from disagreements, and he formed judgments quickly—usually with uncanny accuracy. During one dinner party, he engaged a newly appointed head of school from an independent school to spell out the moral foundations he used in his decision-making. The head of school thought he could deflect attention from this interrogation by lightheartedly talking about consulting his gut and acting on his feelings. Joel would have none of it and insisted on a concrete example. None was forthcoming. He pressed on with heated intensity. As an educational leader, what sources of authority did he call upon, what ethical and theological traditions did he use as a touchstone, and how did he make known the ethical content of his decisions to the larger community? He refused to ease up. He made the point painfully clear: this headmaster had a great deal of serious thought and hard work to do.

The next time we sat down for a meal, I asked him if he intended to humiliate this freshly installed headmaster. He answered, "The man has an enormously important job to do. His failure to engage and to examine the underpinnings of his moral convictions made me angry. Earlier that evening he had identified himself as a Jew. And he had no idea how to tap into his tradition or why it was worth the bother." And so began a long inquiry into the nature of anger and accountability, a subject that we never fully exhausted.

Once again, we circled back to our fathers. Mine turned his anger inward, and he suffered from an unremitting low-grade depression. It was anger drained of all enthusiasm. On those occasions when his rage turned outward, I feared a volcanic eruption that would burn everyone in its path. I think my father feared the same, and so he mostly kept us at a safe distance from his ill temper. Not so with Joel. I realized, somewhat reluctantly, I could not really get close to Joel without becoming deeply familiar with his anger.

We were both keenly aware of the many shapes and sizes in which anger arrives. We both did battle with its neurotic manifestations, the anger that erupted when we strained to control what stubbornly refused our management, and anger that surfaced when we realized we had not taken responsibility for matters over which we had sway. We were intimately familiar with the omnivorous appetites of a bad temper, the ways in which rage swallows everything and everyone within range of its bite. And all because the garbage disposal does not work, or we are faced with an unwelcome interruption, or a whining colleague, or a bout of indigestion. We also knew the distinct anatomy of an anger mixed with fear and uncertainty—a sick child, a suicide, a dreaded diagnosis, a spouse or friend out of reach and in serious trouble.

The challenge was to determine the substance and character of anger, distinguishing the corrosive and dysfunctional variety as opposed to a potent righteous indignation, which holds meaning and purpose. I believe Joel would define this affective response as "serious anger." The violations that triggered this expression of outrage in Joel flared when brought face-to-face with moral indolence. He had exacting standards, and the flouting of basic ethical norms unleashed a storm. He came unglued where cheating, stealing, deception, and betrayal were involved.

Joel maintained that indignation is a righteous response to injustice. Were we to be accepting or indifferent in the midst of suffering, cruelty, and corruption, we would forfeit our own humanity and become accomplices to crimes that echo on high. Ethical lapses have theological implications. Moral violations defile the holy ground on which we stand, and the contamination seeps into the larger community. He paid close attention to the rage in the streets, and the imperative to penetrate its inner character. When, he wanted to know, is indignation righteous, and when is it born of failed bids for power and control? When does anger bespeak legitimate demands for revolution and when is it simply an expression of a resentment kindled when we do not get our way or fail to receive what we think we deserve?

Aristotle once noted: "Anybody can become angry—that is easy, but to be angry with the right person and to the right degree and at the right time and for the right purpose, and in the right way—that is not within everybody's power and is not easy."[1] Joel exhorted me to determine when to hang on to anger and urged me to find ways to put it to constructive purpose. But he also urged me to recognize that there are times to let it go. Few conditions are more enervating than being owned by our anger. I marveled at his capacity to move on after an eruption. He did not cling to

---

1. Aristotle, *Nicomachean Ethics* 2.9.

resentments or allow wounds to fester. He knew the danger of looking back and second-guessing. He was more than willing to own his mistakes and acknowledge his overreactions. He also did not dwell on the grievances or failures of others. He knew that the backward gaze can become a habit that turns the unwary into pillars of salt.

Over the last decade of his life, retirement seemed to blunt his propensity for outrage. Not only was this due to a change in his circumstances, but I think the allure of anger faded as it became popularized. The politicization of anger rubbed off whatever shine it once held. As our country embraced a culture of grievance and became compulsively polarized, the challenges we contemplated required a move away from anger. We agreed the need to diffuse rage posed an urgent challenge, and this subject became a topic for lively discussion.

I spoke of the imperative to love and forgive. He pushed back against my reflexive bromide. To his way of thinking, Christians entertain saintly aspirations, which more often than not remain out of reach. When Christians finally realize that they are failing to love their enemies and are stumbling badly in the footsteps of Jesus, they dare not rage against the one who called them to a life of perfection. But anger will out itself—somewhere at some point. He suspected Christians are at war with their finitude and unwilling to accept the limitations of their earthbound condition. This failure sets them off. Since the frustration must go somewhere, it gives rise to excessive self-incrimination or issues in violence toward those who dare to be different.

Joel claimed Christians set an impossible bar. They are captivated by ideals that pave the way to disillusionment; indeed, they hide behind unattainable standards to avoid the hard work of building an honest relationship—one that includes anger and is attuned to sacred argumentation. He contended my calls for love and forgiveness would exacerbate the conditions of resentment and fuel the fires of an unproductive guilt. Instead, he would settle for the virtues of forbearance, restraint, and mutual tolerance. It is enough for us to be chastened by political defeat, to take the measure of its consequences, to hold fast to our convictions, to muster the resources and energy to resist, and to take bold steps to regroup and regain power. Tolerate the opposition without acquiescence. But for God's sake and ours, leave love out of it.

As far as he was concerned, love and forgiveness invoked categories that struck him as supercilious within our current political context. He thought Christian appeals to love ring hollow and more often than not betray its deeper meaning. Love, he insisted, is too often reduced to a feeling or sentiment, which leads Christians to nestle into a soft-headed abstraction.

He could not imagine how John Lennon or anyone else could insist that "all you need is love." If Joel were to land on a definition, he would most likely endorse the words of British philosopher and novelist Iris Murdoch: "Love is the extremely difficult realization that something other than oneself is real."[2] And that discovery entails hard and resolute labor. He would confirm Murdoch's recapitulation of an Italian proverb: "Between saying and doing, many a pair of shoes is worn out."

On one occasion, he suggested that Christians might consider putting a moratorium on the very use of the word. Instead, he wanted us to substitute words that describe and guide deeds—actions that embody a compassionate performance, what Jewish tradition calls "acts of loving-kindness" (*gemilut hasidim*). Grounded as he was in *halakhah* (Jewish observance), he thought Christians need to be more explicit in spelling out the behavioral implications of love. What he wanted was more attention given to its praxis and less attention to the espousal of vague and threadbare platitudes.

In more sweeping terms, he wondered if Christian notions of "belief" and "faith" and "doctrinal assent" provide a stable foundation on which to build a coherent and cohesive religious community—all the more so when legal guardrails, moral strictures, and ritual observance are systemically undervalued. He was troubled by the tendency of Christians to map out their identities on the basis of propositional thinking, the habit of construing community in terms of ethereal creeds. After reading a good quantity of Christian theology, he wondered if my kin deals with the fact we have a stomach, hands, and feet. Why do we Christians not devote more attention to the ways in which we embody a tradition and give concrete expression to a distinctive form of life? Martin Luther King's leadership should serve as a norm rather than stand out as an exception.

Although his challenges linger in heart and mind, what now strikes me as most remarkable has less to do with the actual content of his critiques than the manner in which he advanced his arguments. Joel was not out to score points or to elevate his own tradition at the expense of mine. He was quick to acknowledge we both had inherited a working vocabulary that was susceptible to semantic exhaustion and trivialization. Guilt, sin, love, and forgiveness had also become fraught categories within his own community, as he was quick to acknowledge.

He turned up the heat in our conversations and pursued sacred arguments because he was committed to helping me identify and think through problems besetting the future of the Christian family to which I belonged. I came away from our meetings with the conviction that he cared deeply

---

2. Murdock, "Sublime and the Good," 51.

about the health and viability of my community—as if he believed that our two traditions are in some mysterious way bound together and that the collapse of one would sooner or later redound on the other. Although divided by a history that had pitted our communities against one another and separated by doctrinal claims that rendered us in no small measure unintelligible to one another, we grew into the uncanny conviction that our destinies are intertwined.

The changes wrought through such a friendship have revelatory significance, and this relationship informed my educational aspirations for the ICJS. Amidst the steps and missteps that go into the formation of friendship, something new breaks into the world, and nothing is ever the same again. It took time for me to realize the nature of this gift and to fathom its institutional implications. Joel demonstrated his trust and respect for me in his refusal to avoid conflict and disagreement. He contested my assumptions and pressed me to peel away layers of confusion, to befriend uncertainty, and to examine the why and the how, the when and the where of my faith. What is faith's content and substance, its meaning and its end? Yet his probing aimed at helping me find firmer ground on which to stand. Insofar as clarity arose, it came as I pushed back and pulled him into a shared struggle. I told him friendship is tethered to grace, and he confessed this category struck him as one more example of fuzzy-headed speculation. No, I insisted; grace is simply an affirmation that the sum is greater than its parts. There is a presence in the encounter bigger and more surprising than anything we could have made for ourselves, a reality that transcends our own devising.

CHAPTER 9

Job and the Question of Suffering

In the early days of the ICJS, I worried over how we could encourage the rabbis to delve into the depths of the Christian tradition. Christian participants had embarked on an uncharted path of study, learning about a history their seminaries and divinity schools sidestepped and contending with a theological triumphalism that bred contempt for those regarded as outsiders. Simultaneously they were discovering a dynamic Jewish tradition that did not atrophy after the destruction of the second temple. Might the rabbis find a theological excursion into Christian doctrine a worthy pursuit, most especially a close examination of those concepts that perplexed or scandalized Jewish sensibilities—such as the incarnation and Trinity?

We extended an invitation to the Baltimore Board of Rabbis and were delighted to host a series of study sessions with a few dozen Jewish leaders from the region. But after a few presentations by several Christian theologians, I noticed glazed eyes and a heavy malaise. The prospect of treading water in a foreign ocean held little appeal and no discernible relevance for their own work. As several rabbinic colleagues told me, "We study sacred texts. We have no appetite for systematic theology. That is something we just don't do!" Nor were the rabbis interested in rehearsing the historical travails of Jews at the hands of zealous Christians. They wanted Christians to learn the anguish of a conflicted past and to examine thoroughly the role the church played in laying the foundations of hostility. However, this was homework that belonged to Christians. They did not want to pile on the guilt or, worse, be enlisted into a pastoral role of helping Christians feel better about their long list of sins. A different paradigm to guide the

Jewish-Christian encounter was required—one that would provoke, if not inspire, all of us to think anew.

In an effort to find a level playing field, the ICJS staff decided to configure a clergy forum and devote the better part of a year to an examination of the book of Job. Since the overwhelming majority of ministers, priests, and rabbis are called upon to care for the sick and dying—and their extended families—we proposed a colloquy to explore how we each read and interpret this biblical narrative. Suffering and death, after all, affect the deepest registers of the human mind and heart; they are the inescapable realities with which all must contend. Every religious tradition proves its worth and reveals its deficiencies in the struggle to wrest meaning out of torment. Suffering gives rise to the fundamental question: are the heavens above us and the ground beneath firm enough to support us? This is another way of asking if the One who creates and sustains the world is really and truly trustworthy.

We approached the book of Job wondering what guidance and wisdom this narrative had to offer, and we wanted to consider how our interpretations of this work might come up short, or even misdirect our caregiving. What are the distinct ways in which Jews and Christians draw upon Job to find meaning in the midst of pain and death, or at least find ways of diminishing its ravages? When and how does the pastoral guidance derived from our respective traditions compound and exacerbate the experience of dislocation and trauma, and when and how do our traditions offer reassurance and wise counsel?

We recruited approximately thirty people—an even mix of Jewish and Christian clergy—into this educational venture. Sessions were held each month, and discussions revolved around assigned segments from Job. Every other month the ICJS invited a scripture scholar, philosopher, or theologian to deliver a lecture and facilitate a plenary discussion. On alternate months, small clusters of participants convened, identified key questions, and then tried to tease out the distinctive ways in which Jews and Christians understood and applied these texts in their congregational work. We configured these small study groups so that Reform, Reconstructionist, Conservative, and Modern Orthodox Jews were evenly distributed among Roman Catholic, mainline Protestant, and evangelical Christians—thereby ensuring that the diversity within and between our traditions was honored.

It was within the context of these study clusters that some of the most surprising friendships were forged. Several years after the programs concluded, I remember a Southern Baptist minister and an Orthodox rabbi telling me that they had consulted regularly in order to find out how they each handled various biblical narratives and dealt with confounding religious questions.

All manner of conundrums emerged over the course of that year, and a few examples will demonstrate the flavor and range of our inquiries. The book of Job hurls a broad range of challenges at the reader, not least the assertion that Job's plight is the result of a bet between God and the *satan* (the Hebrew word for "accuser"). From the start, the story provides grounds for the reader's horror. For instance, the victims of the contest have nothing to do with the question of Job's righteousness; they are collateral damage in a trial adjudicated without regard to their inherent worth or moral standing. From the very outset, God's justice is put in question.

After Job has endured crushing affliction and the loss of his family and wealth, three friends come to console him. "Each man tore his coat, and they hurled dirt over their heads toward the sky. They sat down on the ground with him for seven days and seven nights, no one speaks a word to him, for they saw his pain was very great."[1]

The entire group was quick to acknowledge that Job's friends demonstrate their loyalty and care by coming to the side of their afflicted neighbor and sitting in solidarity with him. The best we clergy have to offer is our presence, a willingness to show up and not look away. Our unswerving regard may be the most powerful gift any of us has to offer. In the words of Simone Weil, the philosopher and mystic whose allegiance was directed to the politically and economically marginal, "Attention is the rarest and purest form of generosity. Absolutely unmixed attention is prayer."[2]

In the case of Job's friends and those armed with good intentions who follow their example, the problems do not really arise until they open their mouths. Most clergy are trained to believe that they have words that will offer comfort and guidance, that they can help the infirm find at least a scrap of meaning in the struggle, that they can help fend off despair with glimmers of hope. A good death—isn't that what everyone wants? But can clergy deliver compassionate and honest assurances that enable the dying to loosen their grip and let go?

---

1. Greenstein, trans., *Job*, 11.

2. Simone Weil (1909-1943) was raised within a secular Jewish family and was deeply attracted to the mystical teachings and eucharistic piety of Roman Catholicism, although she declined to be baptized—for reasons that were rooted in her identification with people regarded as outsiders. Her emphasis on "attention" as a spiritual discipline is most powerfully expressed in her books *Gravity and Grace* and *Waiting on God*. Popova, "Simone Weil on Attentiuon and Grace," https://www.themarginalian.org/2015/08/19/simone-weil-attention-gravity-and-grace/.

One rabbi recounted the experience of visiting the enfeebled father of a congregant—this was one of the first pastoral visits in his career. He approached the man's bedside and parked himself within the father's reach, and soon thereafter heard the faint mumblings of a man on death's doorstep. He leaned his head in closer and explained that he could not understand the words the poor man was uttering. Again the man groaned, louder and more intently than before, but no more intelligibly. Yet another unsuccessful effort followed, and the rabbi turned to his congregant and explained his inability to decipher anything that was being said. So the son bent over his father and asked him to repeat his words. The father obliged, turning to his son and grumbling into his ear. The son then reported to the dutiful rabbi: "Dad wants to know who the f*** you are and what the f*** you want."

On this matter our entire group found rare consensus: the encounter with our own impotence can come as quite a shock. We might do well to bear in mind the adage carved into the back wall of a Quaker meeting house: "Do not open your mouth unless you can improve upon silence."

Divisions began to emerge in response to the question of Job's initial silence, his refusal to follow his wife's instruction to "Curse God and die" (Job 2:9 NRSV). The prologue portrays a righteous individual who insists we cannot accept the good from God without also accepting the bad. Yet the tone is reversed as soon as we engage Job's opening discourse. Immediately we are struck by Job's protests—the intensity of his complaint, the outrage and the defiance in his wish that he had never been born.

In our discussions about pain and suffering, one of my Christian colleagues described his agony in the dentist chair. With the hum of the drill filling his ears, the deep jabbing and sharp sting of the dental instrument digging into the nerve, he recalled the teachings of his third grade teacher, a dutiful nun of impeccable character. He was instructed to "offer it up" always and everywhere, the "it" being the pain. He tried to see the suffering as an opportunity to identify with Jesus and to better appreciate the affliction endured on our behalf. In response, Rabbi Zaiman remarked, "There may be circumstances when we are called upon to suffer on behalf of others or to withstand torment as an expression of fidelity. But do you think God needs or wants your dental pain? What exactly is it you are offering?"

My Christian colleague was quick to insist his predicament certainly did not bear the slightest resemblance to the plight of Job. Yet he did press on to ask what we can learn in the midst of affliction. Suffering often strikes inexplicably, and it demands a response. Perhaps the most important discovery revealed by our vulnerability to pain is that we are not the center of the universe around which everyone and everything is in orbit. We are subject to injury and illness, decay and death. And while our first question is often "Why me?" or "Why must this happen to the people I love?," we may upon reflection see our adversity in a different light.

Job makes it unmistakably clear: calamities are not distributed on the basis of merit. As my Protestant philosophy professor Diogenes Allen once wrote, "When the flow of our self-regard is painfully interrupted, reflection can lead to a new awareness of our limitations, and it may lead to *an act of acceptance* of such limitations."[3] The experience of affliction is profoundly humbling, but paradoxically it enables the realization of our spiritual nature. Submission to unavoidable suffering can lead the afflicted to the recognition that they transcend their physical nature precisely at the moment they acknowledge their material vulnerability. In the words of Professor Allen,

> When nature's negative side is pressed upon us and no direct graciousness is known, it seems that we now have lost all contact with a loving God. . . . The affliction of Christ gives this person reason to accept unavoidable adversities caused by nature as an indirect contact with God. It is to be roughly handled—as was the Son—but still it is to be in the hands of God, even though one is in immediate contact with the harsh side of nature. Because of Christ's affliction we have a way to believe that the Father's concern never ceases, and by our previous actions, we can believe in the divine love even in the midst of adversities when a loving presence is not felt in any way.[4]

Without taking an extended detour into theological formulations that are bewildering, if not scandalous, to non-Christian ears, let me briefly clarify some of the ways in which a good many Christians read Job. Sin is often understood as a condition of alienation, a state of unyielding estrangement that separates us from one another and from God. The horror of the crucifixion resides in the agonizing separation that Jesus endures with respect to God and humanity. Not only have his closest disciples abandoned or betrayed him, but Jesus cries out from the cross, in both Mark and Matthew, the opening line from Psalm 22: "My God, my God, why have you forsaken me?" This is the moment that leads Christians to the interpretation that Jesus has taken on the sin of the world. His physical and spiritual destitution is the embodiment of humanity at the furthermost edge of alienation. And yet out of this desolation springs the affirmation manifest in Jesus' resurrection. God's reach spans the greatest imaginable divide, overcoming the power of sin and the reality of death. Therefore, Christians have often insisted that they remain in God's providential hand even in the midst

---

3. Allen, "Suffering at the Hands of Nature," 184.
4. Allen, "Suffering at the Hands of Nature," 189.

of extreme pain and suffering. They may not experience this assurance in the throes of agony, but the apostle Paul's words reflect a potent conviction: "neither death, nor life, nor angels, nor rulers, nor things present, nor things to come, nor powers, nor height, nor depth, nor anything else in all creation, will be able to separate us from the love of God in Christ Jesus our Lord" (Rom 8:38–39 RSV).

The pastoral practice of instructing sick or dying patients to affirm faith in divine providence and to embrace their suffering as an act of solidarity, which aligns them with the experience of Jesus' crucifixion, may seem analogous to trying to construct a plane when it is already in the air. Professor Allen would have been the first to acknowledge this orientation is not established as an idea the patient first tries on in the throes of suffering. This path into and through affliction is not simply a thought arrived at through logical analysis, but the result of an extended practice, a well-formed habit, a disposition woven into a person's innermost core. The affirmation is rooted in the desire to see, feel, and imagine God in our midst through all the twists and turns of our lives. The practice is consolidated in community through prayer and worship, through the discipline of caring for others, and through a long struggle with doubt and uncertainty.

Some of the rabbis found this aspect of Christian devotion moving. More found these musings strange and unintelligible. A few regarded this spiritual outlook as incommensurate with the lived experience of many patients and wondered how even those grounded in the Christian tradition respond when encouraged to confirm God's presence in the throes of agony. Does this counsel ever compound feelings of despair and hopelessness? What if patients fail to hold on to the belief that God is present in their suffering and they attribute the experience of abandonment to their own lack of faith? Wouldn't this counsel impugn the adequacy of their piety, intensify the sense of isolation, and magnify feelings of guilt? Wouldn't this approach make the Christian counselor yet another of Job's bumbling friends—out to justify God and explain away the spiritual, psychological, and physical dimensions of adversity?

In our inquiries, we returned over and over again to the question: when, if ever, is suffering redemptive? There was general agreement that the contours of our character are profoundly shaped by our tribulations. Without grappling with dislocation and hardship, virtues such as fortitude and wisdom—seen as essential within our traditions—would remain undeveloped. Furthermore, the ordeals people endure are almost invariably occasions for soul-searching, and the pursuit of the underlying cause is an automatic reflex. Most of us reflexively ask what we might have done to deserve the hardships that take us by storm. Christians and Jews alike acknowledged the fact that they are bound to biblical texts that link sin, punishment, and suffering. Time and again the Bible tells us calamities—including plagues and famines—are the result of disobedience.

So much depended on the ways in which the participants read Job and opened themselves to a wide range of meanings within its pages, particularly in the conclusion. A number of the rabbis drew upon a tradition of arguing with God and saw argumentative prayer as the operative dynamic in Job.

While Job's friends seek justifications for God's treatment of Job and decry the possibility that the ways of the Almighty might be unjust, Job holds fast to his innocence. From Job's perspective, God's scourges are unjust, and he mounts a kind of legal defense based on mutual obligations to support his position. He has the audacity to mount a protest and challenge the exercise of divine power because he believes he can marshal the authority of the law to advance his case. Verses 13:7–14:22 reveal the legal framework that levels the gap between these two litigants and is deployed to neutralize the vastly different resources at their disposal.

> Hear my words
> My Declaration—with your ears.
> Here: I am laying out my lawsuit.
> I know I am in the right.
> Who would argue the case with me?
>
> How many are my crimes and my sins?
> My transgression and my sin—tell me what they are!
> Why do you hide your face,
> And reckon me your enemy?[5]

As Catherine Chin elucidates, "The strength of the passage lies in Job's implicit argument that a powerful God can as easily be a bully, a knowledgeable God can be a meddler, a judging God draconian, and an exalted God irrelevant. The author of Job is effective precisely because he does not deny God's virtues, but transforms them into weaknesses through which he can implicitly defame the Deity and through which a powerful argument can be advanced for God's injustice."[6]

The implication of Job's protestations is startling: God has been acting outside the legal, covenantal bounds of fairness and therefore must answer the accuser. Ironically Job mounts his defense from a position of inferiority and complains that God's massively superior power is deployed in a manner befitting a cosmic tyrant who terrorizes the defenseless. The imbalance in

---

5. Greenstein, trans., *Job*, 57–58.
6. Chin, "Job and the Injustice of God," 94.

might and authority heightens God's accountability. In effect, Job has now become the accuser and the examiner.

Job's interrogation of God is not unprecedented. We have already noted Abraham's protest in response to God's decision to destroy Sodom and Gomorrah (Gen 18:22–33). Moses argues with God on behalf of the people who worshipped the golden calf, establishing this people as "Your people" (Exod 32:9–14, 30–34). The psalms of lament, too, contend with divine absence, exhorting God to wake up and come to the rescue (Ps 35:22–23).

This tradition is etched into the Jewish tradition and finds expression in a wide range of stories. One of my favorites tells the tale of the Hasidic master Levi Yitchok of Berditchev, who was revered for his insistent intercessions on behalf of the Jewish people:

> Once on Kol Nidre, the holiest night of the year when all sins are confessed, the tailor, one of the most devout members of the community, was absent. Concerned, the rabbi left the synagogue and went to the tailor's home. To his surprise he found the tailor looking at a piece of paper before him on the table. "What's the matter?" asked Levi Yitzhak. "Oh, everything's fine," replied the tailor. "As I was getting ready to attend the service I made a list with two columns. At the top of one I wrote my name and at the top of the other I wrote, 'God of all the Universe.'
>
> Then, one by one, I began to list my sins. 'Cheated Goldman out of a pair of trousers.' And in God's column I noted God's omission: 'Little girl died of diphtheria.' Then the next sin, 'Lost my temper with my children,' and in God's column, 'I heard there was a famine in another country.'" And so it went. The tailor showed the rabbi the completed list. "And for every sin I had committed during the past year, God had done one too. So I said to God, 'Look, we each have the same number of sins. If you let me off, I'll let You off.'"
>
> But the story does not end there. When the rabbi looked at the paper his face grew red and he scolded his friend" "You fool! You had Him and you let Him go!"[7]

The story often continues with Rabbi Levi Yitchok exclaiming that the tailor's argument provided grounds not just for his acquittal; no, the logic should have been extended so that all of Israel, and indeed the entire world, could be reconciled with God.

While this tale may have been told tongue in cheek, the underlying thrust reflects a practice of seeing oneself in solidarity with the larger community, especially in times of great vulnerability. Furthermore, the

7. As told by Lawrence Kushner in *Eyes Remade for Wonder*, 59–60.

covenantal bond between God and Israel entails mutual obligation—and the cry for help makes a demand that calls forth a response. In the event entreaties fail to elicit help, the imperative of argumentative prayer is to increase the volume and to apply maximum pressure.

The writings of Elie Wiesel offer contemporary testimony to this Jewish tradition. In his groundbreaking novel *Night* and again in his play *The Trial of God*, Wiesel invokes memories of a Jewish community on the edge of extinction. Whether in the death camps during the Shoah or in Eastern Europe while pogroms were ravaging Jewish communities in 1649, the story is told of a handful of learned and pious Jews who decide to put God on trial for allowing his children to be murdered. Witnesses are gathered, evidence collected, and crimes recounted. At the conclusion of the proceedings, God is pronounced guilty. Then one of the talmudic scholars takes notice of the darkening sky and calls the members of the tribunal to their evening prayers. Here is the embodiment of human fidelity that is not contingent on circumstance or God's favor. "Though He slay me, yet will I trust Him" (Job 13:15 KJV).

During the course of our inquiries into Job, the rabbis brought this tradition of argumentative prayer into the thick of our conversations and wondered if there were similar patterns within the Christian tradition. As previously noted, the final words attributed to Jesus on the cross—in both Mark 15:34 and Matthew 27:46—reiterate the lament of Psalm 22 and offer a point of connection with the practice of protestation. However, most of the Christians in our colloquy found it extremely difficult to make the move into an adversarial posture, one that dares to rebuke God for negligence or injustice. Others Christian colleagues found an unexpected comfort in a tradition of lament that had in large measure been neglected or suppressed in their church traditions. My own Presbyterian heritage has placed so much emphasis on the sovereignty of God that the chutzpah involved in reprimanding the divine initially struck me as blasphemous. My family's piety upheld submission as the appropriate expression of religious fidelity. "Thy will be done" was our Christian mantra, and we read Job as a confirmation of our need to capitulate to the Almighty.

After God answers Job—or, perhaps more accurately, after Job is brought face-to-face with the majesty and sovereignty of the Most High, entirely overpowered by the Holy One—the translation of the text that most Christians accept as authoritative validates acquiescence:

> Then Job answered the LORD:
> "I know that you can do all things,
>   and that no purpose of yours can be thwarted.

'Who is this that hides counsel without knowledge?'
Therefore I have uttered what I did not understand,
   things too wonderful for me, which I did not know.
'Hear, and I will speak;
   I will question you, and you declare to me.'
I had heard of you by the hearing of the ear,
   but now my eye sees you;
therefore I despise myself,
   and repent in dust and ashes." (Job 42:1–6 NSRV)

A number of the rabbis were disgruntled with this translation and insisted this handling of the text mischaracterizes Job's response. They commended the translation by the Jewish scholar Edward Greenstein, along with his explanatory glosses:

> Up spoke Job to YHWH and he said:
> I have known you are able to do all;
> That you cannot be blocked from any scheme.
> "Who is this hiding counsel without knowledge?" (Job mimicking God in 38:2)
> Truly I've spoke without comprehension—
> Wonders beyond me that I do not know. (A mock concession)
> "Hear now and I will speak!
> I will ask you and you help me know!" (Job mimicking God in 38:3; 40:7)
> As a hearing by the ear I have heard you,
> And now my eye has seen you. (A mock confession already said in 13:1)
> That is why I am fed up;
> I take pity on dust and ashes. (A figure for wretched humanity)
> (Job 42:1–6)[8]

According to Greenstein, professor emeritus of Bible at Bar-Ilan University—who has spent more than fifty years of his academic career plumbing the depths of this biblical text—Job is "parodying the divine discourse through mimicry" and expressing "disdain toward the deity and pity toward humankind (and not acquiescence)."[9] This reading supports the image of Job as driven to insanity. My impression—often amplified by my colleague Dr. Rosann Catalano—is this: Job is not just an angry rebel, but one who, having seen the face of God, is driven over the edge. Job is submerged in the madness of the seer who has encountered a divine truth that shatters

---

8. Greenstein, trans., *Job*, 184–85.
9. Greenstein, trans., *Job*, 185.

long-standing assumptions and demolishes the norms that make life predictable and secure. No longer bounded by the sanity's unwritten rules and regulations, Job can speak truths with greater accuracy and honesty than a sane and reasonable man could possibly entertain.

This is the madman Elie Wiesel invokes in his descriptions of the prophet who warns of an imminent disaster: the madman who has gazed into the heart of darkness and predicts the arrival of the Nazi invader. The crazed fool who is ignored by his community knows the destructive power of the whirlwind, and the multitude dismisses his vision as delusional.

Once again, we were reminded how much pivots on our translations—and how no translation can be freed from the ongoing demands of interpretation. There is a reservoir of interpretative portraits developed within the Jewish and Christian traditions, and readers are challenged not to submit mindlessly to any one version. The questions raised by Job's concluding speech were freighted with pastoral implications. It's no surprise this was one more issue over which Joel Zaiman and I argued.

My reflexive response to someone caught in the jaws of pain was to invoke the Reinhold Niebuhr "Serenity Prayer"—whether explicitly shared with the anguished patient or internally clenched: "God, grant me the serenity to accept the things I cannot change, the courage to change the things I can, and the wisdom to know the difference."

"So at the bedside of a dying congregant who is suffering miserably, you encourage them to let go? To put themselves in God's hands? To accept and surrender to a higher power?" Joel queried. "That's fine. But how do you really know what cannot be changed, what must be simply accepted? The wisdom to which Niebuhr alludes is in short supply when we are dealing with suffering. And isn't prayer an overture to change what seems unchangeable?"

"Not necessarily. Perhaps we are simply trying to hold on to a sense of gratitude for the life we have been given, the blessings of friends and family, and the wonder of it all. To see the totality as a gift."

"But what if that person is fighting like hell, not going gently into the night, raging against realities that cannot be bent to her will? What if this person feels deep down that God has betrayed her? Doesn't Job offer another option that is true to her experience and worthy of the name 'prayer'?"

"What makes you think God needs or wants our anger? Why is it acceptable to hurl our rage at God, but not to offer up our pain? Isn't this indignation unacceptable because it is rooted in an outsized sense of entitlement?" I answered.

Joel pressed on: "You seem to think God cannot handle your outrage. Your decorum conceals those sides of yourself and your community that you think unseemly and offensive. But this borders on dishonesty—and your self-restraint signals a lack of trust. Your faith in God is guarded and timid. If we are to love God with all our heart, mind, and soul—as you have often insisted—why not bring one's entire self, including our imperfections, our frustrations, and even our demands to God?"

I pleaded: "Even Moses had the good sense to take off his shoes in this encounter with God. I furthermore assume God knows our innermost thoughts and feelings, and I do not see how parading my grievances adds any good to a bleak situation."

He wondered if our approach to God was governed more by fear than love—and suggested that maybe Job was modeling a fearlessness from which both our communities might learn something. We agreed that insofar as Greenstein's Job dares to mock and display contempt for God's providential management, Job crosses a bridge neither one could traverse. At the end of the day, we agreed that Wiesel's talmudic sage had it right. Having convicted God for dereliction of duty, when the time came to put on *tefillin* and recite the evening prayers, the community demonstrated its own fidelity—regardless of God's reciprocity.

Neither of us found consolation in the reversals of fortune at the conclusion of the book. What were we to make of an ending in which God rewards Job with abundance—whether he be a madly unhinged accuser or a submissive supplicant? Families and friends are not so easily swapped, as anyone who has endured the death of a child or spouse can attest. Job would need to be insane, resigned, and/or utterly detached from his previous world not to carry the trauma with him. To embrace a whole new family and celebrate the restoration of his status and wealth would seem to require the gift of amnesia. It was hard for us to imagine Job capable of a deep and abiding trust at the end of the day.

The kinds of exchanges into which Joel and I plunged were commonplace among the participants. The scriptures we explored along with the many layers of distinct—often contrasting and sometimes conflicting—traditions of interpretation generated an intimacy of relationship that took us off guard. The experience entailed a dramatic change in the way we engaged sacred texts, especially among the Christian members. Most of us Christians were raised in an educational setting where a learned professor was called upon to fill empty heads with carefully researched material; we were weaned on practices aligned with textual literalism. As students our job was to acquire the intellectual tools to extract a stable and fixed meaning from the scriptures. Our education was designed to make experts of us, authorities who could then feed their flocks with accurate and reliable explanations.

But in Baltimore our approach to Job destabilized this pedagogy, convincing all of us that scripture holds hidden treasure and multiple possibilities. As stated in the Bablyonian Talmud, Sandedrin 34a, "'Behold, My word is like fire'—declares the Lord—'and like a hammer that shatters rock' (Jer 23:29). Just as this hammer produces many sparks, so a single verse has several meanings." When we study scripture together, the hammer hits the rock and shatters it into seventy pieces—matching the seventy faces of the Torah (*Shivim Panim l 'Torah*). None of us on our own can gather up all the fragments, but in virtue of the unique experience we each bring to the task, different participants will uncover sacred shards that had escaped the notice of others. During the course of the year, the Christian and Jewish participants realized they need to study together because their combined discoveries enabled them to assemble a more comprehensive and incisive understanding than would have been possible had the book been the exclusive province of a solitary interpreter or a single tradition.

This exuberant and fractious style of inquiry did not negate the insights emanating from rigorous biblical analysis. Yet beyond the exegetical methodologies, we experienced an approach that defamiliarized our readings of the text and challenged the Christian tendency to seek refuge in abstractions—as though correct thinking and definitive conclusions are the keys to unlocking divine mysteries. In the context of shared text study, we were discovering that our understanding may be more deeply tied to embellished storytelling than metaphysical speculation. Sustained engagement with a sacred narrative, coupled with risk-taking, an openness to disruption, and a playful suspension of dogmatic certainties, opened a new door. The Jewish Israeli writer Amos Elon once noted how Jews and Christians are accurately described by Muslims as "People of the Book," meaning that they live in a house of paper. Our collaborative study disclosed the resilience and the fragility of these building materials, and the discipline of reading scripture together became foundational at the ICJS for many years to come.

CHAPTER 10

Bill and Judith Moyers and the Genesis Project

While the ICJS was launching the scripture forum in Baltimore, Rabbi Burton Visotzky was venturing outside the hallowed walls of the Jewish Theological Seminary in New York City, where he served as professor of midrash. In a variety of settings with a diverse array of professionals from a wide range of religious backgrounds, Dr. Visotzky was choreographing small group study sessions and setting the stage for participants to learn the art of scriptural interpretation. He focused the groups' attention on the book of Genesis, introducing them to the rambunctious wrangling of the rabbinic sages and nudging his recruits to plunge into biblical waters. Word traveled that Visotzky was orchestrating the best conversations in the city.

Bill and Judith Moyers caught wind of the excitement. Raised a Southern Baptist and ordained a minister, Bill Moyers's career moved into politics and then veered into journalism. Both Bill and Judith were uncommonly qualified to recognize the blessings and the curses lodged within the Good Book. Bill expressed deep concern about the fact that Americans no longer seemed to have a treasury of stories and myths that they shared and that bound them together—not that our country was ever fastened to the same interpretations! Yet there were once biblical narratives that a large percentage of the population drew upon and argued about. Our citizenry had a shared vocabulary that enabled it to engage in civil discourse and, at our best, discover one another's humanity.

Whether this binding tradition was tethered to nostalgia or a more stable ideal of the common good, Moyers saw a unique opportunity to team up with Burt Visotzky to produce a ten-part television series entitled *Genesis: A Living Conversation*. This was in 1996, and the project represented an unprecedented undertaking by the Public Broadcasting Service (PBS). The format featured biblical scholars from Jewish, Christian, and Muslim backgrounds as well as artists and novelists, lawyers, and other professionals. The series brought men and women, Black and Brown and white people to the table. Each episode included seven interlocutors conversing with one another and plumbing the depths of a single narrative from Genesis. The exchanges were sweeping in scope and unconventional in style. Consensus was neither sought nor achieved. Instead, each story accommodated multiple understandings—provoking spirited disputes. It was a celebration of pluralism revolving around a book all too often deployed to impose uniformity.

The scale of the project required massive funding, and the effort to secure the requisite monies was greatly facilitated by Lisa Goldberg at the Revson Foundation and Rabbi Rachel Cowan at the Cummins Foundation—and the resolute creativity of Judith Moyers. They knew which trees to shake. In the process of garnering the funds, they pulled together a remarkable coalition of enthusiastic supporters.

Rabbi Zaiman had developed a close relationship with Lisa over the years, and he had urged her to attend a few ICJS programs illustrative of our approach to scripture study. One of these programs featured Noam Zion, a master teacher at the Shalom Hartman Institute in Jerusalem. Lisa was captivated by a pedagogical approach that demonstrated the ways in which a biblical story gets refracted through Jewish and Christian traditions, yielding a panoply of feelings and ideas. She concluded that our educational organization was ideally poised to serve as an innovative partner in the development of educational resources that would move the conversation from the television screen into the living room. I was hired and tasked with the job of configuring a study guide for the Genesis series.

In cooperation with Lisa and journalist/author/editor Sandee Brawarsky, we mapped out an ambitious publication to embolden individuals and groups to grapple with the big questions in these stories. We recruited an eclectic band of contributors, and the resulting assemblage of commentaries broke the spell of textual familiarity and encouraged folks to enter the fray. Once the container was broken and a multitude of voices started to demand attention, participants began to recognize they also had a stake in these stories—the never-ending task of discovering what these narratives mean and how their claims endure.

Well known are the problems with television, not least the fact that many productions render the viewer passive and sluggish. The Moyers series on Genesis intended to overcome this malaise by pulling together an uncommon assortment of commentators. The sweep of the Moyers cast was designed to inspire disinterested spectators to put down their remotes, climb off the couch, and find settings where they could become active participants. Each episode was an hour in duration, and the multiplicity of viewpoints packed into each session offered many interpretations. But most of all it was the diversity of the troupe that turned out to be pivotal in our efforts to engage new audiences.

While the staff and board of the ICJS had managed to recruit a handful of Black leaders over the years, it was Bill Moyers's production that opened the door to a far more robust and expansive orientation. The African American contributors highlighted the degree to which these biblical narratives shaped their communal imagination and offered refuge from the dominant white culture. Until this point, many of the African American ministers I had tried to enlist in the work of the ICJS had been unmoved by my appeals. Separation and distance were vital in bolstering a distinct religious and ethnic identity—indeed the Black church and mosque may have been the only major institutions where de facto segregation lifted up and celebrated the unique talents and aptitudes of African Americans.

I also discerned another troubling dynamic. A great deal of our attention was given to an unflinching examination of antisemitism. A number of the African American ministers with whom I met insisted this was primarily a white European problem. They were not about to take the fall for pathologies not of their own making. Yet they too, I argued, relied on scriptures in which an anti-Jewish bias is deeply etched. They too were entangled in a culture that sanctioned and reinforced anti-Jewish prejudices. And here I encountered strong pushback. From the perspective of many of my African American colleagues, the problem of antisemitism had for the most part been overcome, while white racism flourished. They insisted the power and influence exercised by Jews in this country demonstrated the extraordinary progress in neutralizing this particular bias.

What became apparent in these exchanges was the extent to which a zero-sum logic operated. In general, African American colleagues believed attention directed to the plight of Jewish people turned the public's eye away from racism. I think these ministers had concluded white America had a very limited ability to reckon with suffering. It was more convenient for Americans to focus on a problem that had to some extent been addressed rather than confront the relentless racial dysfunctions deeply embedded in American life. The ICJS therefore registered as unwittingly complicit in sidestepping the most urgent and pernicious structural defect in the nation—the legacy of white supremacy.

But thanks to Bill and Judith Moyers, the ICJS was able to begin a new chapter in these relationships and pursue a more forthright reckoning with these historic challenges. The African Americans featured in the series highlighted the dynamic creativity and interpretive talents within a rich and vibrant tradition. The production set a table among equals and reassured members of the Black church that their voices would not be dismissed or ridiculed. This was turf where they had laid an undeniable claim.

These considerations factored into the configuration of our study guide as well. Yet the medium of a television production continued to pose a confounding problem. We worried that all the talking heads would exhaust audiences, and that they would conclude nothing of significance could add to the highbrow exchanges. Our challenge was to excite and embolden viewers so they would enthusiastically join the conversation and become engaged contributors. To this end, we collected a potpourri of quotations to trigger reflection; crafted short essays to open up avenues for further exploration; mixed in lively comments from a wide assortment of writers, philosophers, psychologists, and scripture scholars; and framed evocative discussion questions. What was originally envisioned as a modest compendium evolved into a wide-ranging book entitled *Talking about Genesis*.[1] In collaboration with Doubleday and PBS, more than one hundred thousand copies were printed and distributed around the country.

To launch the Moyers series and propel the study guide in Maryland, the ICJS configured a project we labeled the Genesis Project. We recruited ten synagogues, ten African American churches, and ten predominantly white churches to participate in a six-week series. Each congregation was charged with the task of recruiting ten members, and they were linked with two of their counterparts, thereby forming ten working circles. Each week participants would venture to another part of Greater Baltimore with other members in their triad or serve as the host. Some three hundred participants were crisscrossing the city, going to places where they had never stepped, and meeting people they would never have encountered otherwise.

Bill Moyers traveled to Baltimore to kick off this initiative, and the opening event attracted an audience of more than 1,200 people. In addition to the congregational project, we enlisted a diverse cross section of public and independent secondary schools to select students to participate in a six-week series. We also conducted study sessions in retirement communities and local colleges. At the conclusion, we held a jamboree to which all three hundred participants in the congregational project were invited. There was a remarkable outpouring of shared experiences, surprising discoveries, and

---

1. Public Affairs Television, *Talking about Genesis*.

evocative questions for ongoing exploration. The bonds forged through this program formed a foundation for future congregational projects, becoming another pillar of the ICJS.

The buzz generated by this venture rippled outward. One of the memorable expressions of this project took place in a maximum-security prison in Jessup, Maryland. In collaboration with the prison librarian, Rabbi Zaiman, Reverend Grady Yeargin (an African American Baptist colleague), and I were invited to facilitate study sessions among a group of twenty inmates. So began an astonishing six-week pilgrimage. Gaining access to the interior of the prison was an ordeal. I remember the echoes, the din of voices bouncing off cinder block, the cloying aroma of disinfectant, the maze of locked doors and winding corridors, and the spirals of razor wire encircling the entire complex. There were forms to fill out, metal detectors to negotiate, and skeptical guards who made it clear we were wasting our time. I do not know if the anxiety bubbled up from within or emanated from the sullen and distrustful glances that came at us from every direction. There was the knot in the stomach and a growing apprehension we really had nothing worthwhile to offer.

The three of us were escorted to a barren chamber with only a few small and dingy windows hung at an altitude limiting the view to the sky. The incessant flicker of florescent lights overhead kept us in the glare. A perimeter was formed out of metal folding chairs, and the three of us took our seats as the inmates shuffled into the circle and dutifully found theirs. The group was evenly divided between white and Black, and nearly every participant bore the markings of a tattoo. Some emblems were resplendent in design and workmanship; others were crude and ill defined. I found myself facing across the circle a mountainous white man in a black T-shirt and ragged jeans. He was scarred with a rough-hewn cross, one jagged line running across his forehead while the vertical stroke twisted down to the bridge of his nose—clearly not the work of skilled artist. His shaved head, jacked body, and unblinking scowl commanded attention. The man seated alongside of me must have detected my feeble attempts not to gawk and whispered in my ear that the gentleman opposite me was a satanist.

What passed through my mind was the conviction they were going to have a lot more fun with us than we with them. We three were fresh meat. We were the ones about to receive an education. As I struggled to get my bearings, I could not help but notice that the group was segmented into clusters apparently defined by race and political creed—and a predetermined seating arrangement maintained this ordering.

After going around the room and sharing our names, Joel, Grady, and I reviewed the ground rules for our conversation. We underscored the fact we had no expectation of reaching a definitive understanding of these stories. We then read the story of Adam and Eve (Gen 2:15—3:24).

Our attention was initially directed to the consumption of the forbidden fruit. I argued this act of disobedience is accurately described as "the fall." The quest was not simply a bid for knowledge, but an attempt by Adam and Eve to achieve independence, to displace God, and become a law unto themselves. Joel argued Adam and Eve were boldly taking a step into adulthood. Of course, they were seeking independence. Knowledge comes with a price, and their conduct was a bold move. God knew, and indeed wanted them to take risks. It was time for them to grow up and leave the confines of their garden home. Grady suggested the sin was not the result of consuming the forbidden fruit, but the refusal to take responsibility for their action. They scrambled to redirect God's attention, projecting the blame on others. Adam and Eve tried to cover up and conceal their deeds long before they had stitched fig leaves together.

For the remaining hour we did not need to utter another word. Our new students took over. They not only surprised us but I believe they surprised themselves. They were accustomed to having the Bible wielded against them. Its words were routinely invoked to reduce them in size and stature. It functioned like the wagging finger of a punitive judge certain of their guilt and poised to deliver a harsh sentence. The sacred scriptures, they made it known in subsequent conversations, were all too often enlisted by their teachers, clergy, and the larger culture to put them in their place and keep them in a state of exile.

Suddenly, then and there, the rules of the game were changed. They quickly realized they could push back. The first man to speak argued God had set up Adam and Eve. The game was rigged from the outset. Lord Acton was right: "Power corrupts, absolute power corrupts absolutely." The heads around the room nodded until another man interjected. He did not believe the story was primarily concerned with fixing blame on a couple whose curiosity incited them to test the boundaries. He saw "the myth" as a penetrating description of the human predicament. What the story revealed was the impact of our deeds, the way in which the good and bad we do ripples outward from one generation to the next. We live in the aftermath of mistakes that are passed along and then normalized in our families and communities. Without grasping the magnitude of the inheritance, children are punished for the iniquity of their parents. The blunders of one generation becomes structural, systemic, and fixed—and we don't even recognize the underlying roots of our alienation. This comment generated disagreement and struck some as an evasion of responsibility. We can't put the blame on our parents for our own shortcomings.

The conversation took a different tack when another participant wanted to explore the question: what, if anything, comprises "forbidden knowledge" and can the genie, freed of confinement, ever be put back in the bottle? How about the discoveries that made possible the nuclear bomb? Or the technological innovations that enable us to clone and engineer a new generation? Is innocence irretrievably lost—and are we still biting down on the prohibited fruit?

They went back and forth about the eviction from the garden. Did the punishment fit the crime? Was banishment a penalty that offered the means for correction, or was it damning payback, an unending punishment that would define humanity's fate ever after?

When, two hours later, the three of us climbed into the car to drive home, we marveled at the intensity of the conversation. They had read and interpreted the story as though something crucial was personally at stake. They had picked up each other's comments and handled each other's views carefully. They did not so much argue with one another as with the text, and this approach afforded them enough distance to avoid offensive provocation. The bald-headed giant whom I initially found so intimidating was soft-spoken and thoughtful. I marveled at his handling of the narrative as if he were holding a mirror, which might enable him to see things about himself and the world more clearly.

The tenor of this first conversation continued for the remaining sessions. The same men returned week after week, thoroughly prepared, having watched the relevant segment of the Moyers program and absorbed the substance of our study guide. I imagine the stories from Genesis invited such spirited conversation because we could all see ourselves reflected in the leading characters. Almost all of them were deeply flawed and entangled in damaging rivalries. Cain and Abel, Noah, Abraham, Sarah and Hagar, Isaac and Rebecca, Jacob and Esau, Rachel and Leah, Joseph and his brothers—all were blemished. All embodied imperfections that made survival precarious. And yet this is the mythic ancestry from which we sprang. More surprising was the claim that human frailties and failings are material with which God's purposes could still be worked. So, if God does wonders with such raw human matter, perhaps something worthwhile and enduring can be done with us.

In his discussion of fifth-century Byzantium, scholar Peter Brown notes how peoples within East Roman society—not only Christians but also Jews and pagans—shared a common preoccupation: the imperative to maintain a dynamic connection between heaven and earth. "Modern people tend to worry about whether or not God exists. East Romans worried about the exact opposite: Did God know that *they* existed?"[2] My impression is the incarcerated students in this Genesis group had more in common with the East Romans than their contemporaries on the outside. They had in large measure concluded the community at large did not care if they existed. They felt discarded and treated like rubbish impossible to recycle or redeem. They were kept out of sight, and the condition of invisibility forced them to question if their very existence really mattered to the world at large.

Clearly, some sought solace in the belief they counted in the eyes of God. Others were far more circumspect in their theological speculations, and their imprisonment left them little to feed on but doubt. Yet I believe those who embarked on this odyssey found themselves in a conversation that bound them and us to our ancestors and a global community of readers. In a small way for a brief stretch, we were pulled into an encounter with the big questions, joined with peoples far beyond the barbed wire, wrestling with the human predicament, and struggling to wrest order from chaos.

What emerged through our encounters with Genesis was a glimpse into an alternative way of engaging and embracing our differences. There was a realization, however inchoate, that what sets us apart—our incongruities, our idiosyncrasies, our irreducible singularity—adds depth and breadth to the world. Difference is a promise, a blessing, not just a curse that inevitably leads to conflict. During the course of this shared inquiry, the most potent discoveries more often than not came from those with whom we imagined having little or nothing in common. In this communal encounter there was a sense of the sacred, the feeling we were engaged in something bigger than ourselves, that what we thought and what we said and how we acted actually and truly mattered in the grand and wondrous scheme of things.

In the words of Brian McLaren, "As we listen and enter into conversation [concerning biblical texts], could it be that God's Word, God's speaking, God's self-revealing happens to us, sneaks up, surprises and ambushes us, transforms us, and disarms us—rather than arms us with 'truths' to use like weapons to savage other human beings? Could it be that God's Word intends not to give us easy answers and shortcuts to confidence and authority, but rather reduces us, again and again, to the posture of wonder, humility, rebuke, and smallness in the face of the unknown?"[3]

Was this wishful thinking? Was the inmates' experience nothing more than a momentary distraction? Perhaps for some of them, but not for me

---

2. Brown, "Other Rome," 35, https://www.nybooks.com/articles/2022/02/10/the-other-rome-peter-brown/. Brown is professor emeritus of history at Princeton University.

3. McLaren, *New Kind of Christianity*, 93.

or my two teaching partners. We were compelled to reconsider what constitutes a learning community, how the boundaries are established, and who we need to be around in order to think a new thought. From my initial immersion in the Job colloquy to the work with Bill Moyers and the varied Genesis study groups, I experienced over and over again the generative power of sacred texts to bind together the most motley conglomerates of people. My rabbinic colleagues often insisted the serious study of our scriptures is a treasured form of prayer, and this became a conviction I came to share.

CHAPTER 11

The Jewish Scholars Group and *Dabru Emet*

When the Institute for Christian & Jewish Studies (ICJS) was first launched, I shared with many of the Christian trustees the concern that a close examination of the history of Jewish-Christian relations would evoke backlash. We anticipated defensive reactions from ministers and their congregants who would construe our inquiries as an assault on the integrity of Christianity. Christian clergy who saw themselves as the defenders of the faith and suspected our critiques lacked respectable scholarly justification soon confirmed our apprehensions.

In anticipation of resistance, Charlie Obrecht, who was serving as the head of the ICJS board, reached out to a group of Christian scholars previously supported by the National Conference of Christians and Jews (NCCJ). This assemblage of academics featured Protestant and Roman Catholic luminaries who had devoted their lives to disarming anti-Jewish biases embedded in their traditions. They charted paths into theological terrain long avoided by the mainstream, sometimes putting their careers at risk. The pioneers in this field included distinguished theologians, historians, and biblical scholars such as Paul Van Buren, Walter Harrelson, Eva Fleischner, John Pawlikowski, Roy and Alice Eckardt, Franklin Littell, Clark Williamson, Mary Boys, Norman Beck, and Eugene Fisher, among others. This group was looking for a new home, and the ICJS enthusiastically became its sponsor.

Known as the Christian Scholars Group on Judaism and the Jewish People, this academic coalition met twice a year in Baltimore at a conference center administered by St. Mary's Seminary and University. Members presented papers, tested ideas, offered constructive criticism to one another, and agreed to provide intellectual backing and guidance to the ICJS. Some of the most daring scholarship in the field of Jewish-Christian relations was first vetted within this group.

The first Jewish scholar on the staff of the ICJS was Rabbi Shira Lander, now a professor and the director of Jewish Studies at Southern Methodist University. On one occasion, Shira hosted a dinner gathering that changed the course of the ICJS. Among others, she had welcomed Dr. Michael Signer (1945–2009) to her table. He had been one of her seminary teachers at Hebrew Union College before migrating to the University of Notre Dame to become the Abrams Professor of Jewish Thought and Culture. The two of them were musing about the vital role the Christian Scholars Group played in grounding the work of the Institute for Christian & Jewish Studies. If this collection of Christian academics was rigorously contending with the anguished history of Jews and Christians and providing a foundation on which to build new and affirmative understandings of Judaism and the Jewish people, perhaps the time had arrived for a group of Jewish scholars to explore some of the ways in which Jewish identity had been influenced through its encounters with Christian thought and culture. In light of official proclamations ratified by several prominent Christian denominations that denounced antisemitism and called for a change in the relationship, perhaps the time had come for Jews to reexamine its religious posture with respect to Christians and Christianity. Might the Jewish community move beyond the constraints placed on the Jewish-Christian dialogue framed within the traditional Orthodox Jewish community, most especially the positions articulated by Rabbi Joseph Soloveichik and more restrictively fortified by Rabbi Moshe Feinstein?[1]

There were increasing numbers of Jewish scholars and rabbis who inveighed against the defensive reflexes that consigned Jews to the role of victim and froze the larger Jewish community in a fearful and distrustful crouch. They insisted many of the most creative moments in Jewish history occurred when there was robust—if limited—engagement with the surrounding non-Jewish culture. Therefore, the proposal felt vital and urgent.

---

1. Soloveitchik's prohibition on interfaith dialogue was elaborated in the paper "Confrontation," in the 1964 issue of *Tradition*. While acknowledging the value of addressing social and ethical problems together, he maintained that theological dialogue fails to affirm the incommensurability of each faith and puts Jews in an untenable bind with their neighbors. The quest for reconciliation furthermore amounts to betray of the millions of Jews who were murdered in the Shoah. See West, "Soloveitchik's 'No' to Interfaith Dialogue." Rabbi Moshe Feinstein amplified this condemnation, arguing the dialogue is a disgrace to God's name and a "rapprochement with idolatry." See Ellenson, "Jewish Legal Authority."

The time had come to bring together Jewish scholars to explore the ways in which the dynamics of accommodation and resistance went into the making and remaking of Jewish identity within the rapidly changing context of North America.

Joel brought the vision to Lisa Goldberg at the Revson Foundation, and she garnered the funds that enabled the ICJS to host a pioneering investigation, which we referred to as the Jewish Scholars Project. Michael Signer became the point person for this venture, and he deployed his powers of persuasion to assemble a working group of approximately twenty-five academics that included many of the preeminent Jewish scholars in North America.

Participants met three times over the next two years (1997–98) and explored some of the vexing challenges in the field of Jewish-Christian relations. Yet the presentations were pitched to a rarefied audience and held little promise for touching a broader public. To anchor this initiative within the larger Jewish community, a different intellectual trajectory was envisioned. A working group of four Jewish scholars (Michael Signer, Tikva Frymer Kensky, Peter Ochs, and David Novak) was formed to develop and implement a project with three prongs: a public statement directed first and foremost to the larger Jewish community, a volume of essays to model the academic discipline of Jewish-Christian studies, and a congregational primer that would enable Jews and Christians outside the academic guild to explore and lay claim to the distinctive character of their religious traditions. Three publications emerged from the venture: "*Dabru Emet*: A Jewish Statement on Christians and Christianity," *Christianity in Jewish Terms*, and *Irreconcilable Differences?*—the latter two volumes adeptly edited by Rabbi David Sandmel, the ICJS Jewish scholar.[2]

I had the privilege, along with my colleague Dr. Rosann Catalano, to attend all the sessions that went into the crafting of "*Dabru Emet*," which translated from Hebrew means "speak truth." The statement challenged the larger Jewish community to recognize that many Christian denominations were confronting the legacy of anti-Judaism and owning up to the complicity of their traditions. The authors wanted to break the spell of silence and passivity that stunted Jewish participation in the dialogue with Christians. They aimed to provide the basis for a new level of Jewish-Christian engagement, one that would not shy away from serious and sustained theological inquiries.

---

2. "*Dabru Emet*," https://icjs.org/dabru-emet-text/; Frymer-Kensky et al., eds., *Christianity in Jewish Terms*; Sandmel et al., eds., *Irreconcilable Differences?*

Observing the proceedings that led to this document, I learned firsthand how kosher sausage is made! Nearly every claim was subjected to interrogation. Points were argued rigorously, often with a sharp-edged intensity. Whenever positions hardened and movement ground to a standstill, I wondered if the whole enterprise would go up in flames.

Then something extraordinary happened. One of the Jewish scholars made a fist, pounded a beat on the table, and broke into a *nigun* (a wordless tune). The others immediately joined the melody and filled the room with song. After a few moments, the group returned to the discussion. This happened at several critical junctures; after chanting a *nigun*, sometimes those present would make concessions, and sometimes they would put the debate on hold and move to the next point. This pattern was repeated often enough to leave a lasting imprint on me. These Jewish scholars, who were fearless in the face of passionate disagreement, were also utterly confident that even the most insoluble of conflicts was not going to rupture their shared commitment.

Lamentably, "*Dabru Emet*" does not make explicit the internal debates beneath the textual surface. To be sure, there are gaps and silences within the actual text that soft-pedal the most contentious theological divides within as well as between our religious communities. Many of the issues beneath the surface of the text remain undeveloped and unsettled. Yet the statement is misconstrued if read as an immutable testament. *Dabru Emet* is an interdenominational Jewish document, not a magisterial declaration that sets down apodictic truths and commands settled norms. If read in the spirit in which it was composed, its claims will be contested, subjected to interpretation and reinterpretation, denounced, refined, and embellished.

In response to "*Dabru Emet*," I heard the familiar litany from rabbinic colleagues—Christians do theology, not Jews. Jews inhabit sacred texts, and they discern the holy by joining the rollicking and interminable conversations of their ancestors. Yet the debates that arose in the wake of this publication demonstrated that the theological task is inescapable. To map out the distinctive character of the Jewish community, to clarify for its own community and the world at large the values, practices, and sensibilities that animate Jews, and to participate in the critical debates about the democratic ordering of our society—this work demands theological engagement.

"*Dabru Emet*" was first published in a full-page ad in the *New York Times* and the *Baltimore Sun* on September 10, 2000.[3] It generated considerable notoriety among individuals and communities devoted to interreligious relations—and garnered the signatures of more than two hundred

---

3. See full text of "*Dabru Emet*" at https://icjs.org/dabru-emet-text/.

rabbis and Jewish scholars. The reception among Christians was particularly positive because it broke a long silence, signaled a new opening for vigorous theological exchanges, and raised a range of issues that called for ongoing examination. Despite this document's far-ranging dissemination (translated into a dozen languages) and the ensuing conferences that explored its significance in North America, Europe, and Israel, the statement did not register as required reading in most synagogues.

While many readers today may miss the groundbreaking character of this statement, at the time there were some blistering criticisms mounted and some heated disputes provoked. Many of the rebukes, articulated most notably by Jon Levenson and David Berger, pointed out challenges that remain flash points in the Jewish community.[4] Some of the clashes in which I became ensnared or witnessed are worth reviewing.

There was a meeting of the Baltimore Jewish Council on "*Dabru Emet*," attended by several Orthodox rabbis; they were particularly at odds with the first affirmation of this statement:

> **Jews and Christians worship the same God.** Before the rise of Christianity, Jews were the only worshipers of the God of Israel. But Christians also worship the God of Abraham, Isaac, and Jacob, creator of heaven and earth. While Christian worship is not a viable religious choice for Jews, as Jewish theologians we rejoice that, through Christianity, hundreds of millions of people have entered into relationship with the God of Israel.

The Orthodox rabbis in the room were scandalized by an assertion suggesting Christians also worship the God of Israel. From their perspective, this pronouncement failed to acknowledge the theological chasm separating our two traditions. They insisted that Christian doctrines of the incarnation and Trinity are not just incompatible with the truth of Judaism but fall into the category of idolatry. They falsify the oneness of God and his transcendence. On more practical grounds, they saw this assertion as a gesture dismantling the wall of separation. If we worship the same God, then why not worship together? Or worse, what then is wrong with intermarriage among Jews and Christians?

Their alarm was heightened by the complicity of liberal Jews in the so-called betrayal of their tradition. The Jews who endorsed and promoted "*Dabru Emet*" were denounced by these Orthodox leaders as quislings who

---

4. Levenson, "How Not to Conduct Jewish-Christian Dialogue," https://www.commentary.org/articles/jon-levenson-2/how-not-to-conduct-jewish-christian-dialogue/; Berger, "Some Reservations about a Jewish Statement," https://www.ccjr.us/dialogika-resources/documents-and-statements/analyses/dabru-emet-berger.

threatened the integrity of Judaism. The authors and signatories of this document were sliding into the dominant culture and imperiling the future of Jewish people. In their efforts to advance harmony between Christians and Jews, this statement was viewed as deepening divides and exacerbating tensions within the Jewish community. What made this especially troublesome was the fact that this initiative had the backing of learned and committed Jews across a wide denominational spectrum.

While these tensions were palpable in the room, I was eager to understand the fault lines as seen through the eyes of these Orthodox rabbis. I asked, "If Christians do not worship the God of Israel, whom then do they worship? Do Christians worship the wrong god, or do they worship the right God wrongly?" They responded that Christian worship falls into the category of *avodah zarah*, which is roughly translated "strange worship."

I noted that the authors were careful to distinguish between Christians and Jews on this point. If Jews were to become involved in Christian worship, which includes participation in their rituals and prayer, they would fall into the practices outside the boundaries of acceptable conduct. This kind of behavior would indeed entail *avodah zarah*. However, might it be the case that what is anathema for Jews is permissible for Christians? After all, Christians as well as Jews identify God as the Creator of heaven and earth, who guided the Hebrew people out of Egypt, delivered the Torah to them, and entered into a covenantal relationship with them. Do not these overlapping affirmations put Christians in a category that differentiates them from pagans? This was a position taken by at least some Jewish medieval authorities, and the view has been reaffirmed by other Orthodox scholars today.

To the question "Do Christians and Jews worship the same God?," the answer seems to be both yes and no. I suggested the equivocation etched into the Jewish tradition might open up fertile grounds for further inquiry and discussion.[5] But my Orthodox interlocutors wanted none of it. They regarded this first affirmation as a dangerous concession, if not a capitulation, to a hegemonic tradition robbing them of their distinctiveness. They read *"Dabru Emet"* as a diplomatic overture that blurs and amalgamates vital differences and, however unwittingly, paves the way to cultural and religious assimilation.

However, I wondered: "If Christians fall into the ranks of paganism, do Jews have any moral, if not theological, obligation to educate them and to help them see the error of their ways? If the sin of idolatry amounts to a repudiation or grave misrepresentation of the one true God, the error entails dire consequences not just in this life, but in the world to come. Are there

5. See Goshen-Gottstein, "God between Christians and Jews."

not responsibilities to help the stranger in distress? In turning away from serious engagement with Christians—which necessarily includes matters of theology and ethics—are these Jews not turning their backs on God, who made all of us in the divine image? How exactly are the Jews to serve as 'a light to the nations?' (Isa 49:6)."

I imagine my Jewish interlocutors walking in the sandals of Jonah.[6] Just as Jonah recoiled at the prospect of coming to the rescue of imperialist Nineveh, some Jews would rather end up in the belly of a big fish than deliver Christians from the wrath of God—and for understandable if not justifiable reasons. Jonah knew the Ninevites as mortal enemies. If they repented and avoided the destructive punishment of the Divine, they would live another day to inflict great harm on the Jewish people. Jonah's flight from his prophetic conscription reflects his unwavering solidarity with his people. To show Christians the path out of their idolatry might lead to their repentance or even conversion—a path that has all too often proved a very mixed blessing. Or, it might enable Christians in the long run to once again prey on the Jewish people and threaten their survival.

Then again, the grounds for protesting theological encounters with Christians may be simpler. Experience has often shown that Christians are so convinced of their own righteousness and so committed to the truth of their dogmatic claims that they would not grasp the rope tossed to them. History has demonstrated that they would rebuff and resent any attempt at rescue. Better not to poke, provoke, or attempt to save a malevolent giant—or invite Christins into their fold!

The depth of the distrust and fear that shapes the worldview of some segments within the Jewish community is seldom understood or appreciated by the vast majority of Christians. The intensity of this antipathy was most powerfully expressed in response to the fifth affirmation in "*Dabru Emet*":

> **Nazism was not a Christian phenomenon.** Without the long history of Christian anti-Judaism and Christian violence against Jews, Nazi ideology could not have taken hold nor could it have been carried out. Too many Christians participated in, or were

---

6. A caveat: The history of Christian interpretation of Jonah has often served polemical purposes. Christians have used the story to cast Jonah in typological terms as a prefiguration of Jesus (crucifixion is equated with being tossed into the sea; three days in the belly of the fish is linked to Jesus' death; and the ejection of Jonah from the fish signals Jesus' resurrection). Or, Christian interpreters have presented Jonah as a prototypical Jew whose ethnocentric obsessions blinded him to the needs of other peoples. In contrast, I find Jonah's response emblematic of the ways in which all of us are inclined to resist God's dreadful mercy and to protect our own.

sympathetic to, Nazi atrocities against Jews. Other Christians did not protest sufficiently against these atrocities. But Nazism itself was not an inevitable outcome of Christianity. If the Nazi extermination of the Jews had been fully successful, it would have turned its murderous rage more directly to Christians. We recognize with gratitude those Christians who risked or sacrificed their lives to save Jews during the Nazi regime. With that in mind, we encourage the continuation of recent efforts in Christian theology to repudiate unequivocally contempt of Judaism and the Jewish people. We applaud those Christians who reject this teaching of contempt, and we do not blame them for the sins committed by their ancestors.

Daniel Goldhagen's *Hitler's Willing Executioners* framed a worldview shared by many.[7] He maintained that the seeds of genocide were planted in the teachings of the early church, and an unbroken line can be drawn from Golgotha to Auschwitz. While many Christians are eager to differentiate historic Christian anti-Judaism from modern antisemitism, the boundaries are permeable. The extent to which the classical teachings of contempt map onto Nazi propaganda is enormous. Holocaust scholars such as the Jewish historian Raul Hilberg have juxtaposed Nazi legislation with official church decrees, and the overlap should give pause to anyone who denies a profound connection.[8] Strictures against Jews occupying positions of authority in education, medicine, the military, the government, and the judiciary have antecedents in the canon law of the Roman Catholic Church, as well as the official teachings of other Christian denominations. Interactions such as marriage between Jews and Christians—indeed, almost every form of economic and social intermingling—are at various times and places condemned in official Christian proclamations.[9]

In March 1998, the Roman Catholic Church issued a document by the Pontifical Commission for Religious Relations with the Jews entitled "We Remember: A Reflection on the Shoah." This proclamation strives to come to terms with the legacy of the Holocaust, and it stands resolutely in opposition to antisemitism and racism. Yet the document advances a claim that strains to differentiate historic Christian anti-Judaism from modern antisemitism. It declares: "The Shoah was the work of a thoroughly modern neo-pagan regime. Its anti-Semitism had its roots outside of Christianity and, in pursuing its aims, it did not hesitate to oppose the Church

7. Goldhagen, *Hitler's Willing Executioners*.
8. Rittner, *Holocaust and the Christian World*, 63.
9. See an extensive compilation of official documents and charters in Chazan, ed., *Church, State, and Jew in the Middle Ages*.

and persecute her members also."[10] The exculpatory language is a troubling deflection of responsibility and points to unresolved challenges.[11]

Christian attempts to come to grips with the Shoah are often both confused and confusing, as illustrated in an icon entitled *Captive Daughter of Zion*, by Brother Robert Lentz, OFM (see figure). The commentary that accompanies this sacred image notes: "If Mary had lived in Nazi Germany, Mary would have been thrown into a concentration camp with other members of her race. Jewish Mary is the archetype of the Christian church, a church that stood by silently while her people were being exterminated. This icon is an act of repentance for Christian indifference, then and now."[12] Surrounded by barbed wire, Mary wears the yellow star of David, used to identify and stigmatize Jews, while Jesus is wrapped in a prayer shawl holding a Torah scroll. The icon enshrines a fact all too often ignored: Jesus, his family, and his disciples were all Jews. The image is intended to serve as evidence of a spiritual transformation and an admonition to never again stand by in silence.

Captive Daughter of Zion

10 See the full text at https://www.bc.edu/content/dam/files/research_sites/cjl/texts/cjrelations/resources/documents/catholic/We_Remember.htm.

11. See Kertzer, *Pope at War*, 461–71.

12 See https://trinitystores.com/collections/captive-daughter-of-zion-rlcdz.

This sacred portrait can serve as a profound expression of solidarity that binds Christians and Jews to a common ancestry and evokes a sense of a shared destiny. Yet the icon also raises some unsettling questions. Does the imagery offer yet another example of Christians expropriating Jewish symbols and laying claim to a history that does not belong to them? Does the icon unwittingly falsify the history by positioning Mary—who in traditional Roman Catholic teaching is known as "the Ark of the Covenant"—and by extension the church on the wrong side of the barrier? Is a supersessionist bias manifested in an image of the church, symbolized by Mary, who not only surrounds but encompasses the Jewish child and the Torah scrolls? More egregiously, does the icon transmute Mary and Jesus into Jewish martyrs and suggest that the death of Jews can be fitted into a Christian paradigm and read as a mysteriously redemptive sacrifice for humankind? If this is a stretch, does not the icon at the very least imply, if not explicitly declare, that the true church is also a victim of the Nazi regime alongside the Jewish people? Or, in the words of "*Dabru Emet*," "If the Nazi extermination of the Jews had been fully successful, it would have turned its murderous rage more directly to Christians."

The treatment of some Roman Catholic priests in Poland and members of the Confessing Church in Protestant lands offers evidence to support this speculation. Yet, according to Rabbi Jim Rudin, former National Director of Interreligious Affairs at the American Jewish Committee, the statement in "*Dabru Emet*," and presumably the assertion in "We Remember," offer a "misleading at best, and dangerous at worst" false equivalency, namely, "the undeniable Nazi attempt to kill every Jew in the world and an unprovable historical prediction that the same murderous rage would be aimed at Christians in general."[13]

What surprised me in numerous conversations over the years was the extent to which many Jews were quick to conflate Christian anti-Judaism with Nazi antisemitism. While Goldhagen's scholarship has been judged by his peers as seriously flawed, there are many who share his verdict that Christianity was in large measure aligned with the eliminationist policies of Nazi Germany. A significant cross section of Jews has come to believe that Christian affirmations are ineluctably built on the negation of Judaism and the Jewish people and that this hate is woven into the DNA of Christian communities. These Jews have concluded this enmity is a problem that no one can fix.

The scholars who crafted "*Dabru Emet*" wanted to remove this obstacle, because there is no point in entering into a relationship with people

---

13. Rudin, "While the Messiah Tarries."

who, deep down, are out to destroy you. If Nazi ideology and Christian theology are singing from the same hymnal, Jews have good reason to denounce and avoid dealings with both as mortal enemies. And yet, the script that permanently locked Christians into the role of oppressors and cast Jews as victims is a defective and dysfunctional account of the past, one that fails to offer any nuance or acknowledge the creative agency of individuals and communities who affirmed their differences and practiced love of neighbor.

Beyond the confines of our insular religious enclaves, there are promising developments exemplified among scholars, clergy, and lay leaders. The dialectic of change and continuity is giving shape to a new paradigm. The ongoing tension, the mix of accommodation and resistance out of which identity is given form and substance, discloses the complexity within and between our traditions and reveals emerging possibilities for change. During those months when "*Dabru Emet*" was hammered out, I caught a glimpse of a reorientation in our religious traditions, a move in the direction of openness and respect that signals a reformation as dramatic as any seen in human history, a willingness to live gratefully and generously in full awareness of our irreconcilable differences.

The unbearable truth is that nothing in our lives is permanent. We live in a world of contingency and change, and every haven is vulnerable to blight and decay. As the story of Jonah reminds us, the established habits that split the world in two and divide people into warring camps is, in fact, a betrayal of a deeper aspiration—the vision where "nation shall not lift up sword against nation, neither shall they learn war any more" (Isa 2:4; Mic 4:3).

"*Dabru Emet*" issued a challenge to all those—Jews, Christians, and Muslims—who walk in the footsteps of Jonah. What does it take for us to see the imprint of the Divine in the face of long-standing enemies? Perhaps doubt must worm its way into our settled convictions and jostle us out of our certainties. My Jewish colleagues dared to imagine a different way of being in the world—one that offers the possibility of seeing others from a respectful distance while holding them as partners in the mending of a broken trust. To be sure, the shortcomings and limitations of the statement call for refinement and revision. But even if the words do not adequately demarcate the boundaries that separate and distinguish our religious communities, the affirmations may interrupt habit and instinct polarizing Jews and Christians. They may expose us to unfamiliar and unresolved questions, prompting us to ask anew what really matters to us as individuals, religious communities, and a racially and religiously plural nation.

CHAPTER 12

The Atlanta Project

The Reverend George Wirth was the minister of the Sewickley Presbyterian Church when I attended seminary and then served as the chaplain of the Gilman School. By the time I began my tenure at the ICJS, George had moved to Atlanta to become the senior minister of First Presbyterian Church of Atlanta, one of the most influential churches in the Presbytery of Greater Atlanta.

George and I had stayed in touch over the years, and he took a keen interest as I entered into the field of Jewish-Christian relations. From the outset of this unconventional vocation, he provided moral guidance to me and financial support to the ICJS. While he was tuned in to the academic challenges of the vexed history of our traditions, his devotion to healing the divides was rooted in personal experiences at the Chautauqua Institution and his own community in Georgia.

When still setting up shop at the First Presbyterian Church, he was pleasantly surprised that the first person to welcome him to the neighborhood was Rabbi Alvin Sugarman, the leader of The Temple, Atlanta's oldest Jewish synagogue. The two became close friends and confidants, and they configured a variety of programs over the years that brought their congregations into regular contact. One group that forged strong bonds was comprised primarily of interfaith couples from the church and the synagogue. When George invited me to Atlanta for the first time, this was the circle with whom I met.

For a variety of reasons, this did not strike me as the ideal context in which to launch an inquiry into an anguished history fraught with so many misconceptions. As I had learned from Joel many years earlier, it is hard enough to belong to one community, much less two. Almost all the rabbis with whom I worked refused to participate in interfaith marriages, and their reasoning was simple: statistical evidence has demonstrated the vast majority of marriages between Christians and Jews drift into the secular culture. In addition to the complexities of helping children of interfaith marriages develop a balanced and positive view of both traditions, most couples find it easier to maintain domestic harmony by opting out of active participation in either church or synagogue. They join the ranks of the unaffiliated. The Jewish community has demonstrated extraordinary resilience in its resistance to antisemitism. While capable of fending off hatred, what was then uncertain and remains so today is whether the more liberal and progressive sectors of the Jewish community could be "loved" out of existence.

Given the specific challenges and needs of an interfaith couples program, I was not confident our organization could offer educational encounters that would hold much appeal. The ICJS did not gloss over fundamental differences, revel in the fact we have much in common, or avoid the conflicted legacies that often froze Jews and Christians into adversarial relationship. In contrast to other settings up north, where boundaries were clearly demarcated and religious tensions festered and often broke into the open, the Reform Jews from The Temple and the Christians at First Presbyterian were congenitally gracious and accepting.

This amity had unusual historical underpinnings. From 1929 to 1930, members of Atlanta's Hebrew Benevolent Congregation had embarked on a major project to build a new sanctuary, and they needed a place where they could gather during construction. First Presbyterian Church offered its facilities, and the premises of the church became this Jewish congregation's temporary home. Then, on October 12, 1958, the sanctuary of this venerable synagogue was bombed. Five suspects were arrested and a cache of antisemitic literature was uncovered, some linked to the Christian Anti-Jewish Party. The day after the explosion was a Sunday, and immediately following its worship service the governing body of First Presbyterian again voted to make its facilities available to its Jewish neighbors for as long as it would take to complete the repairs. This act of hospitality was a rare and precious gift. An ethos of hospitality bound these congregations together and disposed both congregations to enter into a creative and trusting relationship.

When I shared the story of the ICJS and my experience with congregations in Greater Baltimore, members of this Atlanta dialogue group—with the enthusiastic support of George Wirth and Alvin Sugarman—agreed to embark on an educational initiative we entitled "Reclaiming the Center." We framed our challenge by noting the religious and political polarization within American society, a trend imperiling a future in which our religious communities could help to heal divisions and contribute to the common good.

Here is how we understood the challenge. On the one hand, many folks, especially the younger generation, continue to walk away from their faith traditions because they find religious education and congregational life close-minded, intolerant, and boring. They do not want to shoulder the institutional burdens of organized religion, get entangled with traditions associated with bigotry and bloody conflict, or spend their time and money on the antiquated preoccupations of their ancestors. Commitment to a religious community had contracted into a spiritual interest in personal fulfillment, the promise of individual gain without the communal pain. The unaffiliated—more often than not our highly educated children and grandchildren—are content to drift into a secular culture where they feel liberated from the constricting authorities of the past and their burdensome institutional demands.

On the other hand, many others are reaching a very different conclusion. They fear the erosion of religious certainty, the demise of family values, the unraveling of the dominant social order, and the loss of cultural privilege and status. They are embracing a religious life that promises answers and delivers a reassuring sense of confidence, even superiority. These individuals are settling into a defensive if not fundamentalist stance, learning to combat any and every idea that is not homegrown. They see the world at large either as dangerous and hostile, a threatening environment from which they must retreat, or, more commonly, as a world of apocalyptic struggle where they are called to join in a cosmic battle to defeat an implacable and sinister enemy. Our challenge was to help our communities resist the gravitational pull of these dueling narratives.

The clergy and lay leaders from the two Atlanta congregations recognized that the chasm between these trends was widening and posed not just a threat to the integrity of their respective traditions, but a risk to the health of our democratic order. Apart from involvement with communal organizations such as churches, synagogues, mosques, and other houses of worship, where are individuals to develop the habits to sustain altruism and the discipline of compassionate outreach?

The "Reclaiming the Center" project offered an educational alternative built on the axiom that we can never see ourselves clearly until we learn to see ourselves through the eyes of those who differ from us. It was designed to enable Jewish and Christian participants to discover solid grounding within their own religious culture by paradoxically making an unfamiliar leap—landing them in close proximity to their religious neighbors.

Over three years, approximately two hundred Jews and Christians from these two congregations joined together for six consecutive weekly sessions. Each gathering began with a shared meal at either The Temple or First

Presbyterian, followed by intensive study. At the outset of each meeting, two leaders—a Jew and a Christian with firm footing in their traditions—set the stage for an examination of a key biblical narrative. After they briefly delivered some commentary to put the selected passage into a broader historical and literary context, table facilitators were given a handful of questions to spark small group discussions. Each group included an even mix of eight to ten Jews and Christians. They pondered what the biblical story meant to them personally and how it lived within the imagination of their own community, and they took note of the unresolved questions that emerged during their conversations. The exchanges were guided by discussion leaders who made sure no one dominated the meeting and the views of all were heard. The evening concluded with some brief reflections from the two presenters, with the task of (1) showing how these stories took on different meanings when the times and conditions changed, and (2) highlighting some key places where Jewish and Christian readings either intersected or diverged.

Over the next few years, the Reverend Joanna Adams and Sherry Frank, two experienced veterans of the Jewish-Christian encounter, joined our efforts and coordinated this project in Sandy Springs, a suburb of Atlanta. They brought together congregants and clergy from three churches and three synagogues, thereby multiplying the impact of the initiative in the region to include more than two hundred additional participants.

This program also allowed the ICJS to build on the legacy of "*Dabru Emet*" by launching a colloquy with the Union Presbyterian Theological Seminary in Richmond, Virginia. This cohort met six times over the course of two years. The regulars ranged from Jewish and Christian professors to rabbis and ministers to seminary students. Each session featured two distinguished visiting scholars who delivered presentations on that meeting's central theme. Once again, a remarkable mix of scholars gave precision and rigor to the inquiry.[1]

The title of this venture was "The Scandal of Particularity," derived from Søren Kierkegaard's lexicon. Given the cascade of news about clergy abuse, the reference to "scandal" understandably raised eyebrows and generated some confusion. Yet the thrust of this inquiry was daring and aligned with intellectual responses in a variety of academic disciplines. In disparate intellectual circles, there had been a serious breakdown of confidence in the power of reason and rationality to achieve universal agreement. Each of our traditions makes particular theological claims that appear not only unintelligible, but scandalous to the other. These core assertions are more often

---

1. Two journal publications devoted entire issues to this colloquy. See *CrossCurrents* 59.2 (June 2009) and *Interpretation* 64.3 (October 2010).

than not the source of consequential misunderstanding between Christians and Jews. Our task was to explore these issues and see what we each might discover about ourselves as well as the other by plumbing the depths of these contentious issues.

For example, Christians make the claim that God was incarnate in a particular person, Jesus of Nazareth. He is held as a manifestation of the divine presence in a way that distinguished him from every other human being. Christians insist on his irreducible singularity. His uniqueness cannot be universalized, and this revelatory assertion therefore contradicts the normal boundaries of reason. As already noted, this assertion registers in the hearts and minds of Jews and Muslims as unintelligible at best, blasphemous at worse—and the claim is no less scandalous within the context of modern secular thought precisely because it defies the logic of modernity. The problem expands when attention is directed to foundational assertions about the meaning of being a "chosen people" or "the elect," statuses that have traditionally been professed by both Jewish and Christian communities.

Another claim with scandalous potential is the affirmation that the land of Israel is holy, a traditional Jewish view and one often shared by evangelical Christians (who developed the designation "Holy Land" from its very minimal biblical use). The sacred character of this piece of real estate is understood as categorically distinct. According to rabbinic teachings, the divine presence is manifested in this place in ways that elevate it above every other place on earth.[2] Furthermore, Jewish tradition includes teachings that insist Jews can embody a richer and holier life by dwelling within Israel. There are religious observances that make no sense apart from living in this land. Yet assertions of Israel's special sanctity offend the rational norms of modernity and assign a dangerous—as well as scandalous—status to a hotly contested territory. How can one piece of turf be uniquely linked to the transcendent and rationally regarded as any more sacred than anywhere else? From a Christian perspective, many note that God created the entire earth and therefore to ascribe sacred significance to this one land is to take a leap in the direction of idolatry, mistakenly attributing an aspect of the Divine to a finite reality.

These kinds of theological claims set us apart and define the distinctive character of our traditions, and the underlying affirmations are not easily translated into categories that cohere with modern sensibilities. The challenge was to explore the degree to which we could construct analogical bridges to enable deeper understanding of one another's core affirmations.

---

2. See "Land of Israel in Classical Jewish Sources," https://www.myjewishlearning.com/article/the-land-of-israel-in-classical-jewish-sources/.

The point was not to arrive at agreement or to explain away the disjunctures between our communities. Instead, the endeavor was intended (1) to identify and neutralize those habits of mind that lead us to elevate ourselves at the expense of the other, (2) to turn our gaze outward to consider how the particularity of our own traditions might be understood by the world at large, (3) to consider how our distinct traditions might serve to challenge prophetically the prevailing assumptions of our secular society, and (4) to open ourselves to the questions and judgments of our neighbors—secular and religious—out of the conviction that this engagement with the other might equip each of our religious communities to work for the betterment of a fragile and fractured world. Atlanta provided an invaluable testing ground for educational programs initially developed in Maryland. More significantly, the Atlanta community pressed our organization to expand its reach and confront complexities that could not be avoided or denied.

I will lift up and elaborate on three of the issues in the coming chapters that came into sharp focus and remain pressing concerns around the world. First, the Palestinian-Israeli impasse continued to impinge on our conversations, all the more so as Muslims became integral to our deliberations. Many mainline Protestant denominations were offering resolutions highly critical of Israel, and the condemnations of Israel by Orthodox and Roman Catholic communities in the Middle East also gave urgency and import to the problem. Sharp critiques from Anglicans affiliated with Sabeel and Lutherans such as Mitri Raheb were giving Protestants a denunciatory voice. What role might Jews, Christians, and Muslims play to move beyond polemical attacks and break the grip of a zero-sum logic that insists one group cannot triumph without the defeat of the others? How might we generate learning that leads to a more comprehensive understanding of the historical and political context while simultaneously offering models for constructive and empathetic disagreement?

Second, the exclusive focus on Jewish-Christian relations felt increasingly parochial, especially after 9/11 and the ensuing outburst of Islamophobia. Rather than invite Muslims to take a seat at a table of Jews and Christians already arranged for a predetermined agenda, how might we configure educational initiatives that establish all three communities as full and equal participants? What kind of educational resources would provide a balanced yet challenging basis for the creative interplay of our three traditions?

Third, we live in a world where religion and politics are intertwined. Religion is often fused with ideological agendas that exacerbate the polarization of societies. The majority religion often exercises its power and status in ways that marginalize or demean minority traditions. Do public prayers have a place at football games or presidential inaugurations? Do our religious traditions have a vital role to play in a secular democracy? How might a society cherish and advance the noblest of its religious ideals without simultaneously unleashing its worst impulses?

By going to Atlanta, the ICJS was challenged to adapt to the ethos of a very different city. The questions and concerns that arose from the encounter prompted the ICJS to ask new questions and respond to the needs and desires of a culture with distinctive sensibilities. The participation and support that came from Atlanta enabled the ICJS to take innovative steps to explore the unsettled and unsettling complexities of "*Dabru Emet*." The friendships forged in Atlanta made possible the development and implementation of curricular resources and opened the door to creative engagement with the Islamic community. The expansion of the boundaries and the unanticipated surprise of communal learning in a new setting proved pivotal as our organization embraced a change in the substance and character of its mission.

CHAPTER 13

The Challenge of Israel

My first visit to Israel was in 1982, and the experience was life changing. My wife, Betsy, had enrolled in a course at the Hebrew University to study the history of the Middle East, and I participated in a seminar for educators and professors at Yad Vashem, the World Holocaust Remembrance Center. When Israel was seen through the lens of the Shoah, much was revealed and much was concealed. The precarious circumstances of the nation came into sharp focus, creating an unremitting awareness that enemies surround Israel and threaten its survival. The legacy of genocide loomed, casting a shadow of uncertainty and insecurity over the political landscape.

I became aware that many, if not most, Israeli Jews regarded the Holocaust during its first few decades as an embarrassment best kept on the periphery of the country's consciousness. The supposition that Jews went to their death like sheep to the slaughter gave resonance and urgency to the national cry: "Never Again." As more and more stories of survivors entered the archives, Holocaust history and literature, films and museums of remembrance proliferated. Undiscovered accounts of armed rebellions and cultural resistance came to light and provided a far more complex portrait. Nazi assaults on Jewish populations varied considerably from country to country as did the response from their Jewish neighbors. Despite stories of righteous gentiles who took heroic measures to rescue Jews, the historical record underscored the fact that acts of courageous defiance were exceptional and grimly rare amidst an ocean of indifference and brutality. Scholars found no neat correlations—religious, ideological, or political affiliations—to characterize the people who took exceptional risks and even sacrificed themselves on behalf of Jews, who were frequently complete strangers. The conviction took hold that Jews must therefore stand up and fight for themselves. They could not trust an apathetic and erratic world that turned its back on their plight. A formidable military was imperative for national survival.

The meaning of the Holocaust and the lessons learned from it have shifted and even reversed course over the years, within and also beyond Israel. There was a time when young Israeli soldiers were taken to the top of Masada rather than Yad Vashem for a symbolic moment of initiation. Yet Masada, the site where Jewish zealots battled far more numerous and better-equipped Roman legions in a valiant first-century standoff, ended in ruin with the collective suicide of the Jewish rebels. Better to die free than be taken prisoner and made slaves.

This indoctrination was loaded with troublesome ambiguities. A story that enshrines soldiers as victims and martyrs did not reflect the ideals of self-sufficiency, strength, and triumph for which younger Israelis were to strive. The story of Masada was eventually supplanted as a paradigm of resistance, and in its place a renewed and revised focus on the Holocaust gained prominence. The themes highlighted at Yad Vashem were recast to profile courage and resistance. The museum became a monument to highlight what is at stake, to make undeniable the magnitude of the destruction, and to set aside a place to grieve the dead. The exhibitions were also configured to situate the Shoah in a broader historical and cultural context, so that visitors could contemplate its contemporary significance for the nation. The Holocaust Center now occupies a prominent place in the consciousness of Israelis and Jews around the world. It is almost unimaginable for visiting dignitaries to avoid a visit to what has become a national shrine.

During the seminar, I can remember poring over curricula designed to inform students about the lessons of the Holocaust in Jewish day schools. Our Israeli coordinators were alarmed that the Holocaust was routinely used to anchor Jewish identity. The underlying message: you may not think of yourselves as Jews, but the rest of the world does, and this country is arguably the only place where you are going to be fully accepted and secure. These educational materials served to root Jewish identity, and solidarity was forged in the fear of a hostile world in a contested land.

Many of my rabbinic colleagues have come to the conclusion that the Shoah should remain an important chapter demanding careful consideration, but it should not serve as the foundation for a healthy sense of religious belonging. In view of the predominant place the Holocaust occupies among many Israeli Jews and Jews around the world, reservations about the ways in which this genocidal assault shapes the Israeli national imagination demand judicious scrutiny. As Michael Goldberg notes in his book *Why Should Jews Survive?*, the Holocaust narrative all too often eclipses the exodus story and thereby overshadows a religious understanding of the values and practices that bind the Jewish community together.[1] Or, as some other Jewish colleagues—educators and rabbis—have argued, the Holocaust needs to be located in a broader and richer story of a people's triumphs and travails. They insist the Jewish people cannot thrive unless they can articulate their core affirmations, expressing and embodying what they stand for as well as what they stand against. A national memory that dwells on the failings of others—the injustices done to them—becomes anchored in grievances and cannot adequately support a robust sense of moral agency.

Rabbi David Hartman, founder of the Shalom Hartman Institute in Jerusalem, once teased me about Christians who arrived in Israel expecting to find shepherds in the fields and a dazzling star in the heavens to light their way. Instead, they found a scrum of Israelis at the airport terminal, elbowing and jostling one another to retrieve their luggage. Expectations of docile supplicants and saintly pilgrims following the stations of the cross collided with the reality of an unruly multitude in the streets where shouting and shoving annulled the rules of etiquette. There is a reason that Jews born in Israel are called *"sabras"*—named after the prickly pear cactus.

While Betsy and I learned to raise our voices when ordering a falafel and to stand our ground when navigating the bureaucracies, we were in awe of the energy and determination we encountered at every turn. We could not grab a bus without finding ourselves in the midst of animated debates. We met fascinating people at every turn and heard stories of individuals who endured harrowing adventures to carve out a home in harsh circumstances. We saw the country through the eyes of Israeli Jews who reinforced a highly romanticized tale of heroic persistence. We were swept away by the national aspiration to rise from the ashes.

Beyond the teeming and narrow byways of the Old City (an area that included no Jews from 1948 to 1967), the building projects were everywhere, and the dream of making the desert bloom was unfolding as more than an advertising slogan. The atmosphere, the landscape, and the soundscape were especially captivating—the blend of the muezzin's call to prayer, the ring of church bells, and Sabbath chants converged with the noisy bartering in the souk, honking horns, and blaring radios. Everything was up front and in one's face—the pungent smell of spices, the brilliant skies and dry summer heat, the incandescent colors of the marketplace, and so many faces old and young who showcased a mind-boggling mix of ethnic backgrounds. Betsy and I were overwhelmed with a sense of time we had never known. The stones spoke with eloquence of ancient days and echoed the virtues of

---

1. Goldberg, *Why Should Jews Survive?*

endurance. And soldiers—both men and women—were everywhere, coming and going, carrying weapons as if they were nothing more than another appendage. The disconcerting presence of the military eventually became a normal part of the national topography, which after a few weeks faded into the background. In retrospect this troubling acceptance of a militarized nation situated us between two conflicting and incompatible narratives, making neutrality an elusive ideal.

Years later, in 1990, while the Maryland Interfaith Project was first unfolding, a generous Episcopalian board member named Toby Pitts offered to fund a study tour for the denominational leaders of our study groups. With the guidance and gracious wit of Dr. A. Vanlier Hunter (a Presbyterian Hebrew scripture scholar at St. Mary's Seminary and University), we scoured archeological wonders, traveled around the country surveying important historical sites, and met with outstanding Jewish and Christian academics and community leaders.

While there were individuals who had urged us during our organization's formative years to delve into the political issues confronting present-day Israel, especially its conflictual entanglement with Palestinians, I argued that we had neither the staff nor expertise to unravel the contemporary tangles. I tried to distinguish a mission grounded in theology and biblical study from one devoted to comprehending the political quagmire and advancing international peacemaking projects. Our nonprofit simply lacked the resources to take on this momentous challenge. I furthermore doubted the involvement of predominantly Christian Americans would prove either welcome or helpful. We were excavating a more distant past and then applying our discoveries within an American context far removed from the Israeli-Palestinian morass.

Whether this hands-off approach was an evasion or an expression of naïveté or a fair appraisal of our limitations, we increasingly found the Israeli-Palestinian conflict posed an unavoidable challenge. The ICJS continued to coordinate study expeditions to Israel over the next two decades, and we increasingly honored the imperative to engage a variety of speakers from a broad range of political and religious perspectives. That said, our travels were designed to keep us at a safe distance from the violence and turmoil on the front lines. Rarely did we venture into Palestinian territory or come face-to-face with the pain and suffering of the occupied population in the West Bank. This insulation tilted our sympathies in the direction of Israel and limited our understanding of the enormous physical and psychological cost of the conflict on the Palestinians.

We were also reacting to accounts in the media that recast the story of David and Goliath. Israel became the military and political giant that was increasingly portrayed as wielding its sword with the intention of decapitating Palestinian leadership. Israel's far superior power was profiled over and against the desperation and helplessness of young boys armed with handfuls of stones. Yet the existential stakes were evident wherever we turned our gaze. The anxieties and anger, the frustration and distrust knew no boundaries. We saw the remains of suicide bombing, and we read the Hamas Charter, where the toxic myth of a world conspiracy was deployed yet again to fuel a mission of obliteration:

> With their money, they [referring to the Jews] took control of the world media, news agencies, the press, publishing houses, broadcasting stations, and others. With their money they stirred revolutions in various parts of the world with the purpose of achieving their interests and reaping the fruit therein. They were behind the French Revolution, the Communist revolution and most of the revolutions we heard and hear about, here and there. With their money they formed secret societies, such as Freemasons, Rotary Clubs, the Lions and others in different parts of the world for the purpose of sabotaging societies and achieving Zionist interests. With their money they were able to control imperialistic countries and instigate them to colonize many countries in order to enable them to exploit their resources and spread corruption there. (Article 22)[2]

The more closely we examined the historical and contemporary dynamics of this struggle, the more we came to see that virtually every political faction had innocent blood on its hands. We and the world at large seemed confined to a binary logic in which good is pitted against evil, democracy is set over and against terror, freedom stands in opposition to authoritarianism. Both sides deployed the dichotomies, hardening the failures of imagination and shaping a landscape of resignation. The dueling narratives of the Israelis and Palestinians with whom we met left us shaken: we could not conceive a viable path out of the deadlock. Neither side seemed capable of envisioning a durable peace that did not end with the other paying a greater price.

---

2. See the full text of the Charter at https://avalon.law.yale.edu/20th_century/hamas.asp. This chapter was composed before Hamas launched its brutal assault against Israel on October 7, 2023. The atrocities demonstrate the rhetoric of the Hamas Charter embodies a commitment to annihilate the State of Israel and eliminate a Jewish presence. These events have once again exacerbated irreconcilable differences around the globe and prompted people to embrace the old dichotomies. The ongoing battle entails dueling victimologies. Justifications for violence abound and render peace an elusive if not illusive promise.

Compounding the complexity was the fact that the Palestinian-Israeli crisis defied even a modest understanding unless the context was enlarged to include other countries and people in the Middle East. Perhaps it was no more than a tedious truism to note that Israel lives in a bad neighborhood, but the reality of hostile neighbors has understandably amplified fears for Israel's survival. Furthermore, the interplay of Christians and Jews had far less traction in Israel and the Middle East than most Americans imagined.

Given the prominent place of the Holy Land in the Christian imagination, it often comes as shock to learn that Christians make up approximately 2 percent of the population in Israel, the West Bank, and Gaza.[3] The Christian population in the Middle East has declined precipitously with the exception of Israel, where a modest increase has been recorded. In view of this demographic reality and the significance of Islam in the region, any meaningful conversation among religious communities must include Muslims.

Our study tours swept us into the hustle and bustle of Israel. Despite the stalemates among competing factions, we met guides and heard experts speak with optimism about the promise of this fledgling democracy. There was more than enough bravado to go around, and a steely resolve to overcome any and every obstacle was on public display. Yet we found another undercurrent, another message etched into the stones: if we were able to still the noise and listen with undivided attention, what we heard coming out of the holy land was the sound of God's weeping. The groan was and remains unbearable, and the cries from this region have evoked a wide range of responses from American Christians, which in turn have reverberated in the larger Jewish community.

Back in Baltimore, we were increasingly exposed to incompatible assessments of Israel and found ourselves pulled in opposing directions. At one extreme, I remember a representative from the organization Christian United for Israel (CUFI) delivering a presentation to the Baltimore Jewish Council. He was aligned with Pastor John Hagee, founder of San

---

3. A report by the Israeli Central Bureau of Statistics was released at the end of December 2021. It reported that the Christian population of Israel grew by 1.4 percent and there are now 182,000 Christians in Israel. When Israel was founded in 1948, there were approximately 35,000 Christians. The overall population growth in Israel for 2020 was 1.7 percent, so the Christian population growth closely mirrors the growth of the entire Israeli population. Christians are 1.9 percent of Israel's total population and that percentage has held steady over the decades. The Christian population in Gaza has declined significantly, while official statistics about Christians in the West Bank are inconsistent. There is no longer a Jewish presence in Gaza, having withdrawn from the territory in 2005. See "Israel's Christian community is growing," https://www.timesofisrael.com/israels-christian-community-is-growing-84-satisfied-with-life-here-report/, and "Why are Christians leaving Palestinian territories?," https://www.catholicworldreport.com/2020/06/19/why-are-christians-leaving-palestinian-territories/.

Antonio's twenty-thousand-member Cornerstone Church and one of the most outspoken leaders of the Christian Zionist movement, who insisted Christians needed to overcome the legacy of antisemitism and argued this approach was derived from a literal reading of the Bible. God has entered into a covenant with the Jews, and the "promised land" remains an integral, indeed indispensable dimension of this covenantal arrangement. He then proceeded to draw a straight line connecting ancient Israel with the modern State of Israel. Pastor Hagee's theopolitical platform left little ground for negotiations:

> God's promises to pour out His judgment on any nation that tries to divide up the land of Israel. Listen to the voice of God as it speaks through His prophet Joel.
> "I will also gather all nations, and . . . enter into judgment with them there on account of My people, My heritage Israel, whom they scattered among the nations; they have also divided up My land . . ." (Joel 3:2, 14).
> God continues expressing His love for Israel, saying, "I will bless those who bless you, and I will curse those who curse you" (Gen. 12:3). This is and has been God's foreign policy toward the Jewish people from Genesis 12 until this day. Any man or nation that persecutes the Jewish people or the State of Israel will receive the swift judgment of God.
> At this very moment, America finds itself bogged down in an unprovoked, worldwide world war with radical Islamic terrorists with no end in sight. America is very vulnerable to terrorist attacks in the future, whose consequences could be much more severe than the three thousand lives lost on 9/11. This is not a time to provoke God and defy Him to pour out His judgment on our nation for being a principal force in the division of the land of Israel.[4]

A good many in the audience were convinced that Israel's best and strongest supporters were to be found among evangelicals who embraced Christian Zionism. They welcomed Hagee's affirmation that the modern State of Israel is a divinely sanctioned continuation of biblical Israel. All the land that modern Israelis had conquered was regarded as God's bequest. The "surrender" of the West Bank (which both these Christians and a fair number of Israel's Jewish defenders refer to as "Judea" and "Samaria") for the creation of a Palestinian state was viewed as a violation of God's biblical plan. CUFI's spokesman backed up his pronouncements by noting the depth of their organization's commitment. In addition to their own ongoing

---

4. Hagee, *Jerusalem Countdown*, 294.

funding of various welfare initiatives, especially the support directed to settlers and immigrants, they were unwavering advocates for governmental military and economic aid to Israel.

A few of my Christian colleagues were in attendance, and we had grave misgivings about the ideological underpinnings of this agenda. One of these ministers identified a thinly concealed agenda and had the audacity to ask, "Aren't you squeezing Jews into a role that relies on an imperial theological script? You harbor the expectation that Jews will be 'completed' at the end of days when they recognize and embrace Jesus as their messiah. What you and your evangelical allies herald as 'the fulfillment' of Judaism ends up with the annulment of Judaism. And doesn't the refusal to acknowledge the integrity and permanence of God's covenant and all that it implies in terms of Torah observance reveal an undercurrent of contempt?"

This pushback generated spirited exchanges, but the words of one Jewish respondent stood out: "Israel has a very limited pool of friends. We are not in a position to be picky. If these evangelicals offer unconditional support for the government of Israel, we should certainly welcome them as reliable allies. They say we will bend our knees when Jesus returns and is proclaimed the true Messiah, but this will happen at the end of days. Well, let's wait and see."

Other Jews in the group shared profound misgivings that Christian Zionists were reinforcing what they regarded as the Israeli government's intransigence. They argued the refusal to enter into genuine negotiations with Palestinians and Arab neighbors would perpetuate a never-ending war. "Land for peace" was an essential aspect for a just and durable rapprochement.

What I found especially troubling was a rabid hostility toward Islam. This Christian Zionist framed a worldview in terms of clashing civilizations, and in this unfolding scenario the Muslims were demonized. Here was a coalition of Jews and Christians primed for global warfare—adherents of the Judeo-Christian tradition pitted over and against their Muslim enemies. The apocalyptic contours of this struggle ruled out the possibilities of compromise and reconciliation, setting the stage for a terrifying conflagration. When I expressed opposition to an ideology that transformed a political conflict into a religious crusade, the CUFI representative pushed back and argued that Iran's nuclear project and the extremism of Hezbollah and Hamas validated his theological assessment. This was an embittered rivalry that could only be resolved by the destruction of one side or the other. And he was quite clear which side God was on.

The Christian Zionist with whom we met was one among many, and I could only hope other representatives within this movement would open themselves to more moderate positions. Yet, in many subsequent conversations with other Christians, Jews, and Muslims, I discovered my anxieties were widely shared. The Christian Zionist portrait of clashing civilizations threatens to turn an uncompromising idea into a reality that shuts down other possibilities and locks not just Israelis and Palestinians, but Jews, Christians, and Muslims around the globe in perpetual warfare. A cramped imagination and ideological obstinacy make a combustible combination.

In the meantime, most mainline Protestant churches and some Roman Catholic advocacy groups were crafting resolutions to single out and condemn Israel. While Christian Zionists simplistically conflated ancient Israel with the modern State of Israel and followed a biblical reading in which the land is promised and given by God to the Jews, most Protestants and Roman Catholics were disinclined, if not antagonistic, to this linkage. They recognized Israel as a modern state like other nation-states around the world, and it could not claim special status or get an exemption from international criticism. When foreign lands were confiscated in war, when military oversight of occupied territories caused devastating human hardship and environmental catastrophe, or international norms were violated, Israel must be held accountable—like any other nation.

The mainline denominations, often in concert with Palestinian partners, repeatedly issued denunciations of illegal settlements, decried the ongoing occupation of the West Bank, and condemned the cyclical pattern of military intrusions into Gaza. Increasingly, critics of Israel called for an alignment with the BDS (Boycotts, Divestment, and Sanctions) movement.

The more strident and radical of Israel's detractors did not root the source of the problem in the administration of borders and military oversight. They maintained the very establishment of the State of Israel by the United Nations in 1947 was itself an illegitimate colonial enterprise, which the imperial powers used as a means to assuage guilt for their own failures during the Holocaust. And they wanted to get displaced persons out of sight. The solution to "the Jewish question" was paid in full by the Arab occupants of Palestine, who had no voice and little power with which to advance their own claims to the land, which it is worth noting was held by Jordon.

Opponents of negotiations cited the repeated failures of the government of Israel to adjudicate the disputes that arose with the seizure of Arab territories after the wars of 1967 and 1973, and they used the impasses to corroborate their indictments of Zionist colonialism. The assertion that Palestinians were too recalcitrant to be a credible and reliable negotiating partner was dismissed as a tactical evasion. Furthermore, the expansion of Jewish settlements in disputed territories amounted to a policy of confiscation that inflicted enormous suffering on Palestinians and imperiled their prospects for a viable future. Israel's obsession with its own security was being used to conceal its own abusive practices and discriminatory policies toward Palestinians. The violence of terrorists was regarded as a predictable expression of despair for which the Israeli government was primarily responsible.

In order to redress the failures of the past, many critics of the contemporary political arrangement now argue for a fundamental change. In view of a history of unjust treatment of Palestinians coordinated and implemented by the current State of Israel, these commentators note the country has reached a crossroads. How can Israel be both democratic and Jewish? Will the process of adjudicating conflicting claims to land and water drive a wedge between the secular ideals of a civil society and the imperative to uphold the nation's Jewish identity? Critics of the status quo propose a single binational state, most likely some kind of federated polity. They declare this transition is the only way out of the impasse. However, a merger of the West Bank and Gaza into this new political entity would entail a radical transformation in terms of its demographic makeup and its current national character. The difference in birthrates between secular Israelis and Palestinians points to a demographic shift that would render Jews a minority population in the not-so-distant future. The prospect understandably triggers considerable pushback.

The language of condemnation used in the denominational resolutions has only grown more inflammatory over the years, and in the 1990s many of these documents were suffused with the charge that Israel is an "apartheid regime." I declared in published commentaries and debates that this polemical approach was more often than not counterproductive. The analogical bridge linking Israel's treatment to the Blacks in South Africa was not only simplistic and misleading, but confirmation in the minds of the far right in both Israel and the United States that the underlying motivation of Israel's critics was to dismantle and destroy the country. What many of my fellow mainline Protestant colleagues saw as "peacemaking" struck me as a recipe for civil war.

Christians have a moral and theological obligation to call out injustice and to support oppressed minorities, and there remain serious and sustained abuses in Israel that warrant censure. Yet it is noteworthy that Israel is repeatedly castigated for its violations while other countries with dreadful human rights records—such as Syria, Saudi Arabia, Iran, Russia, China—escape serious and sustained denunciation. The double standard is frequently cited as evidence that anti-Zionism bleeds into antisemitism, and asymmetrical protestations lead many Jews in Israel and around the world to dismiss the rebukes of Israel as self-righteous and hypocritical.

My problem with the criticisms directed against Israel is primarily rooted in a different set of concerns. Time and again, I found the polemical attacks were wrapped in anti-Jewish tropes with a long and deadly history. The essential elements in these indictments are richly displayed in a congregational study guide entitled *Zionism Unsettled*, configured by the Israel/Palestine Mission Network (IPMN) and disseminated widely in the Presbyterian Church (USA). According to its authors, the ideology that led to the creation of Israel and continues to garner worldwide Jewish support is "inherently racist" (reviving the infamous 1975 UN Resolution 3379). Indeed, "Zionism is false theology . . . a heretical doctrine that promotes death rather than life." This caricature of Zionism makes possible sweeping generalizations about a varied and complex nationalist movement and culminates in the charge that Zionism is a major source of "evil." Echoing antisemitic tropes long used to implicate Jews in a global conspiracy, the authors declared, "the major American Jewish organizations bear considerable responsibility" for a "pathology" that leads to "self-inflicted blindness." Zionism is said to lead inexorably to "ethnic cleansing" and "cultural genocide."[5]

Furthermore, condemnations of Israel are often tied to the conspiratorial notion that powerful Jewish lobbies dominate America's foreign policy, most especially when it comes to its unwavering support of Israel. Jewish organizations such as AIPAC are routinely accused of pulling the strings and advancing the interests of Israel even when these policies betray the core values and commitments of the United States. The medieval fantasy of a global takeover is retrofitted for the defamation of Israel's Jewish supporters. Walter Mead, senior fellow at the Council of Foreign Relations and Bard College professor, has demonstrated the fallacy of this position in terms of not only its historical inaccuracies, but its underlying antisemitic logic. In noting voting patterns within the United States, Mead concludes: "If American Jews controlled America's Israel policy, the U.S. embassy would still be in Tel Aviv, the annexation of the Golan Heights would not be recognized, and the United States would be pressing Israel on settlement policy. . . . Zionism was never an agenda that a disciplined Jewish community imposed on the rest of the world."[6] Mead demonstrates that Zionism has deep roots

---

5 *Zionism Unsettled*, 57, 23, and 53.

6. Mead, *Arc of a Covenant*, 52. A blistering critique of the latest Netanyahu regime has garnered more than three hundred rabbinic signatories and refutes the canard of wholesale and uncritical support among American Jews for the Israeli government. Shimron, "Hundreds of U.S. rabbis protest," https://www.washingtonpost.com/religion/2022/12/28/hundreds-us-rabbis-protest-new-israeli-government-public-letter/.

within American history and continues to depend on both secular and religious gentiles for its power and influence.

What requires more careful examination is how religion is deployed and the role it plays in exacerbating political struggle. For example, Harry Stout, renowned professor of American religious history at Yale, offers incisive commentary on the role of religion in the American Civil War. He shows in chilling detail a process of social transformation that turned a limited war into what he calls "total war." By transmuting a political battle into a holy crusade, the lines between combatant and civilian were erased. Without boundaries to preserve this distinction, the ensuing devastation reached a new and unprecedented scale. Clergy on both sides played pivotal roles as "the cheerleaders," and their religious exhortations ironically helped remove moral constraints.[7] If these observations are applied to the Palestinian-Israeli conflict, the results are distressing.

When Christians deliver invocations or stage exhibitions with the assertion that Israelis are reenacting the crucifixion of Jesus on a daily basis with Palestinian bodies, fuel is poured onto the flames of the conflict.[8] This allegation also has a long and twisted history, hardly one that advances the cause of justice or promotes a vision of peace. To be sure, religious extremism that justifies abuse with exalted verbiage can also be found on the Israeli side and in abundance. Much of the fanaticism stems from the ultra-Orthodox messianism that animated Yigal Amir and Baruch Goldstein and continues to find expression in groups such as the "Hilltop Youth."[9] And the reelection of Netanyahu and his far-right coalition in November of 2022 signals a defection from core democratic principles, including one of the most essential pillars of a democracy, namely, an independent judiciary.

The task is not to establish a moral equivalency or to balance the excesses of one side with outrages from the other. Rather, the issue is the role that our religious traditions are playing in our understanding (or lack thereof) and in our advocacy. The fusion of political and religious commitments makes an explosive mixture, most especially when warfare is framed as an apocalyptic battle between the forces of good and evil. What role then

---

7. Stout, *Upon the Altar of the Nation*, Introduction.

8. Liphshiz, "Norwegian church hosts photo exhibition," https://www.jpost.com/diaspora/norwegian-church-hosts-photo-exhibition-saying-palestinians-are-crucified-daily-680264.

9. Yigal Amir was the assassin who murdered Prime Minister Yitzhak Rabin. Baruch Goldstein was the religious extremist who murdered 29 and wounded 129 Muslim worshippers in Hebron. The "Hilltop Youth" are hardline religious nationalists who maintain that Palestinians are "raping the Holy Land" and must be expelled. See Fischer, "State Crisis," and Semans, "God's Honor, Violence and the State.".

might our religious communities play in tempering the hatred, healing the divides, and promoting reconciliation?

Throughout my time at the helm of ICJS, I grew skeptical of Christian resolutions built in America and lobbed overseas, particularly as related to Israelis and Palestinians. I suspected they would have little impact beyond bolstering Christian self-righteousness. I also concluded that Christians cannot make a positive contribution without engaging their Jewish and Muslim neighbors. Many of Israel's sharpest critics assumed that American Jews march in lockstep with Israel's government, and so they remain within echo chambers that bar entry to Jews, except those few who share their opposition and disillusionment. As Walter Mead noted: "The perception that Israel is a white European settler site encamped on land stolen from brown Palestinians may be crude and superficial, (but) it is widespread enough to make the Israeli-Palestinian struggle intensely relevant to billions of people in past-colonial societies around the world."[10] Within this ideological framework, any compromise sacrifices justice on the altar of an illusory peace.

Meanwhile, Israel's staunchest supporters have matched this hopelessness, and they conjecture that no responsive and reasonable conversation partners exist on the other side. The walls of separation between our religious communities appear insurmountable when it comes to the Israeli-Palestinian conflict. As a result, the failures of divergent religious communities in the Holy Land to learn from one another and to forge collaborative partnerships are all too often mirrored in our own country.

In answer to the unending exchange of accusations and the ensuing despair, the ICJS resolved to develop an educational model that would bridge divides and create a climate of trust among supporters and detractors of Israel—even reaching the vast majority of Americans, who have not a clue how things got so bad and why the mess lives on. The plan was to compose an educational resource that would start with root questions: What makes a particular land holy? To what extent is the sanctity of a place acquired over time? In other words, how are the memories of decisive events planted and cultivated, imbuing the land with sacred significance and shaping hopes for a viable future? Or could it be that holiness is the result of a divine bequest, a place unlike other places where God is instantiated and from whence a community traces its origins and envisions its future? Beneath these overarching questions, the ICJS was eager to explore how and why the land of Israel is sacred to Jews, Christians, and Muslims. What are the distinctive meanings each religious community finds in this land, and how are the competing and often incommensurate claims about belonging and ownership to

---

10. Mead, *Arc of a Covenant*, 584.

be adjudicated? How might sacred space be shared among peoples whose histories are stained with blood and mutual distrust—a land where power is asymmetrically distributed and inhabitants of every persuasion are inclined to think of themselves as victims?

The ICJS recruited a distinguished assortment of scholars to contribute essays that would address these issues and provide a broader historical perspective. The result was a curricular resource that featured exercises and study questions to evoke spirited conversation, bringing crucial issues and unexamined assumptions to the surface. Contributors incorporated a wide range of conflicting political and religious viewpoints into this study guide, making sure that everyone would come face-to-face with positions that made them uncomfortable and with which they passionately disagreed. The success of the initiative hinged on whether participants could accurately and fairly articulate the views of those they strongly opposed.

This was the third volume of our "Reclaiming the Center" project, and we field-tested the materials in both Baltimore and Atlanta. Based on our criteria for success, I must admit we came up short. At this point in our own evolution, the ICJS had yet to redefine the scope of its mission to include Muslims, and it was impossible to achieve balance on a two-legged stool. Yet I think our failure went even deeper. While Jewish and Christian congregants and their clergy were exposed to radically divergent positions and acquired a great deal of new information, the majority of Jews could not relinquish their own commitments and conclusions long enough to get inside the skin of their "enemies." Their allegiances were so entrenched that it was almost impossible to entertain the criticisms of their opponents. The pain and uncertainty and threat of terror attacks undercut the trust essential for durable connection. The stakes were too high, and most experienced the imaginative leap into hostile territory as an assault, or perhaps a betrayal of their core identity. This is not to say that Jewish participants were unable to acknowledge the unjust policies of the Israeli government and denounce the violent extremism of Israeli settlers. They shared the conclusion with their Christian counterparts that the status quo remains untenable. However, at the end of day, we had simply reached a limit, a boundary that few could cross—and this brought home the magnitude of the challenge. The power of empathy hit a wall, and most collapsed from compassion fatigue. At certain points, most of our Jewish colleagues just could not manage to get outside their history and their fear—and the Christians in the room could not identify with this acute vulnerability. Once again, the challenge of thinking a new thought proved daunting.

While Jewish congregants struggled to hear the voices of people whom they regarded as their ruthless adversaries, the majority of Christians had tremendous difficulty comprehending the depth of feeling, the ferocity of the attachment to a contested land, and the existential stakes of the struggle. The inquiry had an academic character, and they stood at a distance, befuddled by the intensity of their Jewish and Palestinian counterparts. Very little in their own experience resonated with the conditions of exile and homelessness. They were simply observers, onlookers viewing a historic collision at a dangerous intersection in another part of the world. The situation was incomprehensibly messy and complex and intractable. Everyone seemed to have it right. Everyone seemed to have it wrong.

Looking back now, from a distance that might offer greater wisdom, I still do not know if it is possible to design an educational program that enables Jewish, Christian, and Muslim participants to see the Palestinian-Israeli impasse fairly and accurately. The pressure is enormous to choose a side. The pattern is replicated endlessly: collect evidence to validate your position and muster ammunition to take down the opposition. Efforts to maintain a sense of neutrality are condemned as an evasion that perpetuates the injustices of the status quo. In this kitchen the temperature gets unbearably hot. Most Jews cannot and will not get out, and most American Christians do not want in. And all the while Muslim participation is required and extremely fraught.

Maybe the best we can do is fail, but fail in the right way and honestly. That may not be such a dreadful thing—to be humbled, chastened, and rendered speechless—at least for a time. I am keenly aware that Israel's supporters believe the quest for middle ground is a cop-out, a refusal to reckon with the existential pressure coming from death-dealing adversaries. From the perspective of Israel's critics, the search for balance registers as an act of complicity that ends up normalizing inequality and perpetuating Palestinian suffering. There is no way to escape the crossfire. I suppose there is truth in the aphorism, "If you're not pissing someone off, you probably aren't doing anything important."[11]

But to reach that point—where we can actually learn from our failures—we need to hear the truth the other speaks and ease our grip on predetermined certainties. It is labor in which I doubt the politicians can offer much help. Nor do I find guidance from partisan groups attacking and defending one side or the other, as though blaming and shaming could spin the world in a new direction. Each side has a deep desire to be heard and believed, and it is this underlying desire that really demands our attention. The conflict is meeting a fundamental need; it is a dreadful way of keeping

11. Attributed to the cultural commentator Oliver Emberton: https://oliveremberton.com/2014/if-youre-not-pissing-someone-off-you-probably-arent-doing-anything-important/.

something alive—a memory of those who have suffered and died and a hope that things can be different.

As best as I can tell, the scholars and clergy, experts and pundits can take us only so far. If we are to get beneath the surface, we will need to listen to those who are often overlooked—Palestinians and Israelis alike—those who are scrambling to stay afloat and are actively searching for stable ground on which to build a secure and decent life. If we were involved with and educated by these individuals and the communities to which they belong, perhaps we would return to our own homes with aching hearts and the unsettling awareness that there is no closure.

The world has grown so small, and the struggles in the Middle East intrude whenever Jews, Christians, and Muslims come together. There is so much to learn, but beyond the learning are the urgent needs and desires of suffering people. Rather than pour so much time, energy, and money into supporting one side at the expense of the other, the moment has come for us to engage the question: what will it take for our different religious communities to come together and together create an economy of mutual blessing? We will need to traverse unfamiliar neighborhoods and glean unfamiliar stories—finding ways to translate our discoveries into building hospitals, schools, community centers, and businesses where the lives of those caught in the battle are lifted up. We certainly cannot change the world if we are unwilling to grapple with those we have neglected, and in the process change ourselves. Instead of divestment, I wonder what kind of investment is required to transform the facts on the ground.

CHAPTER 14

Islam

In the early 1990s, Taylor Branch conducted extensive research to follow up on his Pulitzer Prize winning biography, *Parting the Waters: America in the King Years, 1954-63*. He was keenly interested in the ways Martin Luther King Jr. engaged not only Christian but also Jewish and Muslim leaders. During his investigations, he spent considerable time meeting with Imam Warith Deen Mohammed (1933-2008), the son of Elijah Muhammad (1897-1975), the minister and overseer of the Nation of Islam. Imam Mohammed was a theologian, philosopher, and Islamic thinker who became the national leader of the Nation of Islam upon his father's death. His efforts to reform the Nation of Islam included the rejection of several key tenets, including the claim that Wallace Fard Muhammad, the organization's founder, was divine and his father was a prophet. In 1976, Imam Muhammed disbanded the original Nation of Islam and converted over four hundred of its temples into traditional Islamic mosques. This realignment also entailed a break from the Black separatist position, and a repudiation of the racially divisive teachings later associated with Louis Farrakhan, the current head of the Nation of Islam. In charting a path aligned with Sunni Islam, Imam Muhammad forged close working relationships with mainstream Muslim communities and played a pioneering role in the advancement of interreligious cooperation—including an address to the Baltimore Jewish Council in 1997.

Branch had served on the ICJS board from its early years, and he described its educational vision to Imam Mohammed and some of the leading lights within the community that came to be known as the American Society of Muslims. With the encouragement of both Branch and Imam Mohammed, I gathered a handful of rabbis, ministers, and lay leaders to meet with several Muslim counterparts who lived on the outskirts of Washington, DC. Over the next few months, we met on several occasions to introduce ourselves and explore the possibility of more inclusive educational collaborations.

The first session was particularly memorable. There were twelve of us, and we each introduced ourselves and outlined the concerns that brought us to the table. The Muslim members of the group were particularly interested in learning about the fundamental issues and challenges that framed the Jewish-Christian conversation. The Christian participants described an inquiry into the history of Jewish-Christian relations, a subject previously neglected or avoided in their formal education. They summed up disturbing encounters with sacred texts that upheld anti-Jewish attitudes and behaviors, and presented a brief overview of the ways in which this antipathy deformed church teachings and cultivated the soil on which modern antisemitism grew. They highlighted some creative educational strategies designed to ameliorate the distortions and foster a deep appreciation for the beauty and wisdom of Judaism.

The Jews around the table noted that they were also wrestling with an anguished legacy, and they shared a concern about neutralizing material within their own sacred writings that had generated distrust and sanctioned enmity toward their religious neighbors. They insisted that Jews were also struggling to come to terms with the challenge of religious pluralism and questioned the adequacy of traditional formulations that bifurcated the world into two categories—Jew and gentile. Both the Christians and the Jews claimed this educational enterprise depended upon a willingness to engage their respective traditions self-critically in the presence of the other and to confront those troublesome aspects of their religious communities that continue to foment animosity and engender mistrust.

The Muslims around the table listened intently, and agreed the difficulties rooted in the sacred texts of both Christians and Jews presented serious problems. They expressed gratitude for the opportunity to join an important interreligious conversation, since they were all too often left on the sidelines. Eager to establish common ground and to honor a legacy that bound all three religious traditions, they noted they shared many of the same stories and revered many of the same prophetic messengers in their scriptures. One gentleman went so far as to suggest that a good Jew and a good Christian could in a powerful sense be considered Muslims. "All of us—Jew, Christian, and Muslim—recognize the Creator and Sustainer of the universe and seek to live in obedience to his will," he said. This gentleman went on to claim Islam had absorbed the underlying truth of what it means to be a Christian and a Jew. He believed a good Muslim did not stand in opposition to Judaism and Christianity but was called upon to incorporate the noblest ethical and theological aspirations of both traditions into Islam.

In response, I recalled exchanges with fellow Christians that left me anxious and perturbed. These Christians pointed to the fact that Jesus was a Jew; therefore, anyone who follows in the footsteps of the Jewish Jesus should also claim an allegiance to the Jewish tradition. And so the assertion was made: to be a good Christian, you must simultaneously be a good Jew. What I found distressing in this line of reasoning was the way in which the Jewish tradition was folded into the all-encompassing reality of Christianity. Such Christians were convinced they had overcome the anti-Jewish dispositions of the past, but I concluded this approach was simply another form of supersessionism. Their embrace of Judaism was smothering the distinctive character of Judaism and the Jewish people and was yet another example of the majority culture's erasure of a vulnerable minority. Wasn't this Muslim's efforts to map his tradition onto Jewish and Christian traditions an imperious move—one that ended up denying the integrity and indissolubility of both Judaism and Christianity?

The Muslims were taken aback by this response. They were making a gesture of acceptance, trying to establish the grounds for solidarity and common purpose. And here I was insisting on the non-negotiable singularity of each tradition and more provocatively accusing Islam of imperialistic intentions. The Muslims did not react defensively but indicated we were caught in a misunderstanding. What they saw as a generous affirmation had been misconstrued as a problematic theological disposition. There was clearly more work to do to forge sturdy connections and to overcome what I now regard as our capacious ignorance of one another.

At our next meeting, we directed attention to our scriptures: more specifically, to the task of thwarting texts used to justify the oppression of minorities and valorize warfare against real and imagined enemies. The Jews and Christians cited historical and literary criticism as indispensable tools. By linking the polemical assaults in our scriptures to the cultural conditions of the times and binding the texts to the historical circumstances that gave rise to bellicose invective, the community could take an important step in neutralizing toxic material. What was written and spoken in the distant past may be understandable if we reckon with the conditions that elicited the rhetorical excess. However, that does not justify those who would deploy such texts today to legitimize persecution and bloodshed.

We took note of biblical passages in which a sharp line is drawn between the chosen and the rejected, those worthy of salvation and those deserving damnation—and observed a distinction that, once given metaphysical significance, all too often provided a warrant for aggression. The outsider was dehumanized, transmuted into a monstrous evil, and made a legitimate target for elimination. This dynamic has tentacles that stretch into our scared writings. While both Jews and Christians affirmed the entire Bible as holy, the Jews and Christians in our group maintained some words and teachings carried more weight than others. Indeed, some passages needed to be confined to the margins of the community and assigned a warning label: "Handle with great care. The contents may be hazardous to your health and your neighbor's survival."

Our Muslim partners were quick to acknowledge the problem, and two lines of response followed. One fellow declared that the Qur'an has an altogether different status from the Bible. While the sacred scriptures of both Jews and Christians contain imperfections, the Qur'an is a miraculous gift that corrects the flaws of earlier traditions. Divinely transmitted from the archangel Gabriel to Muhammad over the course of twenty-three years, the Qur'an is itself a revelation that embodies the immutable word of Allah, which is to say its fundamental meaning is unchanging and absolute. Therefore, modern tools of historical and literary criticism used by Jews and Christians have no place in the Islamic tradition.

This viewpoint impressed the Jews and Christians as the basis of a fundamentalism that had done great damage within their own communities. How then do Muslims handle those who wield the Qur'an as a sword and invoke its authority to justify the denigration of others, including non-Muslims and women? Another Muslim chimed in: "The problem does not reside within Qur'an, but stems from misguided and corrupted interpretations. When a Muslim invokes the Qur'an to justify violence, in most cases they are guilty of a serious misreading and a defective application of its teaching."

We went back and forth, or perhaps more accurately, round and round. I remember concluding these sessions—privately—with the conviction that Islam is incurably supersessionist. Furthermore, I suspected these Muslims did not regard their claims to a privileged position as an obstacle to the dialogue. I had a new appreciation for how many Jews must have felt in their encounters with Christians. The underlying message seemed to be that Islam offered a religious path that could correct and complete the corrupted traditions in which we Jews and Christians were lamentably mired. But, reflecting back on this now, I am embarrassed to acknowledge that my judgment, hastily constructed, prompted a dismissive view of Islam. A change in outlook would require far more time and study with Muslims before I discovered the dimensions of contempt that were built into the foundations of my cultural home.

While my Jewish and Christian colleagues had intimations of our own parochialism, we came to the conclusion that a serious and sustained engagement with Islam was ill-advised. In the first place, we were keenly aware of the limitations of our current staff, and we lacked the financial resources and physical facilities needed to bring on a Muslim scholar. We were already straining to meet growing demands for our programs; how could we possibly take on a religious tradition as vast and complex as Islam? In the second place, we had developed a pedagogical method that revolved around text study, and we believed the ways in which Jews and Christians read and interpreted their sacred texts were incommensurate with Muslim approaches to the Qur'an. In the third place, we did not know how to configure a three-way conversation that would be balanced and equitable. To simply invite Muslims to pull up a chair at a table already set for Christians and Jews struck us as inappropriate, if not insulting. And on top of it all, we were keenly aware that encounters between Jews, Christians, and Muslims would drive us into a dangerous intersection where politics and religion collide. When we surveyed the globe, we were overwhelmed by the number of conflicts where political and religious agendas were enmeshed. No doubt the Palestinian-Israeli impasse took center stage. Perhaps the most telling stumbling block emerged when I asked the thirty members of the ICJS board how many of them had a Muslim friend or close colleague. No hands went up. We reached a decision that we already had more than enough to handle in mediating new understandings and durable connections between Christians and Jews. To take on Islam would sink us.

Then everything changed! I was in my office early on the morning of September 11, 2001, busy plunking on the keyboard, when the telephone rang. Rabbi Charles Arian was on the line, asking frantically if I was watching the news. He exclaimed that a large passenger jet had flown into the north World Trade Center tower. Minutes later reports were flooding the airwaves, and images of a second plane smashing into the south tower flashed across the screen. The scenes of collapse—the panic and shock, the chaos and frenzy—were burned into our memories as the horror was rebroadcast again and again and again. The massive explosion, the shower of burning debris, and the faces of traumatized victims were seared into the American psyche. As these events unfolded, another plane circled downtown Washington, DC and crashed into the west side of the Pentagon. The scale of this coordinated assault fired the imagination, and the fear of a world at war soon commandeered almost every conversation. We had no idea what surprises this day and the days to come might hold.

Accounts of the assailants began to circulate wildly, and the faces of the enemy were paraded on an endless loop of televised alerts. Pictures of "Islamic extremists" were merged with battle cries from al-Qaeda acolytes, and the menace echoed on every screen and headlined every newspaper. Although the nineteen terrorists who transformed passenger jets into guided missiles were men, the descriptive category that transfixed most Americans was "Islamic." Were we to understand these religious fanatics as outliers, or were they representative of a powerful multitude irreconcilably opposed to the American way of life? Was this attack the outbreak of what the political scientist Samuel Huntington had described as "the clash of civilizations"?

Ignorance of Islam in America created a vacuum that distrust and hate quickly filled. An Islamophobia industry was constructed almost overnight, and incendiary excerpts wrenched from classic Islamic texts and amplified by a curated sampling of contemporary clerics were invoked as proof that aspirations of global conquest define the heart of Islam. America's attention was pulled back to the Iranian hostage crisis of 1979, and the memory of frenzied Islamic mobs burning American flags, storming the embassy, and seizing diplomats and dignitaries was marshaled as proof of an enduring antagonism. Ayatollah Ruhollah Khomeini and Osama bin Laden were imprinted on the American psyche, and their portraits were offered up as the faces of evil incarnate. Christian commentators such as Pat Robertson, Jerry Falwell, and Franklin Graham (all, sadly, reverends) pedaled bigotry, classifying Islam as a "wicked" and "the source of the violence." The Reverend Jerry Vine piled on and labeled the prophet Muhammad "a demon-possessed pedophile."[1]

The impact of 9/11 on American Muslims inflicted a doubled trauma. Not only were they shell-shocked by the terrorist attack on fellow citizens, but they were convulsed by those Muslims who had hijacked and weaponized their religion. On September 17, 2001, at the Islamic Center in Washington, DC, President Bush assured the nation:

> The face of terrorism is not the true face of Islam. That's not what Islam is all about. Islam is peace. These terrorists don't represent peace, they represent evil and war. . . . I've been told that

---

1. Jerry Vines served as the president of the Southern Baptist Convention from 1988 to 90 and is credited with founding the First Baptist Church's Conference, which attracted thousands of ministers and church leaders around the world. Cooperman, "Anti-Muslim remarks stir tempest," https://www.washingtonpost.com/archive/politics/2002/06/20/anti-muslim-remarks-stir-tempest/4577462f-cd70-458c-9fef-133b5143e144/.

some (American Muslims) fear to leave home; some don't want to go shopping for their families; some don't want to go about their ordinary routines because, by wearing cover, they're afraid they'll be intimidated. That should not and that will not stand in America.[2]

But there was no return to ordinary routines for American Muslims. By the end of October, President Bush had signed into law the USA PATRIOT Act, which legitimized wide-ranging surveillance aimed primarily against Muslims. FBI agents interviewed hundreds of thousands of Muslim and Arab men "voluntarily" from 2001 to 2005. As the columnist Wajahat Ali noted, "The NYPD spent years spying on innocent communities that were seen as a threat simply due to their religion and ethnicity. They uncovered zero terrorism plots. Instead, they found that 'mosques and religiosity are actually associated with high levels of civic engagement and support for the American political system.' The chairman of the 9/11 commission eventually admitted that racial and religious profiling is inherently dangerous and ineffective counterintelligence policy."[3]

A cloud of suspicion and hostility hung over the Muslim community. Hate crimes proliferated. Women who wore *hijab* (head covering) were often taunted and vilified. The popular culture fed on the prejudice and added layers of emotional and physical abuse on top of discrimination and misinformation.

Whenever a terrorist incident occurred, the same questions dominated the airwaves: Where are the so-called moderate Muslims? Why aren't there more Muslim leaders condemning the atrocities? Although there were ample public statements and communal displays to repudiate the extremism, the vast majority of denunciations never made the news. The cultural and political atmosphere was defined by the "war on terror," and there was no space for nuance. Military campaigns in Afghanistan and Iraq pitted "us" against "them." Right-wing pundits and conspiracy theorists fanned the flames, declaiming loudly but with little insight and no compassion.

Most Americans have failed to grasp the seismic shift in attitudes toward Islam and the impact of the demonization. For example, anti-Muslim hysteria gave rise to legal attacks on "*Sharia* law." Since 2010, 217 anti-*Sharia* legislative bills have been introduced in forty-four states, and twenty have been enacted in thirteen states.[4] The measures reveal a profound distortion

---

2. "'Islam Is Peace' Says President," https://georgewbush-whitehouse.archives.gov/news/releases/2001/09/20010917-11.html.

3. Ali, *Go Back to Where You Came From*, 109.

4. https://belonging.berkeley.edu/islamophobia/database.

of *Sharia*, which is better understood as the "guiding principles" for drawing close to God and living a moral life in accord with the Qur'an. *Sharia* literally means "the path that leads to the source of water," and serves to orient Muslims in their daily conduct. As canon law serves to clarify religious obligations among Roman Catholics and *halakha* defines norms to guide observant Jews, *Sharia* orients Muslims on a spiritual and moral path that promotes peace in this world and salvation in the world to come. The core elements of *Sharia* center on practices such as daily prayers, dietary regulations, fasting during Ramadan, and the requirements for charity.

Furthermore, anti-*Sharia* legislation attacks a problem that does not exist. There are no instances in which a US court has applied *Sharia* to resolve a dispute, and Muslim communities in the US acknowledge their duty to abide by the United States Constitution and legal codes. The claim that *Sharia* undermines the well-being of the nation is not only patently false, it generates a deadly Islamophobia, which is illustrated in this initiative from Tennessee:

> The threat from sharia-based jihad and terrorism presents a real and present danger to the lawful governance of this state and to the peaceful enjoyment of citizenship by the residents of this state . . .
>
> "Sharia organization" means any two (2) or more persons conspiring to support, or acting in concert in support of, sharia or in furtherance of the imposition of sharia within any state or territory of the United States. . . .
>
> Any person who knowingly provides material support or resources to a designated sharia organization, or attempts or conspires to do so, shall commit an offense . . . punishable by fine, imprisonment of not less than fifteen (15) years.[5]

The political capital that the far right seeks to accumulate through these attacks has been further reinforced with efforts to portray the extremism of ISIS and related groups as the true character of a religious community with approximately two billion followers. The conflation of Islam with an extremist ideology makes as much sense as equating Christianity with the Ku Klux Klan. Yet the polemical admonitions of former Speaker of the House Newt Gingrich still resound: "We should frankly test every person here who is of a Muslim background and if they believe in *sharia* they should be deported."[6] Former President Donald Trump's advocacy of a

---

5. https://www.capitol.tn.gov/Bills/107/Bill/SB1028.pdf. This bill passed both House and Senate Judiciary Committees on April 26, 2011.

6. Etehad, "After Nice," https://www.washingtonpost.com/news/morning-mix/

ban to prevent Muslims from entering the United States and his false claim that thousands and thousands of Muslims in New Jersey were "cheering" as the World Trade Center collapsed—these patently false assertions advance the view of Islam as the enemy and augment dangerous distortions among a large segment of the American populace.

In light of these developments, the ICJS mounted several educational initiatives to develop a deeper understanding of Islam and to repel the alarming upsurge in Islamophobia. In the late 1990s, I met a Muslim professor from Howard University, Dr. Sulayman Nyang. Raised in the Gambia, Nyang became the deputy ambassador and head of the chancery of the Gambian embassy in Jedda, Saudi Arabia, before pursing an academic career. Although reputedly endowed with a photographic memory, coupled with an exceptional range of experience and erudition, his manner was humble, kind, and generous. In the aftermath of 9/11, I invited him to deliver a series of lectures to inform Christians and Jews about the core teachings of Islam. In addition to offering an overview of the pillars of Islam and a snapshot of some key historical developments, he also managed to dismantle some of the most noxious misconceptions about Islam with diplomatic aplomb. He continued to offer guidance over the next several years even as he battled illnesses that gradually sapped him of life.

I cannot claim a deep friendship with Sulayman, but he was one of those rare people who make one feel a special kinship, the kind of ease and comfort felt around someone you have known over the long haul. More than any books read or documentaries viewed, I once again discovered the best way to encounter a religious tradition is through personal relationship. He was someone to count on. He showed up whenever and wherever needed. In his words and deeds, he demonstrated the dynamic character of Islam, its ability to adapt to different cultural settings and advance a religious community in America without the benefit or domination of priests and clergy. In the United States the responsibility for the interpretation of religious dogma was not dependent on an elite who monopolized control over the tradition. Of course, this more democratic form of governance presented its own challenges, most especially the need for consistency and coherence in a land with a dearth of locally trained and learned Islamic jurists.

What I found most compelling about Sulayman's portrait of Islam was a deep-seated ambivalence about America. On the one hand, he spoke of the welcoming embrace of a country that afforded vast educational options, career opportunities, and active participation in the democratic project. He

---

wp/2016/07/15/after-nice-newt-gingrich-wants-to-test-every-american-muslim-and-deport-those-who-believe-in-sharia/.

noted the freedoms cherished by Muslim immigrants, some of whom were escaping religious persecution in India, genocide in places like Bosnia, and the unbearable hardships of civil war in parts of Africa. The central "problem" was how to respond to the pressures to assimilate, how to preserve and honor the distinctive character of the Muslim family and community. Historically, the path to acceptance involved an alignment with the values and practices of what is popularly construed as the Judeo-Christian tradition, and until recently Islam rarely factored into the national equation. Would the demand to conform combine with intermarriages and hollow out the distinguishing character of Muslim immigrants after a few generations—eroding the various Islamic cultures with their food, dress, music, language, and customs?

Sulayman also spoke about the challenges of overcoming the divides between Muslim groups that were rooted in different ethnic and national experiences, including the gap between Muslim immigrants and Black Muslims who embody a different origin story. Not only did Sulayman alert me to ethnic/national divisions, he brought my attention to the multiple ways in which his fellow Muslims read and interpret their sacred texts and adjudicate disagreements. There are vital historical, theological, and political distinctions to take into account when considering the differences between Shia and Sunni, Sufi and Ahmadiyya, Salafist and Ismaili traditions. There are crucial variations to consider when comparing schools of Islamic jurisprudence. The levels of observance also reveal a vast spectrum. There are traditional and modern, religiously devout and highly secular Muslims. All of which goes to show a tradition with the complexity and diversity found in any great religion.

Sulayman felt the United States offered a context in which Muslims—in all their multiplicity—could make important contributions to their tradition and to the larger society to which they now belonged. The religious and ethnic pluralism in North America was brimming with possibility. Nonetheless, he also shared the belief that Muslims had a conflicted relationship with the United States, which reinforced their feelings of liminality, the sense of being simultaneously outsiders and insiders. Not only were they subjected to the negative attitudes of many Americans, they often found themselves at odds with the country's foreign policies. Instead of championing the noblest ideals of liberalism and democracy, the United States often engaged in global confrontations in Central Asia, the Middle East, South Asia, and Afghanistan with the rationale of combatting "Islamic fundamentalism." This category was malleable and poorly defined, all too often giving the impression that beneath the surface all Muslims were aligned with a global ideology of conquest and so belonged within the enemy's ranks.

Meanwhile, the debacles in Iraq, Syria, and Afghanistan dragged on and took their most devastating toll on ordinary civilians. The passivity of the United States as Russians committed atrocities in Chechnya—in the name of defeating Islamic extremism—did not go unnoticed. A good many Muslims whom I came to know concluded that the democratic and egalitarian ideals we strove to realize on our soil did not seem to apply in our conduct overseas. The American quest for profit and power consistently contradicted the values espoused in our Bill of Rights, and this incongruity substantiated the verdict that our foreign policy was yet another form of colonial imperialism. To them, the record of American military and economic adventures was written in blood, overwhelmingly of Muslim origin.

In this cultural and political environment, the imperative to engage Muslims and expand the educational horizons of the ICJS became urgent and inescapable. The more we surveyed the wider cultural landscape, the more we recognized that Islam was not just an addendum to our organization's mission. Islam was indeed the third leg of the stool, and therefore the ICJS needed to reverse its previous position. Its formative import in the shaping of Western civilization was undeniable, even if largely unrecognized. This position not only grew out of more expansive academic inquiries, but key funders in Atlanta, Baltimore, and Washington gave momentum to an expansion of our mission. In response, the ICJS facilitated mini-courses on Islam, hosted gatherings of Jewish, Christian, and Muslim scholars/educators, and shaped new curricular resources. Perhaps most significantly, the staff and board began to reach out to Muslim leaders in the region in order to explore the viability of redefining the scope of our organization. These investigations made us acutely conscious of major obstacles.

We were active in educational networks that focused on Jewish-Christian relations, and we discovered other enterprises that advanced Christian-Muslim scholarship, most notably the Center for Muslim-Christian Understanding at Georgetown University. While there were more modest efforts to establish programs that brought representatives from all three traditions into creative partnerships, we heard accounts of triangulation—the asymmetries that made pedagogical balance and shared purpose difficult. The methods and the goals of the Christian-Jewish dialogue were already hardwired and all too often diverged from the needs and aspirations of many Muslims.

The monumental exception was the work launched by the University of Virginia professor Peter Ochs and the formation of a discipline known as "scriptural reasoning." This academic enterprise brought together a remarkable array of scholars who demonstrated the promise of rigorous engagement with sacred texts from all three traditions. When refracted through different religious lenses and reinterpreted by small groups of Jews, Christians, and Muslims, rigorous study again yielded surprising insights and also sparked experiences that were transformational and holy—creating an altogether different kind of reading community. These colloquies bolstered our confidence in working with Muslim communities and inspired the ICJS to embark on a new venture.

*

On several visits to Atlanta, I had the opportunity to meet with Imam Plemon El-Amin, arguably the most prominent Muslim dealing with interreligious affairs in Atlanta. Pelmon joined forces with Sherry Frank and Reverend Joanna Adams, whose long-standing friendship and creative endeavors in Jewish-Christian-Islamic relations galvanized a community committed to interreligious learning. The ICJS staff scholars crafted a series of text studies to explore the ways in which Jews, Christians, and Muslims read and interpreted the stories of Abraham, Sarah and Hagar, and Ishmael and Isaac. Our challenge was to explore how these narratives pulled us together and simultaneously drove us apart.

Starting with the figure of Abraham, a coalition of nearly two hundred Jews, Christians, and Muslims from Atlanta examined his portrait in the book of Genesis, proceeded to trace his evolving depiction in rabbinic writings, then lifted up characterizations in medieval sources, and concluded with a snapshot of his profile in modern Jewish thought. Although Jews refer to "our father Abraham," his portrayal in Genesis does not reflect the features of someone traditionally identified as the first Jew. He does not deliver in word or deed the teachings that came to distinguished the Jewish people from their neighbors. Neither Sabbath observance nor sacrificial standards nor dietary specifications—practices and beliefs that later define the community—emerged from his example. The one key exception is circumcision. As Harvard professor Jon Levenson observed, Moses might have made a better candidate as the founder of the Jewish people (which establishes an important contrast with both Christianity and Islam, traditions that link Abraham with the founding of a religion). The prominence given to Abraham is "a little surprising" because "so little of what the tradition instructs Jews to practice can be found in the biblical narratives about Abraham."[7] Furthermore, Genesis does not desist from revealing the morally problematic dimensions of the man—for example, the flagrant deception in presenting his wife as his sister, a fabrication that lands her in Pharoah's household (Gen 12).

7. Levenson, *Inheriting Abraham*, 3.

Abraham is given a makeover in rabbinic lore and emerges as a courageous champion of monotheism who destroyed his father's idols and intuitively practiced the entire Torah.[8] His image was elevated to even greater heights in medieval thought, where he is lifted up as a pioneering sage who discerned the path of truth and justice without benefit of a teacher.[9] As our study groups turned attention to contemporary Jewish depictions of Abraham, the picture became far more conflicted: portrayals in literature, the visual arts, and music, as well as literary analyses, historical renderings, and synagogal teaching, did not yield a consistent picture. Instead, Abraham emerged as a figure who fills the mind with questions and the heart with an enduring ache.

Did Abraham pass or fail the test when called upon in Genesis 22 (a scene Jews call the *akeda*, the "binding" of Isaac) to offer up his son as a sacrifice? Did he pass or fail the test when called to balance the demands and desires of Sarah with the fragile hopes and elemental needs of Hagar, the mother of his first son? What kind of father was he to Hagar's son Ishmael and Sarah's son Isaac, and can we learn from his blunders as well as his daring leaps of faith? In the modern imagination these questions prompted participants to dig beneath the surface of familiar portraits and confront a perplexing figure who passed along a disputed inheritance.

When study groups turned to Christian views of Abraham, the focus shifted in yet another direction. Although the New Testament mentions Abraham more than sixty times, the apostle Paul's depiction proves most essential and most challenging. At issue is the task of determining the community to which the promises of Abraham are bestowed. Who are Abraham's rightful children? What are the criteria to determine divine election—who belongs and who, according to later Christian interpreters of Paul, is excluded from membership in God's covenantal family?

Paul argues that Abraham's righteousness was established before Moses had received the Torah. It was Abraham's trust in God that established a binding relationship, and this demonstration of faith took place prior to his circumcision (Rom 4:11–12). This detail becomes pivotal in Paul's thinking because he maintains Abraham provides an alternative model for covenantal membership. The path to salvation has now been opened to gentiles as well as Jews through faith in Jesus Christ, which means that divine acceptance no longer depends upon the maintenance of those ritual practices that set

---

8. This narrative is also found in the Qur'an, Surah Al-Anbiya 21:59-67. https://quran.com/en/al-anbya/51-67.

9. See Moses Maimonides, Mishneh Torah, *Yad Hazakah* 1.3. Kadish, "How Did Abraham Discover God?," https://www.thetorah.com/article/how-did-abraham-discover-god-the-rationalistic-approach.

the Jewish community apart. Paul's interpretation redefines the boundaries in favor of greater inclusion. Yet future generations of Christians, such as the church father Justin Martyr (c. 100–165), locked the door thrown open for gentiles and shut out those who continued to insist on the requirements of the Torah. The thrust of Paul's argument is deployed to substantiate the claim that biological ancestry and ritual observances count for nothing. Anyone who proclaims faith in Christ becomes a child of Abraham and the true inheritor of the promised blessings. In other words, Abraham is recruited to serve as an agent of Christian supersessionism.

This dangerous trajectory leads many Christians to highlight another current in Paul's writing, one that counters an anti-Jewish platform. The foundational text for this position is found in Paul's Epistle to the Romans, especially chapters 9–11, where Paul insists that "the gifts and calling of God are irrevocable" (11:29). God's fidelity to the Jewish people, the physical descendants of Abraham and Sarah, remains unshakable. God's commitment to the covenantal partnerships is unconditional and absolutely trustworthy. The gentile followers of Jesus do not replace the Jewish people or annul Judaism.

The conclusion of this study unit centered on the representation of Ibrahim (Abraham) in the Islamic tradition. In many respects, Ibrahim—considered the founder of monotheism—occupies an even more important place among Muslims than he does among Jews and Christians. Ibrahim is uncoupled from his flesh-and-blood bond to the Jewish people, and his significance thereby takes on a more universal reach. His prominence stems from his role as an indispensable link in the chain of the prophets, which extends from Adam to the greatest of all prophets, Muhammad. According to the Qur'an, Abraham submitted (Arabic, *muslim*) to God and consistently demonstrated his obedience by embarking on a physical journey from his homeland to Syria, and later, back to Mecca. This odyssey is mapped onto the Islamic practice of the pilgrimage to Mecca known as the Hajj, which is obligatory for able-bodied Muslims to undertake at least once in a lifetime. This spiritual discipline binds the pilgrim to fellow Muslims from around the world and enables Muslims to reaffirm the core commitments of the prophets.

According to the Islamic tradition, Mecca is the site where Adam built the Ka'bah and initiated the Hajj rites. The Ka'bah served as the first and foremost sanctuary testifying to the one true God, which subsequent generations lamentably compromised and corrupted. Ibrahim rebuilt the House of Allah, which later became contaminated with idolatry until Muhammad cleansed the Ka'bah of its impurity. The life and deeds of Ibrahim stand out because he foreshadowed the religious commitments of Muhammad, who restored the true path of holiness, overcoming the iniquity of idolaters and the imperfections of Jews and Christians.

This program brought the group to the discovery that we each consider ourselves full-fledged members of Abraham's family, but like most large families we have our fair share of issues. Beneath the anodyne conclusion that we are all related, we found ample evidence of dysfunctional rivalries. Our Christian ancestors forged a worldview in which each community believed it could not inherit Abraham's promises without insisting that the other siblings had been disinherited. And yet, there was a potent conviction that expanded with each session. We witnessed participants who were exhilarated to engage individuals who came from such disparate religious and ethnic backgrounds and realized we need not follow the polemical scripts that earlier generations passed down to us and could craft a different chapter for the sake of our children and children's children. While all of us also came away from the experience with a humbling awareness of the massive ignorance that sits among us and an overwhelming sense of the work that remains, we left with the settled conviction that we each belonged at the table—and we needed to come back for more.

*

As the ICJS became more involved with Muslim communities and conducted a variety of programs on Islam, the board and staff entered more deeply into spirited debates about the advisability of becoming the Institute for Islamic, Christian & Jewish Studies. We faced considerable resistance from those who feared the challenge of Islam would eclipse our commitment to healing the antagonisms that pitted Jews and Christians against one another. No one doubted the magnitude of unfinished business—the depth and breadth of distortions embedded in our scriptures and our traditions. And yet, when it came time to vote on the expansion, there was unanimity—an uncommon achievement among individuals for whom disagreement came naturally! We simply could not remain true to our founding mission without affirming Islam as integral to our work. The world had changed, and our organization knew from past experience our best and most daring work grew out of turbulent encounters with uncertainty. The commitment to disarm religious hostilities within our frayed society mandated a new alignment with Islam and our Muslim neighbors. The board pledged to raise the monies and hire the staff needed to make this transition possible.

The need and the urgency were underscored when some of our earliest funders pushed against this enlargement and refused to maintain their financial and moral support. They were convinced that Christians and Jews were confronting an implacable foe. In their judgment, the ICJS was naively yielding to political correctness and was failing to reckon properly with a religious ideology implicated in merciless violence and devoted to global domination. We did not track the number of individuals who withdrew their support, but two extended conversations with highly educated and well-respected philanthropists were disquieting. One gentleman who had majored in religion at an Ivy League university informed me that Islam ascribes to teachings antithetical to both Judaism and Christianity. He was convinced the underlying ethos of Islam could not be reconciled with democratic principles. He was well armed with Islamophobic literature, including the works of Ayaan Hirsi Ali. Another disgruntled funder was distressed that our organization was partnering with Muslims, but she was particularly outraged by the decision to make Islam the first tradition mentioned in our title. Despite my efforts to assure her that Muslims were not involved in an effort to eclipse either the Christians or the Jews, she demanded that Islam come last. If we did not become the Institute for Jewish, Christian, & Islamic Studies, she was done with the organization. We never heard from her again. The resistance to Islam confirmed our organization's decision. I suspect that no more than two dozen supporters discontinued their support, but the deficit was offset by many others who stepped into the breach, enabling us to bring talented Muslims onto our board and staff.

There was no shortage of hubris driving this development, which I now look back upon with justifiable embarrassment. To be sure, the board and staff were resolved to expose the tangled roots of Islamophobia and cultivate positive regard for a tradition and peoples vast in complexity and diversity. The proliferation of caricatures had migrated from far-right screeds into the mainstream. The media had cast Muslims into the lead role in terrorist activities, efficiently turning outrage at the murderous rampages into a staple of the American diet. We readily embraced the role of public defender and prided ourselves in dispensing nuance and balance. Yet we also believed the ICJS (now the Institute for Islamic, Christian, and Jewish Studies) could illuminate the shadow side of Islam. Christians and Jews were well acquainted with the deadly repercussions of supersessionism, the exorbitant price paid by both the oppressed and the oppressor when dissent is stifled and justice denied to minorities. We knew all too well the arrogance of those who claim absolute truth and certainty. I imagined we could help Muslims with the problem. We could encourage, even exhort them not to make the same mistakes Christians had made repeatedly.

This conceit was exposed near the conclusion of a clergy scripture forum in the spring of 2017. A group of Jews and Christians had spent the day combing through a selection of passages in our respective scriptures that valorized violence directed against the dual threat—hostile outsiders and mutinous insiders. The group had labored to expose the insidious logic within our sacred writings, and had unveiled instances when these writings were used to justify brutality. We concluded each segment with an examination of the analytic tools—the scriptural, moral, and theological instruments—that could disarm these texts of terror.

I had invited a Muslim scholar to join our colloquy, and she listened intently. As our study group was wrapping up the program, one of the main presenters declared both Christians and Jews had taken important steps to neutralize the incendiary material in their scriptures, and he hoped Muslims would eventually do the same. No one followed up or questioned this observation until several minutes later—when the Muslim scholar unleashed her frustration and disappointment.

We had placed her in the position of being the token Muslim called upon to speak for all of Islam and to apologize for the "backward" condition of almost two billion people. She wanted to know why no one had spoken up to contest this off-handed dismissal of Islam, and she was astounded by the self-congratulatory posture we had assumed. She called out the unprecedented violence in America fomented by Christian nationalists, a bloody legacy that far outpaced the damage wrought by Muslim extremists in our country. She pointed to the religious justifications for the degradation and violence directed against Palestinians, which Jewish zealots in Israel deployed on a regular basis. She scolded the group, exhorting us to dislodge the log in our own eyes before trying to extract the splinter obstructing her people's vision. Shortly after, she stood up and walked out.

The experience reminded us that efforts to fix another's tradition more often than not backfire. I believe this Muslim scholar gave us a much-needed "whack upside the head." Clearly it is best to keep one's mouth shut rather than make sweeping judgments about the shortcomings of another tradition. Yet there is something to be said in favor of making mistakes. Had my colleague avoided the stumble into a notable blunder, our group would have missed an important learning. Almost everyone involved in the dialogue has at one time or another caught foot-in-mouth disease, but this common infection is only healed when aired in public and tended by companions well aware of their own susceptibility.

I regret our bungling that day. Even more, I worry about our all-too-frequent caution, our fear of compounding disorder and giving offense to our religious neighbors. Overly cautious conversation partners go to great lengths to avoid mistakes, and in fashioning a totally "safe space" may unwittingly create the conditions that leave our ignorance and insensitivity intact. Rarely do we get outside ourselves and catch a glimpse of our disabilities without some stumbling and bumbling.

In the days that followed, I sought to understand and appreciate why this Muslim scholar walked out. She had been thrust into an awkward situation and more than likely felt badly about unmasking our presumptions. She may well have resented the fact that she was called upon to defend a tradition under relentless scrutiny—and worse, expected to apologize on behalf of those factions within Islam that she vehemently opposed.

The incident had the trademarks of a micro-aggression loaded with macro-implications, and the experience left this Muslim scholar burned. I imagine her withdrawal reflects a reaction that many other minorities understand all too well. The unspoken rules of many religious dialogues often appear to underwrite another form of colonialism, a strategy for the assimilation of difference in which participants are expected to exchange their distinct beliefs and practices for a bland stew of interchangeable spiritual platitudes. The unacknowledged expectation is that everyone will muffle their distinctions, blend into an acceptable unanimity, and content themselves with insipid pieties. And then an event transpires that makes it painfully clear—we are not the same. We are not commensurate and fungible. Our experiences and circumstances set us apart. In these moments of disruption, a cloud of suspicion forms. We discover the trust built incrementally over years can shatter.

I have been told in recent years that it is not the job of Jews to redeem the failings of Christian theology. It is wrong-headed to assign Muslims the hard labor of educating Jews and Christians about their misunderstandings and distorted cultural memories. Blacks are not responsible for the enlightenment of whites about the enduring legacy of slavery, Jim Crow legislation, and the injustice still maintained in economic and political policies. Public intellectuals, most especially from minority groups, can provide resources to expose the enduring dangers of Judeophobia, the damage caused by Orientalism, and the suffering generated by racism, sexism, and classism. But can the essential learning really be developed without awkward and often painful face-to-face encounters? Can transformation take place when abstracted from the interplay of people who will invariably misunderstand one another?

The heavy lifting required to rebuild the foundations of a just society belongs to those who have long held the purse and occupied the seat of political power and cultural hegemony. I do not disagree with those who place the onus on the white Christian majority in this country and demand meaningful reparations. I also recognize the frustration and disenchantment of those who believe the patterns of avoidance and denial are so deeply embedded in our society that nothing of significance will change. The majority is willfully blind to its culpability. What an indictment that huge swaths of the American public are willing to outlaw any educational inquiries that reveal their own and their children's privileges and make them feel uncomfortable!

This is why I believe the work of forging interreligious and interracial partnerships has an essential part to play in building a society that is not simply tolerant but inclusive and equitable. There are so few spaces where Americans meet and speak across the divides; there are few settings where Americans are encouraged to seek common purpose while learning to honor difference. To be sure, the burden falls on those who are most resistant to change—white Christians—but I have little hope for constructive change if religious and ethnic minorities yield to cynicism and despair, as tempting as that may be.

The move to a more egalitarian and just social order will not take place if people remain sequestered in their enclaves. Those places where people of all genders and creeds and backgrounds meet and press one another to define what really matters to them, what they share and what sets them apart—these places are few and far between, yet precious beyond measure. Experience alone will dispel the notion that religious dialogue is merely a cover for the homogenization of difference. I have some appreciation, however limited by my own social and cultural location, for the reasons a good many individuals relegated to the fringes of American life refuse to show up and risk becoming nothing more than token representatives. Yet disenchantment and seclusion will be our nation's undoing. The old aphorism still holds: either we hang together or we hang separately. We rise up together, or we all go down.

CHAPTER 15

Religion in the Public Square

During my first year at the ICJS, in 1987, I stumbled into a quagmire that turned out to be far wider and deeper than initially anticipated. For many years, Baltimore County had paid tribute to the holiday spirit on its front lawn by placing statues of Mary and Joseph alongside a crèche. To give a more ecumenical flavor to the Christmas cast, the county commissioners of good cheer added layers and layers of plastic figures, including Santa Claus, reindeer, and snowmen. Bright lights illuminated the synthetic fanfare, making the seasonal display glow day and night. The jollification could not be missed if you set foot in downtown Towson.

If the county executive had possessed an incantation to turn kitsch into food, no one in the northern suburbs of Baltimore would have gone hungry. Devoid of this alchemy, I was alarmed that this fusion of religious and commercial iconography was delivering some disturbing messages. I hasten to add my anxieties were partially rooted in a Presbyterian ancestry with strong links to Massachusetts Puritans. They insisted there was no biblical evidence to link Christmas with late December, and they outlawed the celebration of Christmas in 1659, maintaining the ban until 1681. My spiritual predecessors feared these celebrations promoted the sensibilities of rowdy pagans addicted to the intoxication of solstice festivals. My anti-Catholic forbearers objected to customs that enthusiastically embraced a rollicking "carnival." Gluttony, cross-dressing, drunkenness, and lewd public displays may have been fine for Roman Catholics in the "old country," but we New World Protestants insisted our celebrations should be "modest," "decent," "orderly," and above all "biblically based."

Those days of repressed celebrations are now long gone, and I suppose there is reason to raise a glass and say good riddance to yesteryear's constraints. Yet the development may not have brought us to a higher state of spiritual evolution. The commercial takeover of Christmas has given us generations of kids who climb onto Santa's lap to demand lots of stuff they do not really need and that won't make them happier, while their parents plunge deeper into debt and are forced to work overtime. The multitude may dream of "a white Christmas just like the one we used to know," but ends up holding an empty bag full of nothing but disappointments. No wonder the suicide rate spikes every year at this time.

There is no escape from the onslaught of jingle bells, gluttonous consumption, and the ensuing malaise of a bad hangover. Who can find a mall or a dentist chair liberated from the muzak of holiday cheer? Even more problematic, the Christmas dilemma runs deeper and works a darker magic. Those who belong to other religious traditions are pushed to the margins and stigmatized as outsiders. The official holiday calendar coupled with the prevailing customs offer convincing testimony that our religious neighbors are "resident aliens" living in a "Christian" country.

To be sure, the foundational Christmas story tells of a miraculous birth and the good news of an impending reversal in the world order. But a troublesome undercurrent is also embedded in the narrative, one that promulgates an anti-Jewish proclamation. The people from whom Jesus came are the very people who rejected him. "He [Jesus] came unto his own, and his own received him not" (John 1:11 KJV). By turning their backs on the one who came to deliver them, they have sealed their doom as a people alienated from God. The lectionary readings underwrite a narrative of Christian triumph. The arc moves from promise to fulfillment: "Therefore the Lord himself will give you a sign: The virgin will be with child and will give birth to a son, and you will call him Immanuel" (Isa 7:14 KJV). What is anticipated within the Hebrew scriptures is realized with the Christmas story. All the pieces can be found within the Old Testament and, when properly assembled, the messianic expectation points to Jesus. So most Christians at one time or another are predisposed to wonder why Jews do not recognize that their own scriptures offer "proof" that Jesus is their long-anticipated savior.[1]

Those who opt for a more inclusive salutation by wishing others "happy holidays" and "season's greetings" are lambasted for their refusal to honor Christian custom. The forces of secularization and a liberal "cancel culture" are seen as conspiring to drive Christians underground, shaming the majority population for the display of its religiosity. The fact that some

---

1. See Levine and Bretler, *Bible With and Without Jesus*, for an analysis of the texts from the "Hebrew" scriptures that Christians often use to bolster their theological claims.

neighbors may not find Christmas a season of comfort and joy—well, isn't that their problem?

With these concerns in mind and heart, I crafted a letter to the Baltimore County office reminding the public administrators that we live in a nation that declares a separation of church and state. I suggested that many churches in the area already had nativity scenes on their lawns, and these public displays on private property were certainly an appropriate expression of their faith. Moreover, to jumble Santa Claus and snowmen with a nativity scene on government land was at the very least a mixed metaphor. More pointedly, this public spectacle was an act of expropriation that trivialized Christian symbols and domesticated a sacred story loaded with a countercultural message. The exhibition was offensive not just to those who belong to a different religious tradition or no religion at all, but also to those who do not want their religious icons used for banal entertainment.

My efforts to recruit Christian ministers and priests to join this protest were not received with gratitude. One of my classmates from Princeton encouraged me to lighten up and not to make a big deal out of an annual custom that had become a community tradition. My concern about the exclusion of our religious neighbors evoked the response: "In the first place, there are not many Jews in the Towson area. In the second place, we can solve the problem quite simply. All we need to do is add a good-sized menorah to the display." Others reprimanded my proposal as counterproductive. I was throwing shade on the Christian tradition and superimposing "negativity" onto a festive celebration. The concern about an anti-Jewish subplot within the Christmas narrative was a pill most of my colleagues did not want to swallow. They leveled the complaint that our religious tradition was already suffering from diminished self-esteem, and my "exposé" would offer another reason to avoid the church.

Another friend observed, "To a hammer, everything looks like a nail. Ever since your immersion in the Jewish community, you seem to think everything looks tainted with antisemitism."

I had become the grinch who threatened to steal Christmas. My friend pressed me to think through the implications of my condemnation: "Let's say your initiative is successful, and the county removes the nativity scene. What's left? An empty space. While you manage to clear the courthouse lawn of religious imagery, you leave nothing of spiritual significance standing. What remains is the plastic clutter we both find repugnant!"

I pointed out you had only to drive a couple of blocks in any direction to relish a Christmas tableau on a church lawn. He saw greater danger in creating a naked public square. In 2001 we would have occasion to continue our debate when the Alabama Chief Justice, Roy Moore, installed a two-and-a-half-ton granite monument featuring an engraved copy of the Ten Commandments in the rotunda of the Alabama Judicial Building.

The pushback I received from my Christian colleagues released some of the air from my righteous indignation and deepened my perplexity over the entanglements of church and state. Our civil ideals and our religious heritages overlap in significant ways, and don't we lose a sense of vital connection if we outlaw public tributes to this overlapping legacy? Don't we sacrifice a vital source of wisdom passed down by our ancestors if we interpret "freedom of religion" as freedom *from* religion?

In retrospect, I think my resistance to the merging of church and state took a sharper turn after an expedition to the Soviet Union on the cusp of its implosion in 1990. I had been invited by the American Center for International Leadership to configure a group of ten scholars of religion from very different backgrounds to visit the Soviet Union and enter into conversation with our Russian counterparts. While our contingent seized opportunities to escape the watchful eye of our Soviet handlers and meet with religious dissidents, we also had the chance to encounter a number of Russian Orthodox officials, including Archbishop Alexander, the rector of the largest seminary in the Soviet Union, at the ancient monastery at Zagorsk. The archbishop was a large and imposing figure wrapped in a cassock of battleship gray. Dark and penetrating eyes, a massive prickly beard, and a deep, commanding voice—he was a man well versed in the defense of his domain.

After the obligatory exchange of pleasantries, our group asked if any of the Russian Orthodox priests assembled for this occasion saw a resurgence of religious life in the Soviet Union and anticipated greater recognition, openness, and freedom. Their responses were immediate, and they eagerly anticipated positive developments. They envisioned a future in which the Orthodox Church would once again reclaim its authority and revive the religious ethos of the nation. We then asked our hosts to tell us what steps the Russian Orthodox Church might take to protect those who were most vulnerable, those who had been marginalized and lived outside their ecclesiastical canopy. More pointedly, I inquired if Orthodox Christians had a special responsibility to ensure the survival of the Jewish population. This query hit a raw nerve. The archbishop fired back with words difficult to forget.

> Do you think that we have not also suffered? Twenty-seven million lost in the Great Patriotic War. As many as forty million murdered in Stalin's purges. Why single out the Jews for special treatment as though their suffering counts for more? The danger

is that we Russians will cling to our separate ways and fail to overcome our differences. We must move beyond our divisions and find unity in our spiritual journey to God.

Astonishingly, our Russian counterparts insisted a viable future depended upon a nation that fused its political ideals with the religious heritage entrusted to the Russian Orthodox Church without regard to other Christian groups, let alone other religious minorities. The secular project had failed, and they argued Russian Orthodoxy alone provided the indispensable foundation for national unity. Without this religious cohesion, the country would splinter into competing factions and the balkanization of Mother Russia would lead to collapse.

The members of our group warned our hosts about the danger that comes from the failure to separate church and state. If the church becomes too closely aligned with the state, both may suffer stultifying consequences. How can the church speak with a prophetic voice and call out state-sponsored injustices without distance and independence from the political establishment? Do they want to live in a regime where criticism directed against the abuse of governmental authorities is interpreted as an act of disloyalty, if not sedition? Furthermore, we declared the alignment of church and state is also apt to marginalize those who do not belong to the official church. The state wants the church to bless its policies, and the church wants the state to support and serve its own hegemonic interests.

The concerns we raised struck our hosts as either incomprehensible or mistaken. When we spoke of the virtues of pluralism and the benefits of religious diversity, our words evoked grimaces and shaking heads. They regarded the refusal of power and privilege as a dereliction of sacred duty. They viewed our celebration of a multicultural society as evidence of a decadent Western culture drifting into the arms of secularism. In their view, when church and state were properly merged, the nation could uphold norms to protect the integrity of the family and put the interests of the larger community ahead of the individual's selfish demands.

The anxieties that emerged during the course of our meetings with Russian Orthodox clerics have taken on much greater significance in recent times. As I write these words, Russia is mounting a bloody assault on Ukraine. The scale of the violent attack has worldwide reverberations, and the deadly consequences of the incursion are immeasurable. By any rational standard, the invasion is a massive disaster not only to the people of Russia and Ukraine, but to the world economy and the global environment. Russian justifications for this war are rooted in preposterous conspiracy theories that rule out diplomatic compromise and humanitarian interventions.[2] The paranoia and mendacity amplified by misinformation platforms are yoked to a pernicious religious ideology that our delegation witnessed firsthand more than thirty years ago.[3]

The senior hierarchy of the Russian Orthodox Church is validating President Vladimir Putin's war on Ukraine with the accusation that the evil "West" is actually responsible for the hostilities. More troubling is the complicity of the hierarchy within the Moscow Patriarchate, most especially the role played by current Patriarch Kirill. With his blessing, the military campaign has taken on the character of a holy war, a battle pitting the forces of the "Russian World" against corruptions of the West—liberalism, globalization, the so-called predations of the LGBTQ movement, and militant secularism. The ideological roots of this Orthodox fundamentalism draw upon a mythic repertoire called "Russkii Mir" (Russian World), which posits:

> a transnational sphere or civilization, which includes Russian, Ukraine, and Belarus (and sometimes Moldova and Kazakhstan), as well as ethnic Russians and Russian-speaking people throughout the world. It holds that this "Russian world" has a common political centre (Moscow), a common spiritual centre (Kyiv), a common language (Russian), a common church (the Russian Orthodox Church, Moscow Patriarchate), and a common patriarch (the Patriarch of Moscow) who works in 'symphony' with a common president/national leader to govern the Russian world, as well as upholding a common distinctive spirituality, morality, and culture.[4]

The Russian Orthodox authorities in Moscow appeal to a mythic past going back to the tenth century, when Vladimir the Great, the grand prince of Kyiv, was baptized and proceeded to Christianize the Holy Rus. The West, with the military backing of NATO, has sundered this unity, and therefore Russia proclaims itself the true victim in this confrontation. The struggle promulgated and sanctified by both Patriarch Kirill and Putin aims at the restoration of an imaginary and glorified past. The Moscow leadership asserts that the stakes in this life-and-death battle will require great sacrifices.

2. See historian of Russian media Yablokov, "Five Conspiracy Theories That Putin Has Weaponized," https://www.nytimes.com/2022/04/25/opinion/putin-russia-conspiracy-theories.html.

3. As Susanne Langer noted, "A vague longing for the old tribal unity makes nationalism look like salvation, and arouses the most fantastic bursts of chauvinism and self-righteousness." Langer, *Philosophy in a New Key*, 238.

4. Excerpted from "Declaration on the 'Russian World' Teaching," https://publicorthodoxy.org/2022/03/13/a-declaration-on-the-russian-world-russkii-mir-teaching/.

Nothing less than the soul of Russia, and by extension the moral destiny of the entire world, requires a fight to finish. Putin's Russia marches under the banner of Christ's cross, armed with a sacred mission—and the Moscow Patriarchate blesses the imperial onslaught.

It was the American theologian Reinhold Niebuhr who argued almost eighty years ago that "religious nationalisms are not merely 'idolatrous,' but 'demonic,' not only in the theological sense that they involve 'invasion and possession of the self' by a racial and national 'spirit' that makes 'pretensions to divinity,' but also in the material sense that they can unleash apocalyptic forms of death and destruction."[5] It is precisely the apocalyptic contours of religious nationalism that reveal the horrific implications of warfare without constraint—the deployment of nuclear weaponry that weds faith in the world to come with the total elimination of the current global compact. Total war is heralded as the only solution to overcome the malignant source of evil.

I did not need to venture overseas to recognize the dangers of an overweening nationalism. I knew firsthand the mechanisms deployed to justify obedience to the almighty state and to sanction the excesses of holy war. The Vietnam War called into question our most primal allegiances. The ultimate sacrifice that my classmates and I were called to make was not to the Creator of heaven and earth, but to a nation we had grown up pledging ourselves to each morning. Did this fusion of God and country—reinforced in our daily recitations—conceal the tension between two competing and irreconcilable loyalties? While some of my peers clung to the belief that the United States government was embroiled in a battle against godless communism—mortal combat to protect freedom at home and abroad—the great majority had grown cynical and weary of a patriotism that yielded so many body bags. The daring protestations of the Berrigan brothers—Philip and Daniel, both now of blessed memory—framed a weighty choice and, as far as I was concerned, exposed the lethargy and cowardice of the larger Christian community. I arrived at the conclusion, later reinforced by my experience in the Soviet Union: every nation is susceptible to idolatrous overreach—laying claim to a devotion to which God alone is entitled.

Years later, Joel Zaiman and I brooded about the relationship between church and state. He suggested one of the most vexing challenges facing his community was figuring out what it means to be both Jewish and American. His patriotism was more clearly defined and less battered than mine. He was adamant about the duty to fulfill one's civic responsibilities and participate wholeheartedly in the debates and struggles shaping our republic. At the

---

5. Quoted in Gorski, *American Covenant*, 125.

same time, there was no question that his primary loyalty was defined by his commitment to Judaism and the Jewish people. He thought the character of his community hinged on the question: do my congregants think of themselves as American Jews or Jewish Americans?

Once again, we found ourselves in that liminal place where the differences between Joel and me were remarkably similar. We had stumbled into a maze in which many Americans are caught and from which there are no apparent exits. How are we Jews, Christians, Muslims, and other religious neighbors to calibrate and reconcile the imperative to remain faithful to our traditions with the fealty we owe our nation—a nation that obligates us to sacrifice ourselves and our children should the need arise?

To be sure, we are all hybrids, and our identities are multiple—linked as they are to gender, class, geographic origin, ethnicity, politics, profession, food habits, sports interests, taste in music, educational background, leisure pursuits, age, as well as to religious affiliation or lack thereof. Are there no guidelines to help us sift through, balance, prioritize, and resolve the competing claims that these affiliations make on us, individually and collectively?

There are strong centripetal forces that locate one or another of these identity markers as central. In the midst of the current culture wars, we have seen political affiliations, racial distinctions, sexual orientations, economic standings, educational credentials, and religious connections enlisted as key ingredients in the establishment of a stable identity. The elements are often bundled in ways that make them appear monolithic—fixed and secure, unalterable and nonnegotiable. More often than not, the factors that are lifted up as essential and embraced as constitutive emerge in adversarial relationship to the characteristics seen as the basis for another's identity—secular vs. religious, liberal vs. conservative, Republican vs. Democratic, pro-life vs. pro-choice, white majority vs. ethnic minorities, populist vs. elitist, individualist vs. communitarian. Identities get whittled down to a few basic conglomerations and set in opposition to a hostile and threatening antagonist. The constriction of our identities, according to the philosopher and economist Amartya Sen, creates the conditions that make problems combustible.

> Violence is fomented by the imposition of singular and belligerent identities on gullible people, championed by proficient artisans of terror. . . . The alternative to the divisiveness of one preeminent categorization is not any unreal claim that we are all much the same. That we are not. Rather, the main hope of harmony in our troubled world lies in the plurality of our identities,

which cut across each other and work against sharp divisions around one single hardened line of vehement division that allegedly cannot be resisted.[6]

In the process of providing educational opportunities to unravel the tangled allegiances that comprise our individual and collective identities, the ICJS paid particular attention to the overlapping connections most commonly lumped under the rubric of church and state. What began as benign and genial conversations eventually brought us into red-hot exchanges as the political atmosphere veered into hyper-partisanship. The signs of a more rancorous encounter were evident even at the beginning of our inquiries, when the times were considerably gentler and kinder than they are today.

What are the hopes and expectations that undergird the discipline of prayer—as individuals, as religious communities, and as a nation? How can we maintain our footing and honor our particular religious traditions when we step into the public square and link arms with peoples from other religious communities—giving thanks for blessings bestowed, beseeching divine assistance in the face of hardship and tragedy, and owning up to our own and our ancestors' failings? How do our religious and secular leaders speak an inclusive language in public settings when a significant segment of the population regards the ritual performance as alien, unintelligible, inherently exclusionary, if not offensive? Do the dictates of political correctness render public prayer banal and vacuous—nothing more than an empty and anachronistic gesture?

The ICJS developed a course of study that opened up the challenge by exploring the question of prayer. To get at this question, we directed our attention to several US presidential inaugurations and examined the prayers delivered on behalf of incoming administrations and the nation as a whole. For example, Rick Warren, the founding pastor of the Saddleback Church, an evangelical megachurch in California, delivered the following invocation at the inauguration of President Barack Obama in January 2009.

> Almighty God, our Father, everything we see and everything we can't see exists because of you alone. It all comes from you. It all belongs to you. It all exists for your glory.
>
> History is your story. The Scripture tells us, "Hear, O Israel, the LORD is our God. The LORD is one." And you are the compassionate and merciful one. And you are loving to everyone you have made.
>
> Now, today, we rejoice not only in America's peaceful transfer of power for the 44th time. We celebrate a hinge point

---

6. Sen, *Identity and Violence*, 2, 16.

of history with the inauguration of our first African American president of the United States. We are so grateful to live in this land, a land of unequaled possibility, where the son of an African immigrant can rise to the highest level of our leadership.

Help us, O God, to remember that we are Americans, united not by race, or religion, or blood, but to our commitment to freedom and justice for all. When we focus on ourselves, when we fight each other, when we forget you, forgive us. When we presume that our greatness and our prosperity is ours alone, forgive us. When we fail to treat our fellow human beings and all the earth with the respect that they deserve, forgive us. And as we face these difficult days ahead, may we have a new birth of clarity in our aims, responsibility in our actions, humility in our approaches, and civility in our attitudes, even when we differ.

Help us to share, to serve and to seek the common good of all. May all people of goodwill today join together to work for a more just, a more healthy and a more prosperous nation and a peaceful planet. And may we never forget that one day all nations and all people will stand accountable before you. We now commit our new president and his wife, Michelle, and his daughters Malia and Sasha, into your loving care.

I humbly ask this in the name of the one who changes my life, Yeshua, Isa, Jesús, Jesus, who taught us to pray:

Our Father, who art in heaven, hallowed be thy name. Thy kingdom come. Thy will be done on earth as it is in heaven. Give us this day our daily bread, and forgive us our trespasses as we forgive those who trespass against us. And lead us not into temptation, but deliver us from evil. For thine is the kingdom and the power and the glory forever. Amen.[7]

In the aftermath of Trump's ascendancy and the rise of white Christian nationalism, this prayer may appear antiquated and quaint. It certainly engenders nostalgia for a time before Americans became such ferocious culture warriors. To assess the appropriateness of Reverend Warren's words, it is necessary to situate this prayer within a broader historical context and to examine the purpose of a ritual performance consistently included in US presidential inaugurations since 1937.

The act of prayer, given a central role in traditional worship, serves to shape community, instill a worldview, and elevate the virtues that elevate individuals and bind them together. The underlying assumption is that God is actively working to forge a nation and to help it embody the noble ideals of

---

7. Warren, "Invocation," https://www.americanrhetoric.com/speeches/rickwarreninaugurationprayer.htm.

a tradition to which all belong. In this case, Warren was celebrating a landmark achievement, the election of the first African American president, and he cautioned the nation to overcome rivalries and divisions that blind the nation to its common purpose. He exhorted citizens to care for one another and our fragile planet, warning the country that God will hold us accountable for our failings. Challenge and civic duty were grafted onto hopes and aspirations which are widely shared.

While a significant sector of the American populace does not identify or subscribe to the theological tenets underlying this prayer, a diverse citizenry heard Warren evoke sentiments and ethical commitments intended to celebrate, distinguish, and unite. His embrace aimed at the spirit of inclusion. But then Warren pivoted from a general appeal to the specific language and ritual conduct of his Christian tradition. While invoking Jesus as a link that ostensibly connects Jews, Christians, and Muslims, he elided the fact that this figure is regarded in radically different and irreconcilable ways—and thereby falls prey to a supersessionist propensity. Did the purpose of a national prayer break down and exacerbate intractable divisions?

At this point, study group participants were primed to jump into the fray, but our curriculum was designed to situate the issue in a larger framework and add new layers of complexity to the inquiry. The focus shifted to Chicago on the day of September 11, 1893, when the first meeting of the Parliament of World Religions was held. The global assembly attracted a remarkable array of participants including representatives from Christianity, Judaism, Islam, Hinduism, Buddhism, Jainism, Taoism, Shintoism, and Zoroastrianism. The mission of the Parliament was grounded in the conviction that people need to discover and affirm shared spiritual commitments. The hope was "to bring the nations of the earth into a more friendly fellowship" and to highlight "how many important truths the various religions hold and teach in common." At the inaugural ceremony, one of America's preeminent Roman Catholic leaders, Cardinal Gibbons, led the crowd in the recitation of the Lord's Prayer. Interestingly, this prayer became "the universal prayer" and was repeated at the beginning of each of the seventeen days of the otherwise interreligious Parliament. When the proceedings came to a conclusion, the Lord's Prayer was invoked yet again with Rabbi Emil G. Hirsch, the Reform rabbi from Chicago, leading the recitation.

Although initially stupefied by the adoption of this particular prayer, the group leaders in our congregational project provided a careful breakdown of the phrasing and demonstrated a broader spiritual reach than generally assumed. Jakob Petuchowski (1925–1991), a professor of Jewish theology and liturgy at Hebrew Union College, mapped out the parallels and substantiated a surprising overlap:

The Petitions of the Lord's Prayer with parallels from Jewish prayers[8]

Father (our, in heaven)	Our father, our king (liturgical prayer formula)
hallowed be thy name	Exalted and hallowed be His great name in the world (*Kaddish*)
Your kingdom come	May He establish His kingdom (*Kaddish*)
(Your will be done in heaven above as on earth)	Your will be done in heaven as on earth. Grant equanimity to those who revere You (*Tosefta Berakhoth* 3:7) He spoke and it came to pass, he commanded, and it stood fast (Ps. 33:9).
Give us today our daily bread	Satiate us out of Your goodness, and bless our year . . . (*Shemoneh Esreh*)
and forgive us our debt (as we forgive our debtors)	Forgive us, our father, for we have sinned against You (Eighteen Benedictions) Forgive thy neighbor the hurt he hath done thee; and then thy sins shall be pardoned when thou prayest (Ecclus. 28:2).
and lead us not into temptation (but deliver us from evil)	Look at our affliction and champion our cause, and redeem us for the sake of Your name (*Shemoneh Esreh*).

Perhaps the petitions voiced in this prayer reflect a spiritual orientation shared with Jews and may also echo the theological sensibilities of other traditions. Many of the older Americans in our gatherings recalled a time when the school day began with its recitation in conjunction with the Pledge of Allegiance. Yet the linkage of the Lord's Prayer with the Pledge of Allegiance reflects an entanglement of church and state difficult to unravel. Does this combination give voice to a national piety that is coherent and appropriate in a plural society? Does the ritual recitation bind a heterogeneous society together, instill a deep sense of loyalty, and imbue its citizens with divinely sanctioned purpose?

Such questions provoked heated disagreements among Jews and Christians seated around our tables, and the disputes did not necessarily

---

8. Petuchowski and Brocke, eds., *Lord's Prayer and Jewish Liturgy*, 186–87.

congeal on the basis of religious affiliation. Some argued this kind of public performance was needed to bind together a society as polarized and splintered as the United States. In response, a Christian congregant who had clearly imbibed the views of the Duke Divinity School theologian, Stanley Hauerwas, countered that as a Christian he saw himself as a "resident alien" and was outraged at the amalgamation of incompatible rituals. Pledging allegiance to a flag, singing patriotic anthems, and recruiting God as our national ally with the affirmations of faith embedded in the most fundamental of Christian prayers scrambles and confuses the lines separating church and state. This juxtaposition of political and religious recitations conflates religious and national commitments—confirming a problematic notion of American exceptionalism.

A few of the participants acknowledged the surprising confluence of words that rooted Jesus' prayer firmly on Jewish soil, but they still insisted the Lord's Prayer is so deeply embedded in the liturgical practices and the personal piety of Christians that any claim to its universality or its affinity with Jewish worship is misleading and overstated. In reciting this prayer, Christians are following the instructions and example of Jesus. In asking others to speak these words or even to assent passively to the prayer's underlying intentionality, isn't Rick Warren—and others who have mirrored the practice—calling the assembly to follow, implicitly or explicitly, in the path of a person whom Christians declare their Lord? Isn't the recital of a foundational Christian prayer in a public setting a practice that serves to veil religious differences, in effect by incorporating others into the dominant Christian culture?

Strong, sometimes vehement views about the appropriateness of this inaugural prayer opened up conversations about what exactly we are doing when the nation is publicly drawn into the activity of worship. Might the recruitment of the Divine in the service of national purposes come perilously close to idolatry, reinforcing the notion that faith in God is tantamount to faith in country? Or, turned upside down, does this conflation of God and country raise questions about whether it is possible to be a true citizen without simultaneously believing in God—or more precisely, holding the right belief in the right God?

The confounding alignments embedded in our national prayers led to other contentious conversations, including clashing judgments about the placement of the American flag in houses of worship. Does the flag signal the grateful recognition that the US Constitution guarantees our freedom to congregate and worship? Some insisted the American flag belongs in our religious sanctuaries because we should never take for granted the political context that protects and honors the eclectic patterns of religious life in the United States.

Others were more troubled. Does the flag once again imply a well-ordered alignment of interchangeable allegiances—the worship of one entails the worship of the other? What if we placed another flag alongside of the American flag, for example, the flag of the State of Israel or the Palestinian flag? What about the Confederate flag? If we were having the same conversation today, I'm sure we would have asked, how about the Ukrainian flag? There was widespread agreement that the clergy and lay leaders within our religious communities have not taught us to think through how to read and interpret what it means to place national flags in our places of worship. Given the current state of affairs in the United States, is it possible to decipher a national symbol put in the service of so many competing agendas—and at the end of the day arrive at a shared understanding?

From these discussions, I reached the conclusion that national flags do not belong in our sanctuaries. These emblems are loaded with so many divergent meanings that they confuse rather than clarify our orientation to the Divine. Increasingly "The Star-Spangled Banner," enshrined in Francis Scott Key's anthem, is hoisted to give legitimacy to questionable, if not xenophobic, causes and is used to evoke a blind devotion that stifles dissent. To locate the American flag alongside the cross—an instrument of execution used by the Roman state—is not simply a mixed metaphor, but a blending of loyalties and allegiances that are incommensurate. My Christian faith transcends national borders, and the emergence of militant religious nationalism, whether in Russia or the United States, makes any suggestion of equivalent loyalties a very dangerous proposition. This is a point to which I will return shortly.

During our first twenty years, the ICJS was able to choreograph conversations about church-state relations with audiences that held dramatically different political viewpoints. We aimed at neutrality and did our best to extend a welcome to individuals with divergent political positions. Although Maryland has a predominantly Democratic demographic, our programs attracted a more diverse cross section of the electorate. In 2003, I extended an invitation to the popular American Catholic writer and historian Thomas Cahill. Best known for his series of books about formative moments in Western civilization, he packed a synagogue auditorium with people from across the city. I cannot remember much about the lecture, but one comment he made during the question-and-answer segment scuttled the evening. Offhandedly he declared, "For the life of me, I do not know how you can be a Christian and a Republican at the same time." At the time the comment struck me as unfair, out of place, and obnoxious. I bristled at the prospect that our educational mission could be squeezed into a partisan box and aligned with the dogmatic platform of any single political party.

Over the last two decades the world around has us shifted, and the changes in the political climate have made neutrality a delusional ideal. With the ascendance of Donald Trump and his more zealous followers, the tenor of public discourse became increasingly mean-spirited, inflammatory, and polarizing—and religion was increasingly instrumentalized for political purposes. The practice of compromise was dismissed not only as a lost art, but as a failure to stand one's ground and fight to the finish.

The German philosopher Karl Schmitt, who described himself as a "displaced Catholic," once claimed that the most fundamental political determination a nation makes is the distinction between those who are friends and those who are foes. This divide establishes a nation's theo-political identity, and virtue is embodied in conduct that either helps your friends or damages your enemies. One of his most provocative definitions has found its way into the autocrat's playbook: "Sovereign is he who decides on the exception." In contrast to other citizens of the state, the sovereign is not bound by the customs, laws, and moral duties that govern the masses. The sovereign controls the power to step outside the social and political norms with impunity. In this regard, Donald Trump's presidency amounted to a bid for sovereignty. It was not just a political gambit but a metaphysical overture, a claim for an unassailable status that elevated him above his fellow citizens. This unique position has fueled the conviction that he is truly above the law.

The verbiage concerning Trump is already piled high, and there is no need for me to share my own indigestion—other than to confess the grimy fact that he occupied an outsized region in my imagination for several years. This fixation amounted to a kind of addiction, an enchantment, a captivity. Every morning I woke up wondering what new indignity the man had delivered when I had turned my attention elsewhere. Tracking the latest outrage, the vile tweet, the trash talk about enemies real and imagined: it was habit-forming. I was utterly flabbergasted that nothing—no scandals, lies, or deceptions—seemed to stick. I could not help but wonder if he was immune because "he" was really "us." Trump's omnipresence was derivative, and remains so. It was both his uncompromising supporters and his disgruntled detractors who inflated him and pumped air into his tires, wind to his lungs. Congress could put him on trial, but the larger and more costly case could not be prosecuted, or even cogently formulated. We did not know how to impeach ourselves. It is still dawning on us that the most fundamental challenge to American democracy and its moral underpinnings does not simply center on Trump and his Republican acolytes but on the country's citizenry and its vision for the nation.

More alarming than the preoccupation with the crimes and misdemeanors of Trump and his enablers was the disenchantment that took hold, a numbing of the mind and a sluggish acceptance of a new reality. It was shocking to reach a point when I no longer seemed capable of shock. As it dawned on me that I was no longer living in the country I had once imagined a sturdy and secure home, I drifted into resignation. I was no longer surprised by the violation of norms associated with basic decency, and the hardening of my heart was in some ways more troubling than his unrestrained exercise of power. In retrospect, the very act of witnessing the abuses felt like an act of submission. The crime was not confined to the Oval Office, but implicated all of us who did not know how to get out of the bleachers. Far too many of us had become gobsmacked spectators, weary and feeble bystanders.

The world had changed and me with it. Back in the early years of the ICJS, there were many reasons why I resisted the plunge into partisan politics. Not only did we want to pitch a big tent to accommodate people from across the political spectrum, we also wanted to advance a dialogical discipline that increasingly seemed antithetical to the habits of political gamesmanship. Some years ago, the Princeton sociologist Robert Wuthnow wrote a book entitled *The Restructuring of American Religion*.[9] His analysis demonstrated the ways in which political discourse was eclipsing theological modes of conversation and constricting the generosity of collaborative spiritual engagement. When shaped by the ethos of political debate, contentious issues gave rise to rancorous encounters in which sharp lines were drawn, and factions squared off with the intention of taking down the opposition. Resolution only emerged when one side or the other was declared the winner or had seized sufficient power to flatten adversaries. Needless to say, the pedagogical habits that define this kind of interaction contradict the norms of dialogue the ICJS had long sought to establish. In this polarized environment, sacred argument becomes nearly impossible.

On philosophical, theological, and educational grounds, the ICJS resisted the leap into the political crossfire, and we struggled against the social and political pressures that would have us betray the dialogical norms established at our founding. Yet the ideal of impartiality and evenhandedness became impossible to maintain as religion was increasingly weaponized and deployed to valorize one group and demean the other. While both Democrats and Republicans developed an outsized sense of their own righteousness during and after Trump's presidency, the most egregious excess was

---

9. Wuthnow, *Restructuring of American Religion*.

on full display when the January 6 insurrection revealed the underbelly of Christian nationalism in the United States.

The events leading up to this crisis, and the people that planned and implemented the assault, were not simply protesting the results of the 2020 election and the peaceful transfer of power. The roots of this uprising stretched into a long-standing legacy, tapping what the sociologists Philip Gorski and Samuel Perry refer to as a "deep story" of our country:

> America was founded as a Christian nation by [white] men who were "traditional" Christians, who based the nation's founding document on "Christian principles." The United States is blessed by God, which is why it has been so successful; and the nation has a special role to play in God's plan for humanity. But these blessings are threatened by cultural degradation from "un-American" influences both inside and outside our borders.[10]

These two scholars link the emergence of the "deep story" to 1690, when racism, apocalypticism, and nationalism were first fused.[11] This inflection point was defined by a series of wars when Anglo Protestant settlers established the dividing line between white and Black, natives and colonists, Puritans and Roman Catholics. Claims to being the "new chosen people" were invoked to justify the assault on the indigenous population, which some notable clerics of the time regarded as a justifiable reenactment of the Israelites' conquest of the Canaanites. Expulsions and massacres were rationalized as an apocalyptic holy war in which natives were sacrificed to a jealous and possessive God.

Then in 1776 another opportunity to link liberty with equality in pursuit of a democratic ideal was squandered. As Gorski and Perry note, national unity was purchased at the expense of racial equality. The "birth of the nation" and the institutionalization of white hegemony were built on concessions that enabled Northern and Southern states to band together, an achievement resting on the backs of an enslaved Black population. The "deep story" coalesced in the Revolutionary War and the War of 1812, when the historic ties to the English no longer defined the true character of "American" identity. In the heat of these these wars, "religion, race, and action were fused together into white Christian nationalism."[12] Although the Civil War provided yet another chance to recover the ideals of equality, the reversions promulgated through Jim Crow legislation during the Reconstruction era

---

10. Gorski and Perry, *Flag and the Cross*, 4.
11. Gorski and Perry, *Flag and the Cross*, 47.
12. Gorski and Perry, *Flag and the Cross*, 57.

(1865–77) and the dissemination of the myth of the lost cause sustained the white Christian nationalist dream.

When the expansion of the frontier reached the shores of the Pacific, the belief in a "manifest destiny" took on international dimensions. The imperial adventures in Cuba, the Philippines, Guam, and Puerto Rico were construed as noble efforts to liberate oppressed peoples from tyrannical overlords. Violence was seen as an indispensable instrument used to advance the cause of freedom. With the enlargement of territory incorporated into the United States and the management of occupied lands, the US increasingly faced an influx of "foreigners" who threatened to redefine the racial and ethnic contours of the white Protestant establishment. While the boundaries of acceptance were eventually stretched to include white Roman Catholics and some Jews (also accepted now as white), the enemy was increasingly identified as outside infiltrators who stole jobs and diluted the purity of the nation. Treasonous insiders compounded the treachery by opening the borders to "mongrel" interlopers and supporting the enfranchisement of Blacks, Hispanics, and Asians, thereby undermining the racial and religious foundations of the nation. This influx of "aliens" posed a demographic danger with serious political ramifications. The growing diversity of the American populace was increasingly portrayed as a plot to swell the ranks of "radical socialists" in the Democratic Party and advance the ascendance of secular globalists and left-wing elites.

The battle now being waged against an invasion of "immigrants" is not just a political and economic struggle, but a theological contest that has the character of a holy war. Those who espouse conspiracies about the "great replacement" imagine American patriots—overwhelmingly white Christian nationalists—pitted against demonic foes out to strip away essential freedoms, flood our towns and cities with fentanyl, and destroy a hallowed way of life. This worldview depends upon the fusion of religion and politics, and is fueled by apocalyptic premonitions: bedrock commitments that support this nation's theo-political foundations are threatened; the divine commission that makes the nation truly exceptional is endangered; a sacred vocation to overcome the forces of darkness and preserve the blessings bestowed on this "chosen people" is in jeopardy. This has become the clarion call that animated a significant sector of the participants in the January 6 rebellion—and it bolsters a worldview that imperils the future of an American republic grounded in democratic values.

What we have witnessed in recent years is the transfiguration of a spiritual disposition into a compulsively partisan identity. Far too many white Christian pastors are consecrating populist passions and invoking a transcendent authority to sanctify brutal battle. As Tim Alberta, the son of a conservative evangelical pastor, noted in *The Atlantic*, "One rarely needs to read to the bottom of a poll to learn that the religious group most opposed to vaccines, most convinced that the 2020 presidential election was stolen, most inclined to subscribe to QAnon conspiracy theories is white evangelicals."[13]

A proliferation of recent studies suggests the democratic principles of the United States are under attack and the extremist wing of the Republican Party is normalizing the drift into an autocratic state.[14] Until recently scholars and public commentators rarely acknowledged that a particular brand of religion is serving as the handmaiden of this emergent reality. Although the ICJS has opened itself to criticisms of political partisanship, it is no longer possible to avoid the disruptive entanglements of church and state. Not only does this burgeoning religious nationalism tap into racist, antisemitic, and Islamophobic wellsprings, the alt-right movement is enamored of a militancy that valorizes violence. With the extraordinary proliferation of guns in America and a Supreme Court now aligned with the unchecked excesses of the NRA, the prospects of more bloodshed in our cities and at our public gatherings are all too real. The popular media and the internet are choked with diatribes that feed on anger, fear, and grievance. The appetite for rhetorical junk appears bottomless. As a result, we are witnessing an erosion of trust in every institution, a subversion of the discipline and restraint that make negotiation and compromise possible. An unbridled scramble for power and notoriety is increasingly defining the political climate. I worry that the future will mirror the pathologies of the present.

I certainly hope and pray that the underpinnings of our civil culture are more durable and resilient than we imagine, and that our citizenry is wiser and less malleable than the surveys and polls suggest. Yet the careful and exacting exploration of this challenge has an inescapable import and urgency, and so the work of ICJS Protestant scholar Dr. Matthew Taylor demands careful scrutiny.

Matt offers a nuanced profile of the Christian participants in the January 6 insurrection. Representatives from the fastest growing segment—charismatic nondenominational Christians—operate without the institutional checks of an ecclesiastical bureaucracy that might temper ideological extremism. This movement functions with an oddly structured hierarchy, one that delivers controlling authority to so-called apostles and prophets.

13. Alberta, "How Politics Poisoned the Evangelical Church," 33.
14. Whitehead and Perry, *Taking America Back for God*; Stewart, *Power Worshippers*; Gorski, *American Babylon*; Parker, *White Too Long*; Edsall, "Capitol Insurrection," https://www.nytimes.com/2021/01/28/opinion/christian-nationalists-capitol-attack.html.

Having predicted the Trump victory in 2016, they again offered an inspired prediction of a second term triumph in 2020. The fact that Biden won the election signaled a prophetic failure that called into question the reliability and integrity of this charismatic leadership, and the only acceptable explanation was to insist the election was fraudulent. Demonic forces were said to be at work. Support for the "big lie" conspiracy became an article of faith. If the installation of Trump—God's chosen instrument to revive and restore the Christian nation—called for extreme measures, so be it. The gospel truth was not established, nor is it maintained, on the basis of democratic principles. The postmillennial mandate may require the use of violence and the overthrow of elected officials at odds with God's plan. "Move fast and break stuff" has become the mantra of this charismatic vanguard. This radical alignment of church and state poses an enormous challenge to traditions and ideals at the heart of the American republic.[15]

The road from the Towson Courthouse to the former Soviet Union and back to the United States is full of twists and turns, but the distance is shorter than I once imagined. The boundaries between church and state are permeable, and the melding of the two not only produces confusion in the public square but, more ominously, sets the stage for extremism. The outrage over Patriarch Kirill's endorsement of Putin's war against Ukraine must not blind us to the dangers of Christian nationalism at home. Enemies in Moscow are holding up a mirror in which we can see ourselves reflected.

How do we unravel the entanglements of church and state? How do we determine the substance and character of our allegiance to each, and how do we prevent a combustible fusion of loyalties? The challenge of sorting out the relationship between religious and political governance is transnational and is addressed in different ways by different religious communities around the globe. Inquiries into the political and religious alignments of communities here and abroad are urgently needed, and they will no doubt claim the attention the ICJS for years to come. The educational task to unveil the conceits of power and provide an alternative to apocalyptic catastrophe has become imperative.

15. See Matthew Taylor's lectures at the ICJS website: https://icjs.org/events/the-roots-and-reality-of-u-s-christian-nationalism/.

CHAPTER 16

Forgiveness—The Impossible Necessity

The event took place at Chizuk Amuno, the synagogue where Joel served as the rabbi. A sizable cross section of Jews and Christians had gathered for a program featuring a notable scholar whose task was to examine the rise of antisemitism and the legacy of the Shoah. The presentation traced some of the teachings and policies embedded in Western culture that set the stage for genocide, with particular attention directed to the roots of anti-Judaism within the Christian heritage. For many of the Christians in the audience, this historical background was jarring news. They were horrified to discover the degree to which the substance and character of Christian culture was yoked to a polemical assault directed against Judaism and the Jewish people.

One well-intentioned Christian stood up at the end of the evening and claimed the microphone. He announced to the assembly that he was appalled to learn the extent of Christian complicity in cultivating the ground for such virulent hate. He had no idea. He proclaimed a deep sense of shame. In a quaking voice he concluded his confession by entreating the Jewish members: "All I can say is please forgive me and my fellow Christians for all these failures."

His supplication was overflowing with sincerity, but the request jolted the Jewish audience into a stunned silence and left the Christians in the room discombobulated and embarrassed. The discomfort was palpable, and the agitation—or perhaps irritation—was evident in downcast eyes and nervous squirming. No one seemed to know what to say in response, and the spell was not broken until some minutes later an unrelated question redirected the audience's attention—to everyone's relief.

The episode framed a haunting and contentious question that continues to confound individuals, and by extension communities and nations. Can a broken trust be repaired? Can we mend the social fabric in the aftermath of betrayal or recover in the wake of wanton death and destruction? Do our religious traditions offer wisdom and guidance to those who seek to heal both recent and ancient wounds? Do they chart a path to break the grip of anger, resentment, and grievous loss? This we know: there can be no peace in our world unless and until our religious communities change their ways and renounce their quest for supremacy.[1]

Judaism, Christianity, and Islam—each in their own way—locate the praxis of repentance, reparations, forgiveness, and reconciliation at the heart of their traditions.[2] They offer the hope that the sins of the past will not have the last word. Out of the ashes a new and astonishing possibility can emerge; light can pierce the darkness; an unexpected and gracious opening can appear where once only a dead end was visible.

And yet, at that moment of awkward silence, the request for forgiveness fell flat. The audience hit a wall of incomprehension, and all those present were brought face-to-face with limitations that reduced the promise of renewal into nothing more than an expression of magical thinking. What exactly happened, and why had the pursuit of reconciliation evoked so much discomfort? Isn't the work of forgiveness the gateway to genuine change?

In the days following the event, I spoke at considerable length with Joel. He and other rabbinic colleagues were puzzled and disturbed. However genuine the intention, they believed this gentleman had taken them and their Jewish congregants hostage to a Christian conception of forgiveness. Had they refused and declared the request inappropriate and brazen, they suspected their opposition would have confirmed stereotypes of Jews as hard-hearted, vindictive, and merciless. They were frankly uncertain if the appeal was in truth a demand for closure—a strategy to put the past in its place and out of sight. The subtext of his petition revolved around the

---

1 In the words of the Dutch theologian Hans Kung, "No peace among the nations without peace among the religions. No peace among the religions without dialogue between the religions. No dialogue between the religious without investigation of the foundation of the religions." https://quotes.pub/q/no-peace-among-the-nationsbrwithout-peace-among-the-religion-520886.

2. Lamentably, I retired as Islam was being fully integrated into the life of the ICJS and did not have the opportunity to delve into Islamic texts and traditions dealing with repentance and forgiveness—a shortcoming I hope to correct in the future.

conviction that once sin has been publicly confessed and lamented, supplicants can rest assured God will forgive them, and so the Jews were expected to follow suit and do the same.

Forgiveness, the rabbis insisted, is far more exacting and involves more than a momentary flush of remorse. They had the impression that this man's apology was either an empty-handed gesture or came with strings attached, namely, the expectation that pardon was now his due. From their perspective, putting the best possible spin on the occasion, this man did not really know what he was asking nor what he was really talking about when he sought forgiveness. As I hope to demonstrate, to grasp the complexities, it is necessary to consider forgiveness as a twofold process: (1) an internal reorientation that aims to neutralize the emotional impulse to retaliate and even the score, and (2) the external efforts to restore trust between the victim and the victimizer.

In response to Joel, I suggested the pursuit of forgiveness was a natural, almost automatic response to the disruption this man was feeling. The quest for forgiveness resides at the heart of Christianity, and the affirmation of God's forgiveness gives the community its pulse—its purpose and the means for healing broken lives in a broken world. At the beginning of most Protestant and Roman Catholic worship services, the congregation joins in a confession of sin, which is immediately followed with an assurance of pardon—namely, the pronouncement that in Jesus Christ sins are forgiven. Jesus is "the Lamb of God, which taketh away the sin of the world" (John 1:29 KJV).

The Christian obligation to acknowledge our failings and seek forgiveness also occupies a preeminent place because the connection between God's forgiveness and our practice of forgiveness are intertwined and, on close inspection, are laid out in terrifying and demanding detail. To be specific, the Lord's Prayer—routinely recited in public and ecclesiastical settings—makes an unmistakable linkage: we are to forgive others their sins (debts, trespasses) as God forgives us our sins (debts, trespasses), which implies that the failure to forgive others negates the possibility of divine forgiveness.[3] Christians are not only asked to practice forgiveness, they are commanded—or perhaps more accurately stated, condemned—to forgive.

Some notable Christians have superimposed this command onto Jews, and this intrusion also accounted for the friction. Anthony Phillips,

---

3. See the Parable of the Unmerciful Servant (Matt 18:23–35), where Jesus concludes: "'Should you not have had mercy on you fellow slave, as I had mercy on you?' And in anger his lord handed him over to be tortured until he would pay his entire debt. So my heavenly Father will also do to every one of you, if you do not forgive your brother or sister from your heart" (NRSV).

an Anglican and former canon theologian of Truro Cathedral, admonished: "Without forgiveness there can be no healing within the community.... In remembering the Holocaust, Jews hope to prevent its recurrence: by declining to forgive, I fear they unwittingly invite it."[4] What Christians proclaim as an ennobling ideal is here converted into a cudgel to threaten the Jewish community. What makes this reproach outrageous is the manner in which Reverend Phillips takes the Jewish community captive to a Christian notion of forgiveness, rarely realized among it own adherents. Apparently we Christians—or at least some of us—have difficulty forgiving those who refuse to forgive us our trespasses. More egregiously, this reverend holds Jews responsible for any future genocidal assault that might befall them. According to his logic, the victims will become the perpetrators of their own demise—and all because of their failure to offer forgiveness to a faceless multitude on behalf of the millions dead and abused. This view is not unique to Reverend Phillips and exposes a conviction shared by many Christians: the refusal to forgive is judged a morally indefensible and a damnable sin.

Haunted by the facile manner in which many Christians have spoken about forgiveness, I realized a far more intensive examination of the philosophical and theological underpinnings of this concept was required. Without rigorous and self-critical inquiry, I could not imagine how an understanding and a rapprochement between adherents of different religious traditions could take hold.

Forgiveness is an exceedingly generous response to an intentional offense; it is a magnanimous counteraction to a defilement of one's dignity. The trespass strips the victim of power and a sense of agency. The humiliation ruptures trust and fractures a dependable moral order. When perpetrators violate the integrity of their victims, they fail to recognize the other as worthy of regard. What makes forgiveness so overwhelming is the goal of restoration and reconciliation. The work of forgiveness involves the repair and rehabilitation in which both the wrongdoer and the wronged are actively engaged—and transformed.

Forgiveness is not simply a gesture of kindness or an optional labor of goodwill. The Jewish philosopher Hannah Arendt maintains that the practice of forgiveness is indispensable in the formation and preservation of our humanity. Her account demonstrates why this concept and its application holds a central place within our religious communities.

> Without being forgiven, released from the consequences of what we have done, our capacity to act would, as it were, be

---

4. Anthony Phillips's quotation is found in Rabbi Michael Hilton and Father Gordian Marshall's *The Gospels and Rabbinic Judaism*, 151.

confined to one single deed from which we could never recover; we would remain the victims of its consequences forever, not unlike the sorcerer's apprentice who lacked the magic formula to break the spell.[5]

She contends that the practice of forgiveness is foundational for the establishment and stability of human community because this faculty makes possible "the redemption from the predicament of irreversibility—of being unable to undo what one has done."[6] Without this capacity, the only way to *undo* what has been done is by means of destruction—through acts of violence that threaten to overpower humanity. Forgiveness is the practice of mutual release that makes human freedom possible. Without this openness to change, people would be forever bound to an unyielding past. "Forgiving, in other words, is the only reaction which does not merely re-act but acts anew and unexpectedly, unconditioned by the act which provoked it and therefore freeing from its consequences both the one who forgives and the one who is forgiven."[7]

This kind of change entails passage through a narrow gate—what in Hebrew is called *teshuvah* (returning) and in Greek *metanoia* (transformation of heart and mind). The movement is propelled by an array of thoughts and feelings that more often than not we strive to avoid—guilt, shame, shattered dreams, grief, resentment, and defeat. What remains unclear is whether the sort of change envisioned in the concept of forgiveness is really a possibility, an experience people can enact and validate in their own lives.

To work out this challenge, I met with my rabbinic colleagues on several occasions, and they directed attention to sections of Maimonides' *Mishneh Torah* dealing with forgiveness. His analysis makes it unmistakably clear: a praxis that unhinges forgiveness from repentance often carries disastrous consequences for the community. As expressed in a midrash, "He who is kind to the cruel often ends up being cruel to the kind."[8] The person who excuses and forgives the abuser all too often enables and perpetuates the destructive behavior. A facile forgiveness—what the German theologian Dietrich Bonhoeffer calls "cheap grace"—amounts to a failure to hold the offender accountable for the damage inflicted, and so the initial injustice is compounded—as the families and friends of many an alcoholic and inveterate gambler can attest. To get a more detailed perspective, it is worth reviewing the critical stages of repentance Maimonides compiled.

5. Arendt, *Human Condition*, 237.
6. Arendt, *Human Condition*, 237.
7. Arendt, *Human Condition*, 241.
8. *Kohelet Rabbah* 7.16. https://www.sefaria.org/Kohelet_Rabbah.7.17.1?lang=bi.

First, there can be no transformation until offenders recognize the damage for which they are responsible and have a sense of remorse. No repentance without genuine regret. Second, the offender needs to resolve not to repeat the wrongdoing in the future. No excuses or rationalizations. Abusers demonstrate the authenticity of their pledge when they find themselves in similar situations of temptation and successfully resist the repetition of the transgression. Third, the offender needs to acknowledge the harm to the victim(s) and to the larger community directly or indirectly touched by the violation. No repentance without some form of public confession. Fourth, the offender must make amends and take action to repair the damage. No repentance without reparations. As we shall see, this requirement becomes problematic in light of incurable injuries and irreversible losses.

According to Maimonides' codification of Jewish law, the victim is required to forgive the one who asks for forgiveness if all the stages of repentance have been completed. Given the difficulties in overcoming a justifiable grievance, the offending party may need to make this approach as many as three times. Thereafter, the guilty party is no longer obligated to seek forgiveness.[9]

This taxonomy unveils another reason why the supplication of this well-intentioned Christian rubbed my Jewish colleagues the wrong way. He operated with the assumption that one Jew could speak on behalf of another Jew, that Jews in one time and place were interchangeable with Jews in another time and place—and, most egregiously, that living Jews could offer absolution on behalf of the murdered. Joel reminded me of a story told by Abraham Joshua Heschel in Simon Wiesenthal's book *The Sunflower*.[10]

The rabbi of Brisk boarded a train to return to his hometown and found himself in a compartment with several rowdy salesmen. They were drinking and playing cards while the scholar immersed himself in reading and meditation. They had no idea that this nondescript traveler was a distinguished sage, and they became increasingly annoyed by an aloof companion who refused to join their games. Finally, they gave him an ultimatum: either participate in the merriment or they would remove him from the compartment. When the rabbi explained he never played cards, one of the salesmen tossed him into the corridor. The rabbi was forced to stand outside in the unheated passageway for the remainder of the trip.

When the train arrived at Brisk, the rabbi was surrounded by a large and adoring crowd. Only then did the salesman realize his offense. The one

---

9 Rabbi Moshe ben Maimon (1135–1204), known as Maimonides, "Laws of Repentance" in his codification of Jewish law entitled *Mishneh Torah*. https://www.sefaria.org/Mishneh_Torah,_Repentance?tab=contents.

10. Wiesenthal, *Sunflower*, 170–72.

who had thrown the rabbi out of the compartment was mortified and immediately asked for forgiveness. But the rabbi refused. As a result, that evening, this salesman could not sleep; so once again he approached the rabbi in search of forgiveness. And once again the rabbi refused. Still racked with guilt, the salesman returned a third time and begged the rabbi for forgiveness, noting that he was prepared to give his savings to charity if the rabbi would forgive him. The rabbi declined.

The salesman then approached the rabbi's son and detailed his plight. That evening, the son engaged his father in the study of a talmudic tractate that spells out the imperative to forgive a sinner who has asked for forgiveness three times. The son then recounted his encounter with the distraught salesman, and he implored his father to explain why he had refused forgiveness. The rabbi answered, "I cannot forgive him. He did not know who I was. He offended a common man. Let him go to him and seek forgiveness."

I pressed Joel: "The rabbi of Brisk had the opportunity to relieve the suffering of the salesman, a man now willing to make restitution. Yet the rabbi refused. To be sure, the salesman offended 'a common man,' but he had also slighted a particular rabbi. The poor fellow is taking steps to repent, and the rabbi leaves him wallowing in his guilt. Don't you think this rebuff could inflame resentment and bitterness, perhaps even leading him to lash out? People in pain do dreadful things!"

Joel replied: "You certainly would make a lousy Jew if you think guilt is such an unfit instructor. And really! Do you think a rush to resolution would better serve the salesman? You assume forgiveness is a hundred-yard dash when it is actually a marathon. The recalibration of the self and the reestablishment of trust are not accomplished with the blink of the eye."

While going round and round, we were reminded how easy it is to use the same word only to discover we mean very different things and frequently operate with divergent conceptual frameworks. There were so many occasions when we began our conversations with the assumption that an overlapping vocabulary implied a shared understanding until we stumbled into the realization that we were talking past each other. It took a great deal of work to sift through the conflicting arguments about the nature of forgiveness—and plumb the confounding relationship between divine and human forgiveness. The muddle continued to claim our attention, perhaps because the imperative to forgive occupies such a prominent place in both our traditions, but more significantly because we both found the ideal so extremely difficult to practice—or even fathom. I like to think we were making headway, but his death disrupted the project. We never cleared up the confusion we shared or fleshed out the disagreements we tried to honor.

We did, however, agree that greater precision was demanded. Clarity, we often found, may only arise after destabilizing the comforts and certainties built into our common ways of thinking. With his voice still echoing in my mind, I hear him making some fundamental distinctions. For example:

- People often talk about the need to "forgive" when they really mean that we should *accept* or *overlook* or *excuse* the wrongdoing.
- To *accept* something entails an acknowledgement that nothing can be done to change the situation. We accept what is beyond our capacity to transform, an acquiescence captured in popular maxims: "Let it go." "Don't poke the bear." "Let sleeping dogs lie." "Don't cry over spilt milk."
- To *overlook* presupposes a redirection of attention away from the offense, a refusal to get involved, a flight from messy entanglements.
- To *excuse* implies an assessment in which the wrongdoer cannot rationally be held accountable. There are extenuating circumstances demanding consideration, factors paving the way to exculpation. No fault or blame should be ascribed because the harm was not intended. "Accidents happen."

Depending on the context, these responses may prove appropriate, but they are mistakenly confused with forgiveness because these reactions can be unilaterally administered. The person(s) who has suffered damage makes a determination independently and need not interact with the one(s) who would otherwise be held responsible. Joel argued that a sharper delineation of the category is essential to correct the fuzzy, overworked, and misleading ways in which we think about forgiveness. Each of these exculpatory strategies works at a remove from the perpetrator and serves to maintain a safe distance. The relational dynamic is concealed, and we lose sight of the fact that forgiveness revolves around complex and risky interpersonal encounters.

To cut beneath the confusion and get greater clarity on the anatomy of forgiveness, at least two considerations are required. Forgiveness is a different kind of response to an abuse of power. It is an answer to the problem that emerges when one person diminishes the intrinsic value of another. According to the early eighteenth-century Anglican bishop Joseph Butler, the violation of a person's dignity gives rise to resentment, and this defensive impulse assumes two forms. The first reaction is a spontaneous upsurge, a reflexive pushback against an injustice, and a valuable God-given expression of our makeup. This response is frequently described as "righteous indignation" and can animate the quest for justice. The second expression occurs when resentment becomes "settled and deliberate anger,"[11] when it hardens into spiteful thoughts, negative feelings, and sometimes culminates in hostile actions directed against the offender. This kind of resentment takes possession of mind and heart, and the results are often destructive and morally reprehensible. Forgiveness is a response that expels, or at least tames, the obsession to "get even." Forgiveness is at least partially achieved when the victim holds in check the impulse to retaliate, or in Butler's idiom, "forswears" the pursuit of vengeance.

This first feature of forgiveness requires an inner process of overcoming one's passions, most especially the natural impulse to retaliate and even the score. Forgiveness—so understood—is a therapeutic move that refuses to give the wrongdoer any enduring power over the person who has been wronged. It is a declaration of independence, a resolution that aims at self-possession. "I am no longer going to let you, the perpetrator, dictate my mental state. I am no longer going to allow the negative feelings you provoked determine my sense of self. I refuse to let bitterness govern my world." The work has the character of a self-help exorcism—an expulsion of inner demons.

No doubt a psychological reorientation of this sort can help heal deep wounds, and the refusal to fight the same battle over and over again is a noble accomplishment. Resentment often holds a sweet and addictive flavor, and once habituated to a grievance it can become a prized possession, one which offers a cramped, but dependable, comfort. Resentment secures the boundaries separating us from our adversaries. It locks in place an image of the past that creates an unbridgeable divide between the wrongdoer and the wronged, and therefore blocks the prospects for creative reciprocity that can emerge when attention is redirected to an open-ended future. So, the ability to overcome remembered wounds is an important, albeit difficult, aptitude to cultivate.

However, this notion assumes people have control over feelings that involuntarily erupt. This formulation presents forgiveness as a process that enables individuals to recognize that their responses are based on emotions over which they can exercise cognitive control. So understood, a person possesses both the rational capacity and the willpower to neutralize the burning desire for vengeance.

Yet the naked truth is that most of us have limited control over our most intense emotional reactions. Vengeful feelings flare automatically, and in the

---

11. Bishop Joesph Butler, "Sermon VIII. Upon Resentment and Forgiveness," 67, https://www.ccel.org/ccel/b/butler/sermons/cache/sermons.pdf. For a more extensive commentary, see Pagani, "Uses and Abuses of Joseph Butler's Account."

heat of the moment most do not have the spiritual resources to domesticate the emotive outbreak. Accordingly, the challenge is not to repress or master how we *feel* about the persons who did us harm, but to take the necessary steps to control how we act toward them. This more modest conception of forgiveness acknowledges forbearance as an achievement. Rather than struggle to suppress outrage and deny it any purchase, one of the responses embedded in both the Tanakh (the Old Testament) and the New Testament would have us hand over our feelings of hostility and entrust them to God's care. This transfer is grounded in the belief that, as Martin Luther King Jr. said, "the arc of the universe bends toward justice" and a final reckoning awaits the abuser. We need not mount an assault on the offender. A higher authority will administer the sentence and exact a fitting penalty.

Thus far, the rendering of forgiveness has a very limited reach. In most pop psychology, forgiveness is construed as an inner-directed activity, which is motivated by the needs and desires of the one who has been injured. Self-regard shapes and powers forgiveness. This orientation may temper our enthusiastic embrace of vengeance, promote self-healing, and maintain the peace, but this inner-driven pursuit reduces forgiveness to a strategy to advance self-interest. Differently framed, forgiveness is pitched instrumentally along the lines presented by the philosopher Thomas Hobbes (1588–1679). He argued that forgiveness is "only a means of maintaining peace and social order" and an indispensable mechanism for "self-preservation . . . Fear and our desire to avoid pain are ultimately the motivating forces behind forgiveness."[12]

While recognizing that there is both a validity and value built into these formulations, a second pass is required to go beyond the therapeutic and utilitarian dimensions of forgiveness. Another move is demanded to bring out its most important and challenging dimensions, namely, its relational and intersubjective character. Forgiveness requires not only a change of heart, but a willingness and ability to see the wrongdoer in a different light and at least to some extent separate the offender from his offense. The uncoupling of the harmful act from the repentant actor hinges on the belief that people can change. The path of forgiveness opens when the one who has been injured refuses to conflate the immoral act with the person who inflicted the wound, and this distinction may not arise until and unless the work of repentance is well underway. What this kind of affirmation entails is a leap of faith that aims at the repair of a broken trust. Neither the intention nor the act of restoration can be demanded or coerced or even earned, which is why forgiveness is often characterized as a gift.

12. Hobbes, *On Human Nature*, ch. 16, sect. 9.

This understanding leads the Jewish philosopher Vladimir Jankélévitch to portray the event of forgiveness as not just exceptional, but ineffable, miraculous, and supernatural. He insists that the power to forgive is in a fundamental sense beyond us, and so he invokes the category of "grace." There is a shift, a reversal, a reorientation, an opening of mind and heart that we cannot force and that comes upon us when we forgive another—and so the gift of forgiveness not only lands on the offender but also—perhaps more mysteriously—enfolds the forgiver.[13] The act of forgiveness involves the surprising discovery of connection between alienated souls, an enduring bond that points to an unanticipated and open-ended future. This depiction may sound as though forgiveness involves metaphysical sleight of hand, but Jankélévitch's analysis simply suggests the experience touches something beyond our normal state of affairs. Forgiveness creates a condition of reciprocal recognition—and this blessing is experienced as given and not simply an accomplishment of our own making.

So what are we to make of those who in the aftermath of inflicted trauma refuse to forgive? Does the Holocaust along with other genocides precipitate an acknowledgment that at least some atrocities render forgiveness an impossibility? Can sustained resentment and the refusal to forgive ever be considered morally acceptable? These are the questions that the Jewish writer Jean Améry posed in his collection of essays entitled *At the Mind's Limits*, and his observations derail the train of thought that my fellow Christian advocated on that memorable evening at Chizuk Amuno.

In July 1943, Jean Améry was arrested by the Gestapo for distributing fliers for a Belgian resistance movement. He and his compatriots clung to the hope that their anti-Nazi propaganda might convince at least some German occupiers that Hitler's war was madness.[14] After being caught with some mimeographed materials, Améry was marched to Fort Breendonk, where he was incarcerated and tortured. When first arrested, he believed himself prepared for the consequences and imagined himself "a hardened expert in the system, its men, and its methods."[15] Soon he discovered the

---

13. "True forgiveness must involve a real relation with another person. If one merely forgets what the other person has done, or if one allows time to 'heal' the wounds, or if someone simply says, 'enough with this,' then....these acts do not necessarily involve any type of connection with the wrongdoer. . . . If a person forgives in order to overcome hatred, then the wrongdoer himself or herself is not the true concern for the victim, but rather the attempt to overcome hatred is the true concern." Andrew Kelley's Introduction to Jankélévitch, *Forgiveness*, xxi.

14. Améry, *At the Mind's Limits*, 24.

15. Améry, *At the Mind's Limits*, 24.

chasm that separates ideas gained from expository literature from the incomprehensible reality of torture.

Améry was hauled into an area known as "the business room," where he discovered the Nazis conducted their affairs with industrial efficiency. His arms were shackled behind his back and attached to a chain dangling from the ceiling. He was hoisted a meter off the ground. Suspended helplessly with dislocated arms attached to iron fetters, shoulders cracked and splintered, he was horsewhipped. Mind and body contracted, and he was reduced to nothing more than afflicted tissue. "Only in torture does the transformation of the person into flesh become complete. Frail in the face of violence, yelling out in pain, awaiting no help, capable of no resistance, the tortured person only a body, and nothing else beside that. . . . Whoever was tortured, stays tortured."[16]

The grisly details are necessary to counter the reflexive flight into abstraction and bring us back to the core questions. What does forgiveness mean in the face of the unforgivable? Is talk of repair, restoration, and reconciliation utter nonsense in the midst of such atrocity?

Améry offers haunting and instructive commentary on the limits of forgiveness and the place of resentment. He is acutely aware that harboring a grudge does not accord with good psychological counsel or comply with the demands of moral generosity. The world moves on, memory fades, a time comes when people are expected to seize a new day. Améry unflinchingly acknowledges that "resentment is not only unnatural but also a logically inconsistent condition. It nails every one of us onto the cross of his ruined past. Resentment blocks the exit to the genuine human dimension, the future."[17]

Why then cling to resentment? Améry suggests his quest is for neither revenge nor atonement. The trauma of torture afflicts him with a sense of an interminable *loneliness*. And what magnifies this sense of isolation and salts the grudge is the steady erosion of memory that surrounds him, the abdication of responsibility among the living, the ongoing failure to uphold the most fundamental dictates of justice. It is not just the horror of an unremitting trauma that renders him homeless, but the fact that there is no social and political context that would enable an honest reckoning with his abusers and their complacent enablers.

Resentment then is Améry's feeble protest against the natural process of healing, which is to say the indolent surrender to the social and biological annulment of time. Resentment becomes his means of resistance, the

16. Améry, *At the Mind's Limits*, 33.
17. Améry, *At the Mind's Limits*, 68.

disposition that can sustain his revolt against amnesia. What Améry dares to hope—a tenuous disposition to be sure!—is that his resentment will awaken self-mistrust and induce a moral restlessness that goads people and nations to "recognize their acquiescence in the Third Reich (*and the evils of our own time*) as the total negation not only of the world that it plagued with war and death but also of its own better origins."[18]

Améry is suspended between two competing impulses: the imperative to remember the horror and the demand to create a space in which he is freed from trauma—and there is no way to resolve the insoluble dilemma. Resentment is the gateway through which he must pass to reach a morally credible future. Yet the irony, so difficult to comprehend, is that the suspension of forgiveness may ultimately establish the basis for what we might accurately classify as an impossible necessity—a revival of trust and mutuality.

The testimony of Améry and others who have suffered "at the mind's limits" does not annul the value and significance of forgiveness, but it does point to limits which most us would prefer to ignore. If forgiveness entails the repair of a broken relationship, if it restores and honors the dignity of both the wrongdoer and the one wronged, and if it (re)establishes genuine bonds of trust, then the interpersonal dynamics place constraints on the applicability of this concept.

To call upon Japan to forgive the United States for the bombing of Hiroshima—this requirement involves a different kind of labor and yields results outside the bounds of forgiveness. To be sure, a certain level of trust can be instituted. Political, economic, and cultural cooperation can lead to peaceful coexistence among previously hostile nations. Call it strategic prudence, or even a form of reconciliation. This is a worthy achievement, but the negotiated settlements that anchor international affairs and lead to mutually beneficial accords entails efforts distinct from the risky, intersubjective activities that define forgiveness. Forgiveness does not traffic among abstractions or operate among impersonal collectives. As the Shoah makes painfully clear, people cannot restore trusting relationships where none existed or forge connections with those known exclusively through their absence. It is only the living who have the agency to forgive, those who encounter one another face-to-face as individuals, families, and communities. It is in the nitty-gritty interactions of daily life where the process is enacted. Apart from an active web of relations that connects wrongdoers and victims, the work of repair at the heart of forgiveness is impossible.

This more restrictive formulation indicates that forgiveness has a more limited reach than most people might wish. When the audience at Chizuk

---

18. Améry, *At the Mind's Limits*, 78.

Amuno was considering the historical roots of the Shoah, the entreaty of this well-intentioned Christian, which he directed to the Jewish community, may have been understandable, but his plea was a misconstrued expression of remorse. To be sure, it is fitting for Christians to recognize that they belong to a faith community with a long and violent history. They are responsible as Christians to struggle with a legacy that continues to wreak havoc and is being passed along to future generations. However, it is inappropriate and morally suspect to ask one congregation of Jews to offer forgiveness on behalf of others, most especially the murdered masses. Rather than seek the resolution that forgiveness promises, the challenge is to take up the work of repentance and reparations—to build the connections and offer help in healing open wounds and in preventing the repetition of past offenses. This labor takes place over the long haul and does not necessarily bring closure.

Over the course of our struggles, a growing cadre of Christians, Jews, and Muslims at the ICJS came to the conclusion that justice is built from the ground up and may not culminate in forgiveness. Justice requires systemic change, institutional reform, legal battles, shifts in the socioeconomic biosphere, a reconstructed political culture, and far-reaching educational innovation. Antisemitism, Islamophobia, racism, classism, and sexism are too deeply woven into the texture of our society for minor tweaks or quick fixes to repair the damage—and the hard labor of repentance requires an uprooting of attitudes and behaviors firmly entrenched and fervently defended. Why then conclude this inquiry with an exposition on forgiveness?

The answer stems from hard-won experience: my colleagues and I came to the realization that the work of creating a just and equitable society begins at home, at our schools, in the workplace, and in the public arenas where we bump into one another. The quest for justice is anchored in the immediacy of our personal relations, and the struggles first confronted at the local level then orient us to the more unwieldy global challenges.

The work of institutional reformation will never be done without people who have forged connections with individuals who hold conflicting views—neighbors and friends and family with whom they first learn to adjudicate and honor their differences. The imperatives for social and religious transformation rest on our experiences with those who know firsthand the difficulty of rebuilding a broken trust, and who have been humbled by the sense that the work entails costs that we cannot calculate and will remain unfinished. The big picture will remain blurred and undefined without bumping into the obstacles that arise in face-to-face encounters. Those who have confronted the impossible necessities of forgiveness and the ongoing travail of repentance, those who have experienced the forces of intransigence, and those who have learned to persist in the midst of resistance—they are the people best equipped to deal with the structural dysfunctions in our society and the world at large.

*

When scanning the terrain we currently occupy, the temperature feels unreasonably hot. Disillusionment clots the atmosphere. Hopes once inspired and sustained by religious communities are curdling. We are acutely aware that religious fervor continues to fire many if not most global conflicts, and the earth gives irrefutable testimony: it is drenched in blood. Rivalries among believers continue unabated, and the scramble to take possession of the high ground, to seize control, and to proclaim supremacy seems to have no end. The most zealous believers conflate religious and political loyalties all the while demanding and receiving blind faith—and that only adds to the mounting cynicism. Religious fervor, it seems, functions as little more than an instrument to elevate divisive political agendas. No wonder so many young people have become disillusioned with our religious institutions.

In spite of the corruptions and betrayals of our noblest religious ideals, I remember the words of Presbyterian Robert Wood Lynn, who headed the Lilly Endowment for many years. He once observed that the last two institutions to leave a city on the verge of collapse are the corner liquor store and the church. As coming generations define the future, they must ask themselves what will happen if the church, the synagogue, and the mosque are abandoned. Will the liquor store offer sufficient comfort and security? I worry about the collapse and the refusal to contend with the dangerous and deadly excesses that I have reviewed in this volume.

Without those who give of their time, energy, and resources as an expression of their religious convictions, who is going to step into the breach and manage many of the hospitals that care for the indigent? Who is going to run our soup kitchens and food pantries, the parochial schools and treatment centers? How will our citizenry break out of the "iron cage" of self-absorption if our nation settles into the habit of "bowling alone"?[19]

In my rehearsal of these woes and anxieties, I imagine Joel ribbing me out of his deep and abiding faith. He would argue that my tradition believes in the triumph of life over death. Despair is not an option either of our traditions can indulge. To be certain, we cannot escape the burden. He would remind me yet again that we carry the bones of our ancestors and

---

19. See Charles Taylor's *The Ethics of Authenticity*, where the malaise of American individualism is examined in light of Max Weber and expounded in Robert Putnam's *Bowling Alone* in terms of the decline in social capital.

will wander the wilderness aimlessly without a deeper appreciation of the legacy we shoulder.

The younger generation will need to unpack the bequest handed down to them and sort out the blessings and curses that have been passed along. And the great majority may refuse. I don't think Joel sought comfort in numbers. A small remnant is all that is required to embody the practices and keep the dream alive. A community, however small, can demonstrate the sacred discipline of discovering the extraordinary in the ordinary, sanctifying time and place, honoring family and friends, nourishing recovery from broken promises, and fostering a sense of gratitude for a reality much bigger and grander than any of us.

In our separate enclaves, we cultivate the aptitude to repair the ruptures in our lives; we hold fast to sacred stories entrusted to us; we are educated and chastened by the disruptions born of grievance and resentment. After all, we first learn to perform these labors at home and in our communities.

But that is not enough. Not now. Whether our religious communities actually have something essential to contribute to the common good will depend on a leap that we have long avoided or denounced as a possibility. What remains to be seen is whether our religious communities can embolden us to step outside our respective sanctuaries and engage religious and political strangers face-to-face in sacred argument. In this broader public expanse we discover who we and our communities really are. We will step on each other's toes and make offensive blunders. That fact does not justify our retreat into safe and separate enclaves, avoiding the upheaval and confusion that comes when we see the world through the eyes of others. The disarmament of hate and the containment of violence require the realization that the destinies of peoples near and far are interwoven—and as Abraham Joshua Heschel noted: "Spiritual betrayal on the part of one of us affects the faith of all of us."[20]

Christians, Jews, and Muslims; peoples of every race, ethnicity, and sexual orientation; everyone and everything that rises must converge, as Flannery O'Connor proclaimed. Will the ideals of repentance, forgiveness, and reconciliation win our allegiance? Will we make peace with the fact that the labor is our solemn duty, but it has no end? Could a sense of incompletion be the source of both the melancholy and the joy of the human condition?

When I grumble to Joel and complain that there is still so much to do, so little time, and so much resistance, I hear him laugh—that rollicking,

---

20. Heschel, "No Religion Is an Island," 119, https://utsnyc.edu/wp-content/uploads/Heschels-No-Religion-is-an-Island.pdf.

thunderous blast that would lift me off my feet and sweep me away. "Where is your faith?" He then delivers an assuring nudge with words from the Mishnaic tractate Pirke Avot 2:15–16: "The day is short, the work is much, the workers are lazy, the reward is great, and the Master is pressing. You are not required to finish your work, yet neither are you permitted to avoid it."

Afterword

HEATHER MILLER RUBENS

In the United States, the radical experiment in building a multireligious democracy is faltering. All Americans who affirm and value religious diversity need to work together to safeguard the rights, well-being, and full participation of citizens of every religion—and no religion—in our society. We must be brave enough to disrupt and dismantle religious prejudice, and audacious enough to imagine and build new interreligious ways of being with our neighbors. As we look around at our polarized and divided world, the efforts of the ICJS to make our religious differences a force for good have never been more urgent.

The ICJS was founded nearly forty years ago with the following premise: the fear, ignorance, and contempt that exists between people with different beliefs cannot be left unchecked. We can, and indeed we must, work together to dismantle religious bigotry. At the same time, we must also be builders and dreamers of a just interreligious society that weaves together diverse religious and spiritual imaginations. To imagine a more just Baltimore together—to imagine a more just world together—that is the hopeful work of the ICJS. To build an interreligious world overflowing with justice, we need to tell stories that show how our religious differences can become a force for good.

As the stories Chris tells in this volume illustrate, the ICJS has been carrying out this task for nearly four decades and has accomplished great things. Today, we are continuing to do both the hard work and the hopeful work, the dismantling and the building. In ICJS programs and fellowships, we bring people together to study sacred texts and explore different religious beliefs and practices, to share what we hold most dear about our religious traditions, and to ask questions about the traditions of our neighbors. We create space and opportunity for individuals to have meaningful face-to-face encounters with their neighbors and engage in the study of difficult interreligious histories. We invite people to dream new worlds together.

How does the ICJS continue to challenge the prejudice and fear that keep us apart? How do we end habits of religious division? We firmly believe that two ingredients are necessary for citizens to co-build a resilient interreligious society: increased knowledge, and real relationships.

Our commitment to interreligious learning rests upon the conviction that resilient interreligious networks require both meaningful interpersonal connections and interreligious literacy. By bringing scholarly rigor to community engagement, the ICJS facilitates thoughtful, sustained, and demanding conversations among unlikely partners. Who are the people that the ICJS invites to interreligious conversations? Where is the ICJS building interreligious networks?

The ICJS began our efforts by inviting clergy and religious congregations to take a leading role in building an interreligious society. Strong, interconnected religious institutions remain critical to realizing our mission. In recent years, we have reinvigorated our work with religious communities. The ICJS launched an intensive Congregational Leaders Fellowship that brings together both ordained and lay leadership from local synagogues, mosques, and churches who commit to a six-month program focused on building their religious and institutional capacity for interreligious thinking, dreaming, and collaborating with their neighbors. In addition, the ICJS realized that most clergy and religious leaders did not have an interreligious course in their seminary training. To address this need, the ICJS committed to bringing an interreligious lens to theological education in the US. Since 2013, the ICJS has hosted a one-week residential intensive interreligious study course and retreat. In 2022, the ICJS became an affiliate member of the Association of Theological Schools (ATS), and beginning in 2023, now offers this academic course to Jewish rabbinical schools, Muslim theological schools, and Christian seminaries from across the country.

While traditional religious institutions remain key to realizing our organizational vision, the ICJS identified two additional sectors—education and nonprofit—that we believe are critical to building an interreligious society.

We have developed an intensive Teachers Fellowship open to educators from religious, private, and public schools, because young peoples' first impressions of global religious communities and encounters with people who are religiously different occur in the classroom. Over the last five years, seventy educators from thirty schools have completed an intensive ten-month program at the ICJS. We encourage them to think about where religion is already present in their curriculum and help them gain confidence in talking about religion in the classroom. They also learn how to recognize and respond to religious bias and bullying in their schools. Finally, they reflect on why this work is important to do in schools in order to build an interreligious society.

Helping civic leaders and justice makers create a more interreligious public square has been another area of creative and invigorating work. After the death of Freddie Gray Jr. in 2015, the ICJS committed to exploring how interreligious learning could help community groups, nonprofit organizations, and government agencies approach justice-making interreligiously, and encourage more religious diversity in civic conversations. Since 2016, we have had 110 participants from 103 civic and nonprofit organizations that have completed the ten-month intensive Justice Leaders Fellowship. The ICJS helped the Justice fellows think creatively about what it takes to build a religiously diverse public square, gain confidence in talking about religion, and begin to claim a religious voice in their justice-making; and recognize and respond to religious bias and bigotry. While the ICJS staff and scholars lead the sessions, important learning happens between the fellows themselves. They ask important questions of us, of one another, and of the nonprofit sector more broadly as they try to imagine how they might be able to bring an interreligious lens back to their nonprofits

So what does become possible when interreligious friendships flourish? Allow me to answer that question by telling two stories. Both involve Rabbi Joel Zaiman and the work of the ICJS.

A little over twenty years ago, Rabbi Zaiman was leading a group of rabbis from the National Council of Synagogues in regular Catholic-Jewish dialogue meetings with a delegation of American Catholic bishops, led by then-archbishop William Keeler of Baltimore. The bishops and the rabbis had been meeting for several years, doing the slow, hard work of building trust, studying sacred texts together, and having tough conversations around theology and Jewish-Christian relations.

The result of this deep work of dialogue was a 2002 joint publication, "Reflections on Covenant and Mission."[1] This was a groundbreaking statement of Catholic-Jewish relations in the United States. In this statement, Archbishop Keeler—along with some of America's leading Catholic bishops—publicly embraced a radical shift in Roman Catholic teaching. The bishops affirmed that God remains faithful in his divine covenant with the Jewish people. Furthermore, they asserted publicly—for the first time—that

---

1. Consultation of the National Council of Synagogues and delegates of the USCCB Bishops Committee for Ecumenical and Interreligious Affairs, "Reflections on Covenant and Mission," https://www.usccb.org/beliefs-and-teachings/ecumenical-and-interreligious/jewish/upload/Reflections-on-Covenant-and-Mission.pdf.

Catholics should no longer try to convert Jews, asserting the "... evangelizing task no longer includes the wish to absorb the Jewish faith into Christianity and so end the distinctive witness of Jews to God in human history." This statement made headlines not only across the country, but across the world. And eventually this radical revolution in Catholic theology made its way into Vatican teachings, in 2015.[2]

What becomes possible when interreligious relationships flourish? World-changing beliefs become living religious realities for two religious communities. The deep connections between Rabbi Zaiman and Archbishop Keeler, and their mutual commitment to the difficult and serious work of dialogue, made this possible.

I also have my own Rabbi Zaiman story.

As I was finishing my doctoral studies at the University of Chicago in 2011, I applied to be the Roman Catholic scholar at the ICJS. My phone interview with Chris Leighton must have been good enough that he invited me to a second round in Baltimore.

Rabbi Zaiman was present for three parts of my multiday interview—attending a lecture I gave, participating in my teaching demonstration (which was a close study of early twentieth-century texts), and a group lunch at the ICJS library. While much of that interview is hazy in my memory, Rabbi Zaiman stands out clearly in my mind. He asked the most wonderful questions during both my lecture and teaching, questions that were both challenging and complex. By pushing me to explain my thinking further, he gave me the biggest compliment that you can give a young scholar: a serious engagement with my ideas.

Through this experience, I realized the ICJS was a place where I could do scholarship and teaching that matters. I really wanted to work at the ICJS, thus I was thrilled when Chris offered me a job. And when I moved my family to Maryland, one of the first people to reach out and take me out to lunch was Rabbi Zaiman. To my great delight, this was not a one-time welcome lunch, but became something that happened a few times every year. Sometimes Rabbi Zaiman, Chris Leighton, and I went out as a trio, and I was lucky enough to glimpse the deep bond of their friendship up close.

And sometimes I was lucky enough to go out to lunch with Rabbi Zaiman alone, and receive his undivided attention. These lunches did not have much small talk. Rather, we would wrestle with big questions, talking

---

2. Commission for Religious Relations with the Jews, "'Gifts and the Calling of God Are Irrevocable,'" http://www.christianunity.va/content/unitacristiani/en/commissione-per-i-rapporti-religiosi-con-l-ebraismo/commissione-per-i-rapporti-religiosi-con-l-ebraismo-crre/documenti-della-commissione/en.html.

about what mattered most to us and about the books we were reading to find some answers. He always asked after my two young children, my husband, my parents, and about me. He wanted to know how I was doing—really doing—both at work and in life.

In 2015, Rabbi Zaiman invited me out to lunch, and I could tell that he had an agenda for our conversation. He wanted to know if I would consider becoming the ICJS executive director when Chris Leighton retired. I was shocked. And I laughed incredulously at such a proposition. Rabbi Zaiman did not laugh, but waited. I immediately demurred. "This was not in my plans, or even on my horizons," I told him. And Rabbi Zaiman looked at me and said, "Don't say no just yet. Think about it, and we will talk again." I treasure so much the conversations that followed with Rabbi Zaiman—about leadership, about community, and about connecting with people. And I'm grateful that he didn't let me say no to this opportunity to continue the sacred interreligious work that was happening at the ICJS.

So what becomes possible when interreligious relationships flourish? Sometimes we better see ourselves through the eyes of others. Rabbi Zaiman saw something in me that I did not see in myself.

Interreligious friendships can change the world for the better—in ways both big and small.

I hope, and indeed I pray, that the work of the ICJS honors Rabbi Zaiman's memory, and that the friendship between Chris and Joel—which profoundly shaped our organizational ethos—inspires new relationships across lines of religious difference.

Acknowledgements

This book would never have been written without the gentle and insistent prodding of Charlie Obrecht. He believed the story of the ICJS needed to be told, and he brushed aside every excuse I deployed to avoid the task. I am deeply grateful for his persistence, support, and unwavering encouragement. Once I began to reclaim experiences before and during my tenure as the Executive Director, I realized the enormity of this gift—the chance to situate my own story within a bigger and more important narrative. George Bunting was one of the founding members of the ICJS, and his thoughtfulness and generosity combined with Charlie, Bernie Manekin and Rick Berndt to put the ICJS on the map. Thanks to support from George and Jean Silber, treasured friend and horticultural adviser, I was able to enlist a talented editor, Jon Sweeney. Special thanks to colleagues who read specific chapters or the entirety of my manuscript. They offered invaluable counsel, including John Roth, Alvin Rosenfeld, Steven Epperson, Matthew Burdette, Phil Cohen, Deirdre Good, Amy-Jill Levine, Ulrich Grueninger, and Joyce Karpay. The deficiencies that remain are distinctly mine.

These reflections leave out a great many characters who are integral to the ICJS, and the omissions demand repentance and restitution far beyond the scope of this acknowledgement. Dr. Rosann Catalano served as the Roman Catholic scholar at the ICJS for the bulk of my tenure. In addition to her considerable academic talents and brilliance on the classroom stage, she made the ICJS fun and filled our chambers with laughter. The ICJS also benefitted from the talents of several Jewish scholars, including Rabbis Shira Lander, David Sandmel, and Charles Arian. Drs. Adam Gregerman and most recently Ben Sax brought their scholarly expertise into play and set a high bar for academic excellence. There were so many individuals who kept the organization in good working order, most especially Jenny Rothschild, Sister Joan Marie Stief, Valerie Williams, Janis Koch, Bobby Waddail, Laura

Riger, Karen Johnson, Marilyn Powell, Anita Prettyman, Nancy Hagner, and Les Goldsborough.

The founders of the ICJS assembled one of the most exceptional board of directors in all of Maryland. They contributed—each in their own way—to launching an ambitious enterprise and then sustaining it as the organization moved beyond its tender infancy. In addition to the founding chairs, George Hess was one of the originals and his dedication to the mission was second to none. I had the honor of working with severals Board Presidents whose friendship and counsel kept me from going over the cliff: Charlie O., Kathy Hoskins and Frank Heintz (both of blessed memory are among the very finest people I have ever known), Lee Hendler (trusted adviser, dependable friend, and creative wizard), and Joe Langemead (master accountant and theologian). Tom Brown and Kenny Karpay led the Board during the last stage of my tenure They are intrepid explorers of ideas and have become honorary members of the extended Leighton family.

So many other members of the board, visiting scholars, and the larger community made a lasting impression on my way of seeing and engaging the world, and I will spend sleepless nights knowing how many of them did not receive explicit mention within these pages. I would be remiss if I failed to mention several local and national foundations that supported this educational venture. They took a leap of faith and placed their trust in work that offered no assurances of success or longevity. The list of supporters is too long to include all those who helped to launch and sustain the ICJS, but the following certainly made this organization possible.:The Joseph and Harvey Meyerhoff Family Foundation, the Thalheimer-Eurich Fund, the Blaustein Foundation, the David and Barbara Hirschhorn Foundation, the Weinberg Foundation, the France Merrick Foundation, the Shelter Foundation, the Rosenbloom Foundation, the Luetkemyer Family Foundation, the Manekin Foundation, the Rouse Charitable Foundation, the Osprey Foundation—among other Baltimore based philanthropic organizations. The generosity of national foundations also proved invaluable to our efforts, including the Revson Foundation, the Cummins Foundation, the Lilly Endowment, the Bloomberg Philanthropies, the Righteous Persons Foundation, the James and Alice Clark Foundation, the Glenn Family Foundation, and the Whiting Turner Contracting Company. The United States Holocaust Memorial Museum became an invaluable partner on numerous occasions, and the leadership of Sara Bloomfield and Victoria Barnett inspired creative education and rigorous scholarship. The Shalom Hartman Institute demonstrated that collaborative text study is an exhilarating adventure, and Rabbi David Hartman, of blessed memory, and Noam Zion were exemplars of teaching at its best.

ACKNOWLEDGEMENTS

Death has claimed friends, colleagues, and former trustees. Their voices continue to echo in my dreams and noodge me in waking hours. I carry their memory and cherish their enduring influence: Vanlier Hunter, Donna Lee Frisch, Nancy Roche, Bishop Frank Murphy, Sid Silber, Lisa Goldberg, Lois Feinblatt, Joe and Nellie Birnbaum, Jeannette Karpay, Kathy Hoskins, Richard Schifter, Michael Signer, Tikva Frymer-Kensky, Meg Mock, Bernie Manekin, Mel Sykes, Sue Cohen, Mark Loeb, David Hirschhorn, Roy Hoffberger, Richard McKinney, Sister Mary Aquin O'Neil, Redmond Finney, and of course Joel Zaiman.

Good friends kept the sky from falling and that, of course, has made all the difference. I am especially grateful to George Mason whose ennobling friendship calls me to pay exacting attention to those aspects of the world routinely overlooked. Susan Tillett inspired me to write when we first met in the 11th grade, and she has reassured and emboldened me ever since—making possible writing retreats at Ragdale and the Mesa Refuge. John Buchanan and Betsy Buckman were woven into the texture of my family in Sewickley, and they were the best of companions in the making of mischief.

I met Lawrence Farris during my first year at Princeton. He and his wife Pat became family away from family. Larry has read every chapter of this manuscript and offered wise counsel at every turn. His love of irony infused this undertaking with the traces of humor that occasionally offset the forces of gravity.

The ICJS is now guided by a gifted leader and a superb scholar, Dr. Heather Miller Rubens. In conjunction with a staff brimming with talent, she has moved the ICJS to new heights and put the organization at the cutting edge of some of the most exciting and daring work in the field of interreligious study. She gives me hope for the future of what Joel would call "serious education."

The process of transforming a document into a concrete publication requires a special alchemy. My thanks to Matt Wimer, Nathan Rhoads, Jonathan Hill, and Wipf & Stock for their encouragement, guidance, and professional wizardry.

Finally, I cannot imagine how I could have pursued a disruptive ministry without the support of my wife and life partner, Betsy. She kept me anchored in vocational storms and tethered me to the holiness of family. Along with our children—Ben, Hannah, and Sam—and now Cait, Clara and Luke, she has filled me with joy and hope—and taught me the most about what really matters.

Bibliography

Alberta, Tim. "How Politics Poisoned the Evangelical Church." *The Atlantic*, May 10, 2022. https://www.theatlantic.com/magazine/archive/2022/06/evangelical-church-pastors-political-radicalization/629631/.
Ali, Wajahat. *Go Back to Where You Came From*. New York: Norton, 2022.
Allen, Diogenes. "Suffering at the Hands of Nature." *Theology Today* 37 (July 1980) 183–91. https://doi.org/10.1177/004057368003700204.
"American Society for Meliorating the Condition of the Jews." *The Occident and American Jewish Advocate* 1.2 (May 1843). http://www.theoccident.com/Occident/volume1/may1843/meliorate2.html.
Améry, Jean. *At the Mind's Limits*. Translated by Sidney and Stella Rosenfeld. Bloomington: Indiana University Press, 1980.
Arendt, Hannah. *The Human Condition*. Chicago: University of Chicago Press, 1958.
Aristotle. *Nicomachaean Ethics*. Translated by W. D. Ross. Internet Classics Archive, 2000. https://classics.mit.edu/Aristotle/nicomachaen.html.
Berger, David. "Some Reservations about a Jewish Statement on Christians and Christianity." October 2002. https://www.ccjr.us/dialogika-resources/documents-and-statements/analyses/dabru-emet-berger.
Berlin, Isaiah. *Crooked Timber of Humanity: Chapters in the History of Ideas*. Edited by Henry Hardy. 2nd ed. Princeton, NJ: Princeton University Press, 2013.
Branch, Taylor. *Parting the Waters: American in the King Years, 1954–63*. New York: Simon and Schuster, 1988.
Brown, Peter. "The Other Rome." *New York Review of Books*, February 10, 2022. https://www.nybooks.com/articles/2022/02/10/the-other-rome-peter-brown/.
Buber, Martin. *Daniel: Dialogues on Realization*. New York: Holt, Rinehart and Winston, 1964. https://archive.org/details/danieldialogues000bube.
———. *I and Thou*. Translated by Ronald Smith. New York: Scribner, 1958.
Butler, Joseph. "Sermon VIII. Upon Resentment and Forgiveness of Injuries." In *Fifteen Sermons Preached at the Rolls Chapel*, 66–72. Cambridge: Hilliard and Brown, 1827. https://www.ccel.org/ccel/b/butler/sermons/cache/sermons.pdf.
Chin, Catherine. "Job and the Injustice of God." *Journal for the Study of the Old Testament*, December 1994, 91–101.
Chazan, Robert, ed. *Church, State, and Jew in the Middle Ages*. West Orange, NJ: Behrman House, 1980.
Commission for Religious Relations with the Jews. "'Gifts and the Calling of God Are Irrevocable' (Rom 11:29): A Reflection on Theological Questions Pertaining to

Catholic-Jewish Relations on the Occasion of the 50th Anniversary of *Nostra Aetate* (No. 4)." December 10, 2015. http://www.christianunity.va/content/unitacristiani/en/commissione-per-i-rapporti-religiosi-con-l-ebraismo/commissione-per-i-rapporti-religiosi-con-l-ebraismo-crre/documenti-della-commissione/en.html.

Consultation of the National Council of Synagogues and delegates of the USCCB Bishops Committee for Ecumenical and Interreligious Affairs. "Reflections on Covenant and Mission." August 12, 2002. https://www.usccb.org/beliefs-and-teachings/ecumenical-and-interreligious/jewish/upload/Reflections-on-Covenant-and-Mission.pdf.

Cooperman, Alan. "Anti-Muslim remarks stir tempest." *The Washington Post*, June 20, 2002. https://www.washingtonpost.com/archive/politics/2002/06/20/anti-muslim-remarks-stir-tempest/4577462f-cd70-458c-9fef-133b5143e144/.

"*Dabru Emet*: A Jewish Statement on Christians and Christianity." September 10, 2000. https://icjs.org/dabru-emet-text/.

"A Declaration on the "Russian World" (Russkii mir) Teaching." *Public Orthodoxy*, Orthodox Christian Studies Center, Fordham University, March 13, 2022. https://publicorthodoxy.org/2022/03/13/a-declaration-on-the-russian-world-russkii-mir-teaching/.

Edsall, Thomas B. "The Capitol Insurrection Was as Christian Nationalist as It Gets." *New York Times*, January 28, 2021. https://www.nytimes.com/2021/01/28/opinion/christian-nationalists-capitol-attack.html.

Ellenson, David. "A Jewish Legal Authority Addresses Jewish-Christian Dialogue: Two Response of Rabbi Moshe Feinstein." In *After Emancipation: Jewish Religious Responses to Modernity*, 404–9. Cincinnati: Hebrew Union College Press, 2004.

Etehad, Melissa. "After-Nice, Newt Gingrich wants to test every American Muslim and deport those who believe in sharia." *The Washington Post*, July 15, 2016. https://www.washingtonpost.com/news/morning-mix/wp/2016/07/15/after-nice-newt-gingrich-wants-to-test-every-american-muslim-and-deport-those-who-believe-in-sharia/.

Fisher, Shlomo. "The State Crisis and Potential for Uncontrolled Violence in Israel-Palestine." In *Plowshares into Swords? Reflections on Religion and Violence*, edited by Robert Jenson and Eugene Korn, 61–99. Center for Jewish-Christian Understanding and Cooperation, 2014.

Flannery, Edward. *The Anguish of the Jews*. Mahwah, NJ: Paulist, 2004.

Frymer-Kensky, Tikva, et al., eds. *Christianity in Jewish Terms*. New York: Basic Books, 2002.

Gager, John G. *The Origins of Anti-Semitism: Attitudes toward Judaism in Pagan and Christian Antiquity*. New York: Oxford University Press, 1983.

Gatta, Julia. Review of *Reclaiming Faith: Essays on Orthodoxy in the Episcopal Church and the Baltimore Declaration*. *The Christian Century* 111.23, 751.

Goldberg, Michael. *Why Should Jews Survive? Looking Past the Holocaust toward a Jewish Future*. New York: Oxford University Press, 1996.

Goldhagen, Daniel Jonah. *Hitler's Willing Executioners: Ordinary Germans and the Holocaust*. New York: Vintage, 1997.

Gorski, Philip. *American Babylon: Democracy and Christianity Before and After Trump*. London: Routledge, 2020.

———. *American Covenant: A History of Civil Religion from the Puritans to the Present*. Princeton, NJ: Princeton University Press, 2017.

Gorski, Philip, and Samuel L. Perry, *Flag and the Cross: White Christian Nationalism and the Threat to American Democracy*. New York: Oxford University Press, 2022.
Goshen-Gottstein, Alon. "God between Christians and Jews: Is It the Same God?" In *Do We Worship the Same God?*, edited by Miroslav Volf. Grand Rapids: Eerdmans, 2012.
Greenstein, Edward L., trans. *Job: A New Translation*. New Haven, CT: Yale University Press, 2019.
Hagee, John. *Jerusalem Countdown: A Warning to the World*. Lake Mary, FL: Strang, 2006.
Heschel, Abraham Joshua. "No Religion Is an Island." *Union Seminary Quarterly Review* 21.2 (1966) 117–34. https://utsnyc.edu/wp-content/uploads/Heschels-No-Religion-is-an-Island.pdf.
Hilton, Michael, and Gordian Marshall. *The Gospels and Rabbinic Judaism*. London: SCM, 1988.
Hobbes, Thomas. *On Human Nature*. New York: Oxford University Press, 1999.
"'Islam Is Peace' Says President." The White House, Office of the Press Secretary, September 17, 2001. https://georgewbush-whitehouse.archives.gov/news/releases/2001/09/20010917-11.html.
"Israel's Christian community is growing, 84% satisfied with life here—report." *The Times of Israel*, December 22, 2021. https://www.timesofisrael.com/israels-christian-community-is-growing-84-satisfied-with-life-here-report/.
Jankélévitch, Vladimir. *Forgiveness*. Translated with introduction by Andrew Kelley. Chicago: University of Chicago Press, 2005.
John Chrysostom. *Eight Homilies against the Jews*. 387. Translation and publication information unknown. https://en.wikisource.org/wiki/Eight_Homilies_Against_the_Jews.
Kadish, Seth. "How Did Abraham Discover God? The Rationalistic Approach." *TheTorah.com*, 2013. https://www.thetorah.com/article/how-did-abraham-discover-god-the-rationalistic-approach.
Kertzer, David I. *The Pope at War: The Secret History of Pius XII, Mussolini, and Hitler*. New York: Random House, 2022.
Kimel, Aidan. "The Baltimore Declaration." *Eclectic Orthodoxy*, November 17, 2014.
Kushner, Lawrence. *Eyes Remade for Wonder: A Lawrence Kushner Reader*. Woodstock, NY: Jewish Lights, 1998.
"The Land of Israel in Classical Jewish Sources." *My Jewish Learning*. https://www.myjewishlearning.com/article/the-land-of-israel-in-classical-jewish-sources/.
Langer, Susanne noted. *Philosophy in a New Key*. New York: New American Library, 1948.
Levenson, Jon D. "How Not to Conduct Jewish-Christian Dialogue" *Commentary*, April 2002. https://www.commentary.org/articles/jon-levenson-2/how-not-to-conduct-jewish-christian-dialogue/.
———. *Inheriting Abraham: The Legacy of the Patriarch in Judaism, Christianity, and Islam*. Princeton, NJ: Princeton University Press, 2012.
Levine, Amy-Jill. *The Difficult Words of Jesus*. Nashville: Abingdon, 2021.
Levine, Amy-Jill, and Marc Zvi Brettler. *The Bible With and Without Jesus: How Jews and Christians Read the Same Stories Differently*. New York: HarperOne, 2020.
Liphshiz, Cnaan. "Norwegian church hosts photo exhibition saying Palestinians are 'crucified daily.'" *The Jerusalem Post*, September 25, 2021. https://www.jpost.com/

diaspora/norwegian-church-hosts-photo-exhibition-saying-palestinians-are-crucified-daily-680264.
Luther, Martin. *On the Jews and Their Lies*. In *Luther's Works*, vol. 47, edited by Franklin Sherman, 268–93. Philadelphia: Fortress, 1971.
Maimonides, Moses. *A Maimonides Reader*. Edited by Isadore Twersky. West Orange, NJ: Behrman House, 1972.
Marissen, Michael. *Lutheranism, Anti-Judaism, and Bach's St. John Passion*. New York: Oxford University Press, 1998.
McLaren, Brian. *A New Kind of Christianity: Ten Questions That Are Transforming the Faith*. New York: HarperOne, 2010.
Mead, Walter Russell. *The Arc of a Covenant: The United States, Israel, and the Fate of the Jewish People*. New York: Alfred A. Knopf, 2022.
Merton, Thomas. *Collected Poems*. New York: New Directions, 1977.
Murdoch, Iris. "The Sublime and the Good." *Chicago Review* 13.3 (Autumn 1959) 42–55. Reprinted in Murdoch, *Existentialists and Mystics: Writing on Philosophy and Literature*. Edited by Peter J. Conradi. New York: Penguin, 1997.
Nirenberg, David. *Anti-Judaism: The Western Tradition*. New York: Norton, 2014.
Pagani, Karen. "The Uses and Abuses of Joseph Butler's Account of Forgiveness." *Southern Central Review* 27 (2010) 12–33.
Parker, Robert P. *White Too Long: The Legacy of White Supremacy in American Christianity*. New York: Simon & Schuster, 2020.
Petuchowski, Jakob J., and Michael Brocke, eds. *The Lord's Prayer and Jewish Liturgy*. New York: Crossroad, 1978.
Popova, Maria. "Simone Weil on Attention and Grace." *The Marginalian*, August 19, 2015. https://www.themarginalian.org/2015/08/19/simone-weil-attention-gravity-and-grace/.
Presbyterian Peace Fellowship. "Zionism Unsettled: A Congregational Study Guide." New York: Curtis Brown, 2016.
Public Affairs Television. *Talking about Genesis: A Resource Guide*. New York: Main Street/Doubleday, 1996.
Putnam, Robert. *Bowling Alone: The Collapse and Revival of American Community*. New York: Simon & Schuster, 2000.
Reinhartz, Adele. *Cast Out of the Covenant: Jews and Anti-Judaism in the Gospel of John*. Minneapolis: Fortress, 2020.
Rittner, Carol, et al., eds. *The Holocaust and the Christian World*. 2nd ed. Mahwah, NJ: Paulist, 2019.
Rivkin, Ellis. *Hidden Revolution: The Pharisees' Search for the Kingdom Within*. Nashville: Abingdon, 1978.
Rosenzweig, Franz. "The Love of One's Enemies." In *Franz Rosenzweig: His Life and Thought*. Edited by Nahum N. Glatzer. Indianapolis: Hackett, 1998.
Rudin, James. "While the Messiah Tarries." *The Forward*, February 22, 2002.
Sacks, Jonathan. *The Dignity of Difference: How to Avoid the Clash of Civilizations*. New York: Bloomsbury Continuum, 2003.
Sandmel, David, et al., eds. *Irreconcilable Differences?: A Learning Resource for Jews and Christians*. New York: Routledge, 2001.
Schramm, Brooks, and Kirsi Stjerna. *Martin Luther, the Bible, and the Jewish People: A Reader*. Minneapolis, Fortress, 2012.

Semans, Don. "God's Honor, Violence and the State." In *Plowshares into Swords? Reflections on Religion and Violence*, edited by Robert Jenson and Eugene Korn, 100–31. Center for Jewish-Christian Understanding and Cooperation, 2014.

Sen, Amartya. *Identity and Violence: The Illusion of Destiny*. New York: Norton, 2006.

Shimron, Yonat. "Hundreds of U.S. rabbis protest new Israeli government in public letter." *The Washington Post*, December 28, 2022. https://www.washingtonpost.com/religion/2022/12/28/hundreds-us-rabbis-protest-new-israeli-government-public-letter/.

Sievers, Joseph, and Amy-Jill Levine, eds. *The Pharisees*. Grand Rapids: Eerdmans, 2021.

Soloveitchik, Joseph. "Confrontation." *Tradition: The Journal of Orthodox Thought* 6.2 (1964) 5–25.

Stewart, Katherine. *The Power Worshippers: Inside the Dangerous Rise of Religious Nationalism*. New York: Bloomsbury, 2019.

Stout, Harry S. *Upon the Altar of the Nation: A Moral History of the Civil War*. New York: Penguin, 2007.

Swidler, Leonard. "Dialogue Principles." https://dialogueinstitute.org/dialogue-principles.

Taylor, Charles. *The Ethics of Authenticity*. Cambridge, MA: Harvard University Press, 1991.

Taylor, Matthew D. "The Roots and Reality of U.S. Christian Nationalism." ICJS mini-course in 3 lectures, delivered November 2–16, 2021. https://icjs.org/events/the-roots-and-reality-of-u-s-christian-nationalism/.

Teter, Magda. *Blood Libel: On the Trail of an Antisemitic Myth*. Boston: Harvard University Press, 2020.

———. *Christian Supremacy: Reckoning with the Roots of Antisemitism and Racism*. Princeton, NJ: Princeton University Press, 2023.

Tiffany, Kaitlyn. "That's It. You're Dead to Me." *The Atlantic*, September 2022. https://www.theatlantic.com/magazine/archive/2022/09/toxic-person-tiktok-internet-slang-meaning/670599/.

Warren, Rick. "Invocation at the First Presidential Inauguration Ceremony for Barack Obama." January 20, 2009. https://www.americanrhetoric.com/speeches/rickwarreninaugurationprayer.htm.

Weil, Simone. *Gravity and Grace*. Translated by Emma Crawford and Mario von der Ruhr. New York: Routledge, 2002.

———. *Waiting for God*. New York: Routledge, 2021.

West, Angela. "Soloveitchik's 'No' to Interfaith Dialogue." *European Judaism: A Journal for the New Europe* 47.2 (September 2014) 95–106.

Whitehead, Samuel, and Samuel Perry. *Taking America Back for God: Christian Nationalism in the United States*. New York: Oxford University Press, 2020.

"Why are Christians leaving Palestinian territories?" *The Catholic World Report*, June 19, 2020. https://www.catholicworldreport.com/2020/06/19/why-are-christians-leaving-palestinian-territories/.

Wiesel, Elie. *Night*. Translated by Marion Wiesel. New York: Hill & Wang, 2006.

———. *The Trial of God*. Translated by Marion Wiesel. New York: Schocken, 1995.

Wiesenthal, Simon. *The Sunflower: On the Possibilities and Limits of Forgiveness*. New York: Schocken, 1969.

Wilken, Robert. "The Jews as the Christians Saw Them." *First Things*, May 1998. https://www.firstthings.com/article/2008/05/jews-as-the-romans-saw-them.

———. *John Chrysostom and the Jews: Rhetoric and Reality in the Late Fourth Century.* 1983. Reprint, Eugene, OR: Wipf & Stock, 2004.

Wiman, Christian. *My Bright Abyss: Meditation of a Modern Believer.* New York: Farrar, Straus and Giroux, 2013.

Wistrich, Robert S. *Antisemitism: The Longest Hatred.* New York: Pantheon, 1992.

Wuthnow, Robert. *The Restructuring of American Religion: Society and Faith since World War II.* Princeton, NJ: Princeton University Press, 1990.

Yablokov, Ilya. "The Five Conspiracy Theories That Putin Has Weaponized." *The New York Times*, April 25, 2022. https://www.nytimes.com/2022/04/25/opinion/putin-russia-conspiracy-theories.html.

www.ingramcontent.com/pod-product-compliance
Lightning Source LLC
Chambersburg PA
CBHW070317230426
43663CB00011B/2159